Our Field in India

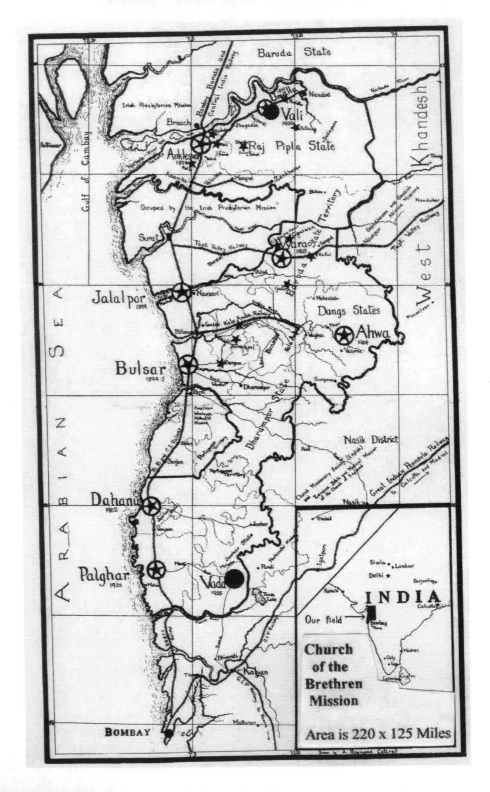

SPLENDOR IN THE DUST

By Lois Shull

Order this book online at www.trafford.com/
or email orders@trafford.com

Most Trafford titles are also available at major online book retailers.

Note for Librarians: A cataloguing record for this book is available from Library
and Archives Canada at www.collectionscanada.ca/amicus/index-e.html

Printed in Victoria, BC, Canada.

ISBN: 978-1-4269-0988-7 (sc)

*Our mission is to efficiently provide the world's finest, most comprehensive
book publishing service, enabling every author to experience success.
To find out how to publish your book, your way, and have it available
worldwide, visit us online at www.trafford.com/10510*

Trafford rev. 8/5/2009

 www.trafford.com

North America & international
toll-free: 1 888 232 4444 (USA & Canada)
phone: 250 383 6864 ♦ fax: 812 355 4082

For Ernie, who carried India in his soul.

Acknowledgements

I would like to express my special thanks to three people. Stanley Crum, a true friend in need, offered his computer expertise and gave many hours to this project. Without his help, this book could not have been completed. Stan's daughter, Hannah Pearson, labored dozens of hours as my unofficial editor, making countless corrections and many suggestions which made the text more readable—especially for people with no prior knowledge of India. I also want to thank my son, Jim, who read and critiqued the text, made suggestions, occasionally offered his memories of events, and helped with the final typing, editing and arrangement of this manuscript.

Foreward

"Quit India!"

The British Raj had been brought to its knees and Indians had reclaimed their homeland. These were turbulent times on the Indian subcontinent. The early years of our missionary work in India, 1946 through 1964, had brought Ernie, our family, and me face-to-face with the birth pains of an emerging nation. Mahatma Gandhi was assassinated, the country was being divided into Pakistan and India along religious lines, rioting and bloodshed were rampant, and the British had, indeed, quit India. Yet shining lives emerged amidst this turmoil of religions on collision course, the formation of a new democracy, clashes between rich and poor, city and village, and the Oxford educated versus those who could only mark an "X" or press an inked thumbprint to sign their name. There remained the long shadow of an ancient caste system and a society which subjugated women to near slavery. But Ernie and I had been called to do God's bidding now and in this place. In truth, both missionaries and Americans were welcomed and well-treated in rural India. The people seemed receptive to the agricultural, educational, medical, and evangelical work to which we had been called. When we left India for good, a growing, self-sustaining church stood in Ahwa, relationships and friendships had been built that survive to this day, and India had taken major steps toward the vibrant society it has become.

Contents

Chapter 1

———•———

Calcutta

Calcutta at last! Fascinating city of mystery, beauty, fantasy, and filth, it was home to temples and palaces, revolutionaries and politicians, holy men and beggars. Congested on the banks of the muddy Hooghly River, one of the mouths of the sacred Ganges, where devout Hindu worshipers from all over India came to bathe in its purifying waters, this largest Indian metropolis, called by Rudyard Kipling "the city of dreadful night" was one of the great religious and cultural centers of the Orient.

An American ship, its heavy cable lashed securely and its gangway lowered into place, lay berthed, like a great, disabled whale next to the sweltering dock. At the top of the gangway a slim, brown haired young woman with a baby in her arms hesitated for a moment, her clear, gray eyes glancing back over the deck of the troop transport, aptly named the Marine Jumper. The registered temperature of 117 degrees Fahrenheit seemed to Lois far too low, considering the blast of burning, pre-monsoon heat rising from the metal deck under her feet.

Marine Jumper! Lois remembered that once during a storm a tilt of 3 more degrees would have capsized the ship. She recalled how this hastily-outfitted, wartime craft had dived into 30-foot troughs and leaped at the crest of each wave that followed, and survived. Nonetheless she felt a twinge of nostalgic reluctance to leave this last bit of America. On Indian soil the future stretched many years ahead challenging and inviting, but also uncertain and strange.

This was not the best of times to be arriving in India. Politically, in early 1946 the British Government, which had been a part of Indian history for the past 300 years, was being pressed by all Indian factions to "Quit India!" Gandhi and the mainly Hindu Congress Party were demanding complete independence from Britain, while at the same time Mohammed Ali Jinnah, of the Muslim League, was immovable in his determination to gain not only freedom from Britain, but also freedom from the Hindu majority Congress, and resolved that the Muslims should have their own separate state of Pakistan. Like a gigantic, seething volcano, the communal antagonism and hatred barely beneath the surface had brought affairs in all of India to a point just below boiling. The British were trying to control the situation, but with only limited success. Nowhere was the intensity of feeling more evident than in the city of Calcutta, where news of atrocities committed by both Hindus and Muslims were being reported daily.

Lois's momentary reluctance to leave the ship didn't arise from any doubt in her mind as to whether they should be coming to this country so full of paradox and conflict. This was a land of ancient and diverse culture, suffering from the nearly insurmountable problems of poverty, illiteracy, superstition, disease, overpopulation, and political unrest. Chalmer, Lois's husband Ernie's oldest brother, and Chalmer's wife Susan, who had worked in the Church of the Brethren Mission in India for years, used to mention in nearly every letter home that the Mission was handicapped severely in its educational, medical and religious work because of insufficient staff.

Now on the threshold of a new life, Lois remembered those days of momentous decision making at the beginning of Ernie's senior year in seminary, when the Mission Board had asked them to consider going to India as a lifetime commitment, to work as educational and evangelistic missionaries. The commission was, "Go to India and share your Christian faith with the people around you, striving to improve conditions wherever you can, concentrating on education, health, and sanitation, meeting every available opportunity for service."

The period of indecision which followed, frequently a very painful one for Lois, for it meant leaving family and friends for many years, had been filled with gathering information and counseling with people who had been to India. Then there had been the complication that they were expecting their first baby in December.

By the time Baby Linda Kay was born, a tiny five pounds eleven ounces, Ernie and Lois were sure that going to India was the decision God wanted them to make.

Lois took a deep breath. That had been four years ago, two years spent in a pastorate and one year in the Hartford School of Missions to prepare specifically for working in India. While Linda attended nursery school, Ernie finished a Masters of Arts Degree and Lois, among other courses, took a full year, four-hour course in tropical medicine and midwifery designed especially for missionaries. Even if she wouldn't need the education for helping the Indian people, Lois reasoned, she would need it in caring for the health of her own family.

Graduation day had been a day Lois would remember vividly for several reasons. It started early with a hurried trip across the city to the hospital, arriving just in time for the birth of curly-haired James David at 7:55 a.m. Ernie made it through the delivery quite well. However, he had to rush back to the University to receive his degree at 9:30. Still the day's events were not yet finished. To add more red to this red letter day, Linda broke out with German measles.

Nine months later they were arriving in Calcutta.

Lois tightened her arms protectively around blond, kinky haired Jimmy, who was waving his tiny hand enthusiastically at the troops lining the railing of the lower deck. Jimmy and his four-year-old sister Linda had been their favorites among the twelve civilian passengers aboard. Their childish play reminded the homesick men of their own children whom they had left behind, not knowing when, or if, they would see them again. It had been good therapy for the troops when Dr. Greenspon, the troops' surgeon, carried Jimmy daily for a walk down to the lowest deck where the men, whose destination had not been revealed, were assigned to crowded quarters. Babbling good naturedly, Jimmy seemed to represent a state of normalcy and the folks back home.

As Lois hesitated, Dr. Greenspon emerged through the hatch, and seeing the woman and her baby about ready to leave the ship, came over to say goodbye. "Hey, Jimmy." The young doctor smiled as he patted Jimmy's seat. "We're going to miss you. You've given a lot of guys a great deal of happiness during these five weeks."

"We'll never forget you, Doctor," declared Lois, her voice a bit shaky with emotion. As she shook the doctor's hand a picture flashed across her mind of Linda lying desperately ill with pneumonia down in the troops' sick bay as Lois sat anxiously beside her, and of Dr. Greenspon's tireless care and concern for the frightened little girl. No doubt he had saved her life, for pneumonia at sea was often fatal. "You've been a great friend to all of us. Thanks to you, we still have our little daughter. We can't ever thank you enough, Doctor. We pray that you, and all the men aboard, may soon be able to return to the States and your own families."

Dr. Greenspon nodded agreement. "As they say in some countries, 'go with God.'" Giving Jimmy another pat, he turned with a spring in his step toward the stairs leading to the bridge.

From her high vantage point on deck, Lois looked down onto the busy Calcutta dock, where she could see Ernie, holding Linda's hand, working his way through the congestion of people, animals and carts toward the gangway. Moving closely behind him to avoid being separated, hurried an American lady about forty years of age, wearing a pink skirt and a neat, white blouse, her long dark hair braided and pinned attractively around her head like a crown. A returning missionary with six years of experience teaching village girls in the Mission Boarding School in Vyara, Gujarat State, Kathryn Kiracofe was now coming back to take an assignment teaching in a vocational school in Ankeleshwar.

As Lois watched the three of them winding their way toward the ship, she thought again how fortunate the Shull family had been to be able to travel with Kathryn ever since leaving Seattle. They had shared so many experiences that she and Kathryn had become like sisters, and the children called this lovely, gentle lady Aunt Kathryn. Due to limited space in officers' quarters on this troop transport, Ernie and the other male passengers had been assigned bunks down in the hold with the troops. Although he spent as much time as he could with the family, it was often Kathryn who helped with the children. On the night that Lois had to take Linda down to the ship's hospital and needed to stay with her five days, it was Kathryn who took over the care of baby Jimmy.

Below on the dock, like a giant, ever-changing kaleidoscope, the shifting crowds slowly made way for the Americans. Lois could distinguish coolies carrying head-loads of luggage, vendors selling trinkets or food, waiting taxis, victorias hitched to emaciated horses, ragged beggars, handcarts loaded with luggage, happy sailors on a few hours leave, and many other strangely-garbed persons whose occupations she could not guess.

Ernie reached the base of the gangway with Kathryn and Linda just as Lois was starting to descend. Glancing up and seeing her, Ernie smiled encouragingly, his intense, blue eyes sparkling with amusement at the picture she made.

In that sea of oriental dress, Ernie looked so American and familiar, mused Lois, his curly, blond hair, sport shirt, and slacks making him stand out like a polo player on a football field.

The gangway swayed unsteadily as Lois, running her hand along the loose guide rope and holding onto her purse, the diaper bag, and Jimmy, descended step by step to the confusion below. It felt good to stand on solid ground again.

"We're out of luck about the luggage in the hold, honey." Ernie wiped the perspiration from his face with his white handkerchief as he glanced up and down the docks where other ships lay quiet in their berths with very little activity observable on their decks. The giant dock cranes, usually so busy lifting and swinging and lowering their heavy cargoes from around the world, stood like giant, petrified fingers silhouetted against the sky. "There'll be no unloading today or the next day. I can't say I blame anyone for not working in this heat," Ernie commented.

Already at 11:00 a.m. the tropical heat seemed unbearable. Ernie and Kathryn had checked the visas and health cards through immigration, but had been stymied later when they found the customs offices closed. Nothing would move until the stevedores came back to work, and that time was indefinite since most of the stevedores, being Hindu, were celebrating the important Hindu festival of Holi, nowhere with more enthusiasm than in Calcutta.

Fifteen or twenty barefooted, scantily-clad men, pushing and shoving each other out of the way, were trying to get the attention of the travelers by gesturing and yelling words that meant nothing to Lois. They pointed to the cabin luggage which had just arrived and was stacked near them and then pointed to themselves, making it clear that they wanted a job carrying the various footlockers, boxes, and suitcases to wherever the Americans might wish to go. They were wearing turbans on their heads and pieces of cloth splashed with some kind of red color draped around their hips. Their bodies and faces had also been smeared with the red liquid, making them look rather sinister and frightening to the unaccustomed eyes of the foreigners. Linda started to cry as she hid her face against her daddy's slacks. Ernie lifted her into his protecting arms to reassure her.

Speaking in a mixture of English and Gujarati, Kathryn took charge. She selected three coolies to carry the luggage to two waiting taxis, the drivers of which wore brightly-colored, neatly wrapped turbans and long beards rolled up and carefully pinned out of the way with large safety pins. They were followers of the Sikh religion, Kathryn explained. It took a full fifteen minutes fitting, and pushing, and changing, to stow away five people and eleven pieces of luggage into the limited space of the two old cars. Kathryn with her past experience suggested that Ernie should ride in one taxi, while Lois, Kathryn and the children should go in the other, a precaution to make sure that all the luggage would arrive at the proper destination, the Methodist House, where traveling Europeans (a term applied to all Westerners) could find reasonably-priced room and board.

As the perspiring taxi driver, a taller than average Indian, came around the side of the car and climbed into the well-worn driver's seat just in front of where Lois was holding Jimmy, he exclaimed cheerfully in English, "Very much work." He shook his head from side to side in a gesture that Lois soon learned meant "yes."

Kathryn looked at Lois and winked. "That's his buildup for asking a larger fare," she whispered.

Disregarding the general protests, Ernie paid the coolies the amount Kathryn said was right and climbed into the second taxi. As the two cars pulled slowly into the line of traffic, the coolies trotted easily along beside, with their hands on the window sills.

"Two rupees, Sahib, two rupees." Then as the taxis began to pick up speed, their calls changed to a hopeful, "Bakshish, Sahib, bakshish." Finally realizing that there was no more money to be had even as a gift, they turned back to the docks.

Chapter 2

————— •• —————

Methodist House

The bulging taxis negotiated the crowded street. Their aggressive drivers dodged bullock carts and horse-drawn, two-wheeled tongas. With their horns blasting, the taxis careened around bicycle rickshaws, carts, scooter-taxis, bewildered cows, coolies with huge head loads, and hawkers selling everything from beetlenut to watches. The burning air coming through the windows seemed to bake the skin. Linda and Jimmy were broken out with a bad heat rash. Lois could feel her wet clothing sticking uncomfortably to her body, but she found the strange and confused scene outside the taxi fascinating, even though she couldn't understand some of the activity.

"Kathryn, look! Everywhere I turn I see people splashed with that red color. What does it mean?" Lois wondered.

"I'm not sure what it means," answered Kathryn thoughtfully. "I know only that it is a part of the worship of the god Krishna, and that it is the Hindu custom to throw colored water onto other Hindus during this festival. It seems to be a kind of fun that Hindus have with other Hindus. The Muslims don't like it very much. It gets even worse sometimes out in the villages when they start throwing cow dung."

Suddenly their taxi came to a screeching halt, and if they hadn't been packed in so tightly, they would have been thrown against the seat in front. Their bearded driver stuck his head and shoulder out the window, and waving his arm angrily in the air began exchanging invectives with other taxi drivers.

Just ahead a massive crowd of Hindus throwing red water in all directions, laughing and shouting enthusiastically, were oblivious to the interrupted traffic. Horns were blowing and irate vehicle drivers were yelling and crowding forward. The white-uniformed officer standing on his high box in the middle of the street was blasting his whistle, but the revelers seemed unaware until four mounted police arrived, expertly maneuvering the holiday crowd to one side, clearing a narrow way for the taxis to move forward. Lois wondered if everyone had been able to get out of the way of those big horses' hooves. As their cab picked up speed the driver, like a chameleon now turned pleasant, remarked over his shoulder in a smooth, tour-guide voice, "Very big day. Much people!"

That's certainly the understatement of the year! thought Lois, who had never seen so much milling humanity, most of whom looked poor and undernourished, in her whole life. She wondered how they could have so much energy and enthusiasm on such a hot day.

The Methodist House was located about a half-hour's drive from the docks. Built flush with the street, it was a large, two-story, four-sided building with an extensive, grass-covered court-yard in the center. This was filled with cultivated flower beds of red and yellow cannas and two gold mahor trees, their large, orange blossoms and wide branches making an inviting, shady space for a children's play area. The open courtyard was surrounded by apartments and rooms accommodating a day school, a small dispensary, and living quarters for the workers as well as guest rooms for travelers. To enter the compound the taxis passed through an iron-grilled gate in one side of the building, opened for them by a uniformed gate keeper, who swung the gates shut immediately behind them.

The comparative quiet of the enclosed compound was a welcome relief from the noisy street outside. The cabs pulled up in front of an open verandah on their right, and above the first open door was a sign which read "Manager's Office." A rather formidable English lady with her hair pulled back tightly and fastened in a knot on the back of her head, rose from behind her desk as they entered the room.

"Good afternoon. You must be the Shull party--you are later than we expected. We were led to believe that you would arrive in time for chotahausery (midmorning snack), but that food is no doubt spoiled by now," she informed them with a rather pinched smile, leaving the impression that they had at the least broken all rules of good etiquette and at most spoiled valuable food that could have been given to the hungry.

"But no matter. The next meal will be tiffin (lunch) served at 1:30. Would you please try not to be late to meals for the sake of the servants." Then noticing the taxi drivers still waiting she said, "You had better pay each of your drivers three rupees since you came from the docks . . . No, that's enough!" she told the drivers who had followed the Americans into the office and had ready protests on the ends of their tongues. However, recognizing an iron lady when they met one, they unloaded the luggage without further objection.

There was no doubt that Mrs. Smythe was very efficient, Lois had to admit. Calling two servants to help, she had their luggage down the hall and into a rather crowded room, and Kathryn into another room with a roommate before they knew it.

As Lois set Jimmy down on the bed she noticed that the one window in their room had up-and-down iron bars about three inches apart and a thin, white half-curtain hanging motionless in the midday heat.

Flipping on a wall switch that controlled a most welcome overhead fan, Mrs. Smythe straightened her shoulders. "We try to save as much electricity as we can here. Be sure to turn off the fan and all the lights before you leave the room." Lois could almost hear her own father telling her the same thing when she was just eight years old.

Linda climbed up on the bed beside Jimmy and grabbed his leg as he was about to roll over the side onto the hard floor, at which interference Jimmy began to yell lustily.

"Mrs. Smythe," Lois picked Jimmy up again to stop his crying, "The children are hungry. They ate breakfast at 8:00 this morning and it's an hour and a half until the next meal. We would appreciate it if they could have something--perhaps milk and toast to help them until the meal is served."

"We don't do special orders. The servants are too busy for that. But--perhaps in this case--I'd better prepare something myself and send up a tray. As I said, we don't do special orders." Not waiting for a reaction, she turned back through the swinging half-doors into the hall. Ernie and Lois listened to the diminishing sound of her footsteps on the floor tiles in the hall, then they looked at each other and laughed.

Ernie observed with a twinkle in his eye, "You know, we like to meet interesting characters. You can see Mrs. Smythe stands on principle. One has to wonder how long she has been running this guest house--perhaps too long--no doubt all during the war, and no chance for a furlough since." Before long the tray arrived with not only toast and milk, but orange juice as well.

The 1:30 meal turned out to be an uncomfortable experience. Mrs. Smythe at the head of the table, a brass bell at her fingertips, directed the two white-uniformed bearers as they offered dishes of food to each of the ten guests. The amount of food in each main dish seemed inadequate to serve eleven people. Each guest had to mentally proportion the food in order that the last person served would not be slighted.

Linda and Jimmy were the only children present, and as the meal of creamed eggs and toast progressed, their manners, movements and mouthfuls along with the near misses were watched carefully. Someone observed that having lunch with children at the table was interesting--back home in England parents usually fed the children early. The prevailing atmosphere of disapproval, and the feeling that Americans in general, their manners and customs, were quite a few notches below the British culturally speaking, made Lois feel uneasy during the entire meal.

Later as they were walking back to their rooms Lois told Kathryn about her impressions of their hostess.

Kathryn smiled. "Well, don't let it upset you," she advised. "There are people like Mrs. Smythe in every country, protecting their egos by hanging on to imagined superiorities. Really, I've found most of the British to be very friendly and I admire them in many ways, even though there have been a few incidents here in India that were not admirable."

They stopped for a moment just outside the swinging doors to the Shulls' room where Ernie and the children, who had gone on ahead were moving around. They heard Linda's excited voice, "Let me, Daddy. I know how to turn on the fan. Let me."

"Okay. But you're too short. Here, let me hold you up." There was a slight pause, then the two watching the ceiling fan through the wide space above the doors saw the long blades begin to move.

"In a climate where midday has such intense heat as pre-monsoon India, one can see why most people take this time of day between lunch and 4:00 o'clock tea as a siesta. Exercising much in this weather could be dangerous, especially to newcomers."

Ernie looked over the doors. "Kathryn, what do you say to you and me going at 4:30 to begin picking up some of the supplies we will need for our trip across India to Bombay. We won't be able to get everything in one day."

"Yes, let's get that done as soon as we can; then when the luggage is released from customs, there will be nothing to keep us from leaving Calcutta. You are going to be too late for the beginning of language school at Mahableshwar as it is, but we will do our best."

"Just be back in plenty of time for dinner," warned Lois with a smile. "We don't want to be punished for being late."

With his teddy bear in one arm and his thumb in his mouth, Jimmy was asleep by the time Ernie laid him on his pillow. Linda begged for her mother to read her a story, but her eyes were closed before page three, her long, blond lashes curling softly on her flushed cheeks and her curly hair wet on her forehead.

Lois laid the book on the table and crossed the room to the extra-wide cot where Ernie was dozing. She slipped off her sandals and lay down beside him, resting her head on his reassuring shoulder.

"It's funny, but I feel excited and frightened at the same time. That mob of people this morning could have turned ugly very quickly. The Indian people are not very fond of Westerners right now, as you could tell by their yelling, 'Quit India!'"

Ernie's arm tightened around her. "That's true. You can feel tension in the air," he agreed thoughtfully. "But the exciting thing is that in the next months, maybe years, we will be able to watch the birth struggles of a new, independent nation. It's inevitable that it is going to happen, you know. I only hope that it can be brought about peacefully."

Ernie and Kathryn left in a taxi a little before 4:00. The children awakened in ample time to have their hot faces and hands washed before the high tea was served in the main dining room by the two uniformed Indian bearers, each wearing a hat fashioned with a stiffly-starched, fan-shaped cloth on the top. As Lois lifted Jimmy into the wooden high chair and helped Linda climb onto a chair, she was most grateful for the large electric fan turning slowly above them. Mrs. Smythe poured. Carefully removing the hand-embroidered tea cozy from the large white teapot and laying it on the corner of the table, she poured the first cup of tea and handed it to the bearer on her right who served it to the guest at the foot of the table, then she poured the second cup. Everyone watched as the ritual proceeded. It took some time to serve all the adult guests. When the bearer moved to set a cup at Linda's place, Lois waved it away. Mrs. Smythe raised her eyebrows.

"I see the children are not drinking tea. They will have to learn if they are going to live in India. Would they drink lemonade if I have the bearer prepare it?" she asked, with a hint at the extra work involved.

"Yes, thank you, Mrs. Smythe. That would be better for the children than tea," Lois replied.

In a few minutes the lemonade arrived. Then plates of small peanut butter sandwiches, cookies, hot mix, peanuts, and golden slices of papaya were offered to each guest by the bearers. Lois saved two sandwiches and two cakes for the children to eat later, since dinner would not be served until 8:00 o'clock.

"Let's go for a walk in the compound, Linda," Lois suggested later when tea time was finished. Carrying Jimmy and holding Linda by the hand she went out to stroll among the flame-colored flower beds. Near the center of the court as they walked by the gold mahor tree, Linda spied a wide seed pod about eighteen inches long and picked it up to examine it. Turning it over to look at the back, she was delighted to hear the dry seeds inside dancing around. She shook the pod vigorously, captivated by her new toy; then, wanting to share her discovery, went running to Jimmy and put the smooth-surfaced pod into his hand, giving it a shake. Jimmy was pleased with the sound he could make with his new rattle. Then Linda found another seed pod for herself.

As they strolled on, they passed near the entrance gates. The sounds of shouting and angry arguments in the street outside drew Lois's attention. She could see crowds of people carrying signs and moving about. Ernie and Kathryn had not yet returned and she felt apprehensive for their safety, even though they had gone in a taxi. It was unfortunate that their arrival in India had come just at Holi festival time when emotions were already running high because of the political situation. It would take three days for them to cross India by train and another half day to travel up the coast from Bombay to Palghar where they were to be temporarily stationed in the same big bungalow with Chalmer and Susan. Although she had never met Ernie's brother and sister-in-law, for Chalmer and Susan were in India before Lois became a part of the Shull family, she felt that they were like her own brother and sister, and that arriving in Palghar would be almost like going home.

Ernie and Kathryn were only moderately successful in buying supplies for their trip across India. Not only were many of the shops closed, but the crowds in the streets, many of them unruly, made it difficult to get through, even with a taxi. They kept the taxi with them on hire, afraid that if they let it go while they were shopping, they would not be able to find another when they needed one.

Ernie arrived back at the Methodist House as Lois was preparing to bathe the children before dinner, and gave her a helping hand. They cautioned the children to not get any of the water in their mouths, for it had not been boiled. This was especially hard for Jimmy, since he loved to chew the washcloth. Linda agreed to help watch Jimmy. The children liked the big wash tubs provided for bathing, especially the exciting tinny sound they made when Linda and then Jimmy pounded a block against the side.

Freshly dressed and hungry, the Shulls took the children down to dinner, which proved to be a disaster. The meal consisted of a highly-spiced soup followed by rice and hot curry with an Indian bread called chapatti. Even though they were hungry, the children would eat only a small bit of the bread. Upon Lois's request one of the bearers brought two bananas for the children.

After the meal, Mrs. Smythe, admirably doing her duty, informed Lois that the children should be fed alone when they would not disturb the adults. Lois felt rebellion welling up inside her. *That might be the British way, but it certainly wasn't the American way*, she fumed. However, there were more important aspects to be considered. They were going to be guests in this house for only a few days and besides, they needed the advice, information, and experience that Mrs. Smythe could give them. So Lois held back her anger.

For the remaining time they stayed in Calcutta, Lois prepared food for the children in the main kitchen, a most inconvenient place with charcoal burners for heat, and huge, heavy, brass vessels for cooking pans. Still, with this arrangement she was able to give the children simply-prepared, unspiced food at more accustomed hours. The cook, once Mrs. Smythe left the kitchen, cooperated in many little ways, which made her task easier.

By the time dinner was finished the children were nearly asleep. Ernie and Lois carried them to their room and laid them on their cots. The heat was stifling, for the air had not cooled with the coming of darkness. Gratefully Ernie flipped on the ceiling fan. They breathed a breath of relief as the air began to stir around them.

"It's a shame we have to put these mosquito nets down and cut off what little air there is," commented Lois as she began to unfold the net hanging over Linda's cot, holding it carefully to avoid its swishing into the little girl's face. As she began to pull the net out to the four corners of the cot, she stopped abruptly.

"Ernie! Look at this net--it's full of big holes! It will never do. Why, it's worse than nothing. It would only trap the mosquitoes inside." It flashed through her mind that malaria was one of the great killing diseases of India, and using a good mosquito net was one of the best ways to avoid getting the disease.

Ernie quickly dropped the net hanging over Jimmy's bed. "Well how do you like that. These holes are big enough to let in big June bugs," he exclaimed indignantly as he threw the net back above the cot. A quick examination disclosed that the other two nets were in a similar condition.

"This won't do." Ernie's jaw set in a determined line. "I'll go down to the office and pick up four other nets," he said as he went through the swinging half-doors. He was gone only a few minutes, and when he came in again Lois looked up expectantly.

"Bad news--they don't have any other nets, and it wouldn't be wise, all things considered, to go out to a bazaar and try to find some. Besides the outside doors and gates have been locked for the night because of the demonstrations going on all over the city."

Lois sank dejectedly down on the side of the bed thinking westerners, who are supposed to know about such things, would be more concerned about health measures. "I'm glad we've been taking those nasty prophylactic aterbrin tablets for several weeks. They should be some protection." While trying to think of a solution, she suddenly remembered two packets of American, rustproof safety pins she had bought in New York at the last minute and stuffed into the bottom of the big, catchall diaper bag just in case there was need. Well, this was trouble, and the safety pins might just save the day--or more to the point, the night.

She jumped up and threw her arms around Ernie's neck, nearly throwing him off balance as he caught her. "I've got a great idea!" she exclaimed.

"That's good, honey, but I hope all your great ideas don't hit me with so much impact," he grinned.

"Oh, be serious! I'm trying to solve a health problem. Do you remember those safety pins I bought at the last minute in New York?" She hurried on not waiting for his answer. "It may take us a while, but let's pin all the holes shut."

It took over an hour to mend all the breaks in the children's nets and that used up all the pins they had. They breathed a sigh of satisfaction as they tucked the nets securely under the mattress pads. Hopefully the slowly moving air from the ceiling fan would help to keep mosquitoes away from themselves.

With their immediate emergency solved they became aware of the increasing sounds of angry, yelling voices outside their window. Although they could not understand the languages being used, the wrath and hate were inescapable. Quickly, Ernie flipped out the light, then crossing to the window he opened the wooden shutters, which had been closed by servants earlier in the evening, and pushed back the curtains. The end of one of the cots stood partially beneath the window. Lois climbed on her knees beside Ernie to look out anxiously through the bars. The scene in the street a few feet below was bedlam. Hordes of men whirling iron bars, knives with curved blades, and cruel, long bamboo truncheons called "lathis" about their heads, seemed to be gathered into groups. The atmosphere was ominous. The Hindus were throwing red water, some laughing and taunting, and others angry and challenging.

A half hour passed with little visible change, but the couple in the darkness just inside the window could feel the growing tension. No police appeared to disperse the rabble. It was obvious that the conflict outside was building towards explosion.

"What would happen if they saw us up here?" Lois asked uneasily, shifting an uncomfortable knee from the iron rod which formed the foot of the cot. "Maybe we should close the shutters."

"Nothing would happen to us. They are too busy hating each other to care about us," commented Ernie as he slipped a reassuring arm around her. "Look out there and to your left; do you see that large group of men wearing those gray fur hats? Do you hear them? They are shouting something about Pakistan. That's the independent country the Muslims want to create instead of remaining one united India. That group is about to do something--I'm not sure what."

Instinctively Lois drew back as she noticed the group who, instead of carrying bamboo sticks and iron rods, were holding long, steel blades that flashed threateningly in the light from the street lamps. They were working their way down toward the wall near the window when one of the Hindu revelers, in a mad gesture of disrespect, threw big splashes of red water over the leading two fur-hatted men. A fierce snarl rose from the incensed group.

While Lois and Ernie watched helplessly, the two disgraced Muslims, dripping red and yelling like frontier tribesmen, grabbed the offending Hindu and dragged him from the center of the crowd toward the wall. Knives flashed. People screamed and scrambled to get out of the way of death.

Because the Moslems had dragged the Hindu directly below the Methodist House window, neither Lois nor Ernie could see what actually happened next. They heard screams of terror as people scrambled to get out of the way, and saw the long knives raised high in the air and then brought down with great force, like woodsmen wielding axes. Fighting broke out among a number of groups, and in the melee that followed, the fur-hatted knife-wielders, who had taken their revenge, melted away into the chaotic background, like striped tigers in a shady jungle.

After some time the harried mounted police arrived, whistles blowing and night sticks swinging. On this holiday night there were hundreds of disturbances throughout the city and too few police units to handle them. They rode into groups to break up the fighting, and made an effort to get the crowd moving on down the street. Observing a large group of wailing Hindus at one side, three police worked their way over toward the wall of the Methodist House. There, guarded by a number of blood-splattered men, was what appeared at first to be a crumpled bundle of bloody rags. The policemen pushed the men back with their sticks. Lois listened as they shot staccato questions at the people standing near, demanding answers that nobody seemed to have. In the end they learned very little although they had written down pages of information.

Finally the police gave permission and three men who had been standing guard when the police arrived stooped to lift the bundle of rags. As they shambled away from the wall, their clothes and hands covered with the murdered man's blood, the hanging head and the slashed throat made a grizzly midnight spectacle to the watchers in the window, unreal like a scene in a horror movie. With the police efforts the massive crowd like a mammoth juggernaut had finally started moving down the street.

Turning away from the window, Lois sank down on the bed, her face in her hands.

"Honey, how can we ever live in a country like this? What can you or I ever do to help solve problems as huge and many faceted as India has? It's one thing if you can risk something and have a chance of success, but what we've witnessed tonight makes our being here to help India seem utterly hopeless! How can we, with our college educations and our midwest, small town, American culture acquired skills, help India, when it seems she's dying from self-inflicted wounds?"

The strain in her voice brought Ernie's attention immediately back to his wife.

"Darling--aren't you forgetting a few things?" he soothed, taking her into his arms as she sobbed. At that moment she wanted nothing so much as to go back to the States on the next ship.

"What we saw tonight was brutal extremism and savage violence," Ernie continued. "Historically this has not been true of India. Comparatively speaking, it has been a gentle country. And don't forget, we are not taking on the whole job alone. God has brought us here with something specific for us to do. We don't know what it is yet--but we will know when we need to know. Remember too that there are many forces at work in this country trying to bring about peaceful change. Look at Mahatma Gandhi and his following. His message is brotherhood--and freedom--and peace, although it is not welcomed by everyone." Ernie offered her his handkerchief which she accepted gratefully.

"Come now," Ernie reasoned. "We are responsible for only what we can do to help--not to right all the wrongs of India. Look at me!" He ran his finger along her cheek. "Where is all that courage I know you have so much of?"

"It's in mighty short supply right now," Lois confessed with a weak little smile. "I know that God doesn't make mistakes, but it does seem to me that He made a mighty poor choice in choosing me for this job. I'm sure there are dozens of other people who would have been better." She sighed with a little catch in her throat.

"Oh, I don't agree with you there. God made a good choice when he chose you. The Indian people will love you because you will love them. We'll live a day at a time and have complete faith in His guidance. Now let's pray a little prayer before we sleep and leave the responsibility for helping us work things out with God." Much later they slept.

Chapter 3

—•—

Touring

It was nearly two hours after sunrise the next morning when Lois slipped out of bed, and after a quick bath and dressing in a cool cotton dress and sandals, she went to find the kitchen and boil water for Jimmy's morning formula. The kitchen was down a short hall from the dining room, and as Lois came to the door she heard a lively conversation going on in a language she couldn't understand. The cook and his helper were preparing food at a metal-topped table, while the two bearers were arranging the morning trays of orange slices, hot toast and marmalade, and tea to be served to the guests in their rooms. *That would have been nice--to have tea and toast in bed,* thought Lois as she walked over to the man who appeared to be the head cook.

When the men became aware of her presence, all activity stopped as they stared--a guest in the kitchen was still unusual. Ignoring the attention she was getting, Lois stepped over to a very old faucet above a chipped sink in the corner, laid her hand on the faucet, then pointed to a big, brass kettle steaming on a charcoal fire, and finally to herself. She felt very frustrated because she couldn't speak their language.

Immediately everyone seemed to relax. The men smiled and the head cook shook his head from side to side in that characteristic motion which Lois now recognized as 'yes.'

"Yes, you can have," he agreed, and he hurried to help her with the unwieldy, heavy pan of boiling water. Apparently he didn't mind her being in his kitchen at all.

By the time Lois returned to their room with Jimmy's warm bottle, Linda and Ernie were just finishing the food on their trays. The street outside their window seemed to have only ordinary activities and there were no traces of what had happened the night before. Ernie had called a taxi and was preparing to go to the customs offices again to check on when they might expect their luggage to be released. He glanced down a list of things that had to be done before they could leave Calcutta.

"We'll try again to find shops open where we can buy supplies, and after that we may have time to visit the botanical gardens. The one here in Calcutta is very famous because it has the largest banyan tree in the world. They say this one tree is 1,000 feet in circumference."

"May we go, Daddy?" asked Linda eagerly.

"Of course, we'll all go and take Aunt Kathryn," smiled Ernie, whose interest in nature was unbounded. Somewhere in their luggage were supplies furnished to him by the American Museum of Natural History in New York for collecting natural history specimens for the museum, and Ernie intended to add to his own collection as well through the coming years. Dr. Steggarda, his anthropology professor at Hartford, used to say, "Ernie, collect, write, keep up your interest in wildlife--it will make you a better missionary."

As Lois laid Jimmy back on his pillow and placed the bottle in his reaching hands she looked anxious. "Are you sure it's safe to take the children out after what happened last night?" she questioned as she glanced out the window at the seemingly unconcerned people going by.

Ernie picked up his briefcase and started toward the door. "You are right about not taking any chances with safety, but they told me at the office that these kinds of sporadic incidents have been occurring in Calcutta for the last three months without interrupting ordinary life and business. They say that we will be fine if we hire a taxi for the whole day and avoid dense crowds." As he pushed the door open he added, "I'll be back as soon as I can--very soon if the offices are closed."

Lois poured herself a cup of tea from the small pot on her tray, surprised that it was still quite hot. She sat down on the bed beside Linda and listened absent-mindedly as the little four year old turned the pages of her book, telling the story word for word as if she were reading. When the story and her cup of tea came to an end, she gathered together the family's dirty clothes they had worn the day before and prepared to wash them by hand in the galvanized tub in the bathroom. She was glad she still had a cake of American soap she could use. Digging in the diaper bag she located the rope that had been her clothes line all the way across the Pacific, up through the China Sea and across the Indian Ocean and the Bay of Bengal. On the Marine Jumper the steward had placed hooks so she could zigzag the rope across the cabin. She wished she had Mr. Heinz to help her for a few minutes right now. She found a slatted stool in the bathroom and by moving it around she was able to climb up and find opportune places to fasten the rope--around a bar in the high window, over the handle of a locked door, over a mirror hook, back through another window bar and onto a transom post. In the middle of all this creative activity Kathryn came in and offered to watch the children while Lois did the washing. They talked over the plans for the day and then the happenings of the night before. Kathryn had been aware of all the noise outside, but she hadn't known about the murder, although she wasn't very surprised in light of the intense animosity between the Hindus and the Muslims.

As soon as Lois finished hanging the clothes she went to the kitchen to bring food for the children's lunch. By the time Ernie returned just before the 11:00 o'clock breakfast bell, Jimmy had gone to sleep for his nap and Linda was playing with her doll.

Talk during the meal was mostly about the murder and the violence in Calcutta. Many of the guests had heard the noisy crowds in the streets, but they had been unaware that there had been a murder until their morning tea trays arrived.

"Well, I don't know what's going to happen in this country. It certainly was safer for everybody, including all the Indians, before all this push for independence," declared Mrs. Bradford, who had been living in Calcutta since the death eight years before of her husband, a British Major. "I think Mr. Gandhi is a lot to blame for making people think they could manage this country without the help of the British army. Just look what would happen if the British really turned over power to the Indians. How long do you think Europeans would be safe?" Mrs. Bradford looked very indignant just thinking about it.

Janice Trent, a middle-aged Australian missionary nurse who had arrived at the Mission House from up country the evening before, shook her head doubtfully. "That isn't true in our area--Gandhi's influence has been a moderating one, channeling potential violence into peaceful efforts. It's the radical elements that are causing the trouble. These young men seem to resent Mr. Gandhi and his nonviolent approach. They say that if everyone followed Gandhi, India would never gain her independence."

"I realize that these are troubled times, but I wish we could depend more on the loyalty of our own people," complained Mrs. Delmont who had been staying at the Mission House for over a year supposedly making arrangements to return to England. The plans never seemed to work out. "Servants are so unreliable. Why, I heard that our own gatekeeper here was found asleep this morning at 4:00 o'clock! Why, we might all have been murdered in our beds!"

Deciding that it was time for a change in the topic of conversation, Mrs. Smythe commented dryly, "Oh, I don't think we were in any danger. I would have disliked missing the afternoon tea next Tuesday at the Heatherston bungalow. They say Mrs. Heatherston is very charming. She has just come out from London to join her husband, who is a Captain stationed here in Calcutta, you know, and we are all invited to her tea."

The Americans, being newcomers, took no part in this conversation, and were relieved when the meal was finished. They were ready half an hour later when the taxi which they had hired for the day arrived, and armed with a lunch and an extra baby bottle, they headed toward the botanical gardens. When Lois noticed that their driver was another turbaned, bearded Sikh, she was glad. Like their driver from the docks, he proved to be a congenial, English-speaking tour guide, familiar with all parts of the city and its history and traditions. Ernie sat in the front with him and carried on a running conversation, enjoyable and informative. As they drove out through the Mission House gates, the driver asked permission to take them past a few of the famous places in Calcutta before they went on to the gardens.

"I am Padam Singh," he informed them as he swung the car out into the traffic. "I tell you everything!" His excitement and enthusiasm were infectious. "We go past the finest building in all of Bengal--The Victoria Memorial. All people want to see."

The taxi turned into streets so crowded it was impossible to move forward with any speed. The evidence of poverty and overcrowding assailed their senses--pressing mobs, streetcars with passengers clinging outside the windows and doors, sidewalk hydrants where naked children were bathing, grand old houses carved into tenement warrens. Bamboo and tarpaulin lean-tos built against walls and buildings were covered with a patina of filth. Here and there shrouded, still forms of sleepers lay on the sidewalks or in stairways. As they turned into a dark, narrow street, almost like an alley, they saw old women sitting motionless, their frail arms holding begging cups. As their taxi was forced to stop by the shrill whistle of a uniformed traffic officer, allowing the heterogeneous traffic to move a cross direction, two congenitally deformed beggars, misshapen and mute, shuffled up to the windows on either side of the car.

As Ernie reached in his pocket for some coins, Mr. Singh held up his hand in warning. "Don't give money here or there will be many more climb on taxi--not go away."

"Jao. Jao." he yelled at the beggars shaking his fist in the air. Just then the light changed, and seemingly with no thought for the beggars, the driver sent the car forward with a jerk.

Lois looked quickly through the back window to see if anyone had been hurt. They seemed to be uninjured, however, for they were hurrying to the window of another car.

"These conditions are terrible," she exclaimed. "Mr. Singh, isn't anyone trying to help those poor people?"

The driver shook his head from side to side in agreement. "Yes, many people help, but there are too many beggars. Hindus give money to make their gods happy. Soon we finish this street and come to Victoria Memorial."

And, sure enough, as they turned the corner a dazzling scene stretched before them. Across an open, green "maidan," with a beautiful fountain playing in its center, stood a magnificent, marble palace, a monument to Calcutta's British past. There was a huge, central dome surrounded by colonnades, with a winged figure on its peak. Nestled just below the colonnades forming the four corners, slightly smaller domes, pointing their marble peaks to the sky reminded Lois of pictures she had seen of the magnificent Taj Mahal. The pool surrounding the playing fountain reflected like a mirror the detail of its beauty.

The Americans gazed in awe at the majestic structure, its impact greater because of the streets of squalor through which they had just passed.

"That is truly a beautiful structure," Ernie said as he gazed at the domes gleaming like giant pearls in the sun. He turned to the smiling Indian driver. "You can be proud of such a fine national monument."

Mr. Singh looked pleased, and yet his expression showed doubt. "You Americans?" he asked irrelevantly.

"Yes, we are from the United States," Ernie answered, wondering what the connection was.

"British people not like Americans. They rule their country and they rule our country. They build nice places and do some nice things. But this is our country--they should go home now." The driver was earnestly trying to get them to understand the Indian point of view."

Ernie thought a moment. This was hardly the time for a political discussion, and yet he wanted to assure Mr. Singh of their sympathy with the Indian cause.

"I have a feeling, Mr. Singh, that the time when India will be independent is not many months away. Mr. Gandhi is a great leader--I hope the people of India will follow his teachings about nonviolence."

The Sikh turned to look at Ernie, his eyebrows raised questioningly. "Maybe," he responded enigmatically.

Ernie glanced over his shoulder to see how the children were doing and noticed that they were getting restless. "I wish we had time to go inside to see the historical exhibits here, but the children would get too tired. I think we had better go to the botanical gardens now."

"Yes," smiled Padam Singh, shaking his head from side to side. "Now we go."

Twenty minutes later they arrived at the arched, iron grilled gates to the Municipal Botanical Gardens of Calcutta. Leaving the driver outside to guard the taxi, Ernie, carrying Jimmy, and Lois and Kathryn with Linda between them, entered the gates through an arbor of dark red bougainvillea blossoms.

It was like stepping into a different world--shady, quiet, and cool--with overhead foliage so dense above the red dirt road that it formed a wide, green tunnel. Here and there an occasional ray of saffron sunlight filtered through, catching the brilliance of an iridescent butterfly or the flash of a blossom-headed parakeet. Eventually the foliage thinned, and they walked along a moss-covered, stone wall that had been built to separate what proved to be a special garden from the more wooded areas. As they watched, a rhesus monkey came running along the top of the old wall, his long tail arched behind him. He stopped for a moment silhouetted against the sky and chattered at them in a friendly way.

Linda was fascinated by the monkey. "Is he talking to us, Aunt Kathryn? What do you think he's saying?"

"I wish I knew, Linda. Maybe he's telling us the latest garden gossip. He looks as though he would know everything that happens around here," smiled Kathryn.

A swinging gate in the wall led them into a formal garden, its colorful flower beds planned and balanced, its shrubs trimmed and regular and its wide, grassy areas shining like emerald carpets in the late afternoon sun. In the center of the garden stood a white, latticed gazebo, inviting them to rest a while and enjoy the beauty around them.

"What a perfect place to have our picnic," exclaimed Lois, and everyone agreed. Their food was delicious, and the water from their canteens satisfying, even though it was very warm. In the distance the regular *tuk-tuk-tuk* of the coppersmith, like the tap of a small hammer on metal, rang out monotonously in the afternoon heat. A few other people were beginning to come to the gardens, now that it was mid afternoon.

On a wooden stand under glass they were delighted to find a picture of the famous banyan tree and a map showing just how to reach it. Fortunately it was not far from the gazebo.

Ten minutes later they came to the outer trunks of the tree. It was like a gigantic umbrella having two hundred thirty handles extending down to the ground, with a main trunk thirty feet in diameter. There was very little undergrowth, but many long, trailing aerial roots of various lengths which had not yet reached the ground, and if these living ropes were not cut off, they would become more trunks. The fascinated Americans strolled among its trunks, staying on the clearly marked paths. It was like being in an enchanted forest.

"Do you know how the banyan tree got its name?" asked Kathryn as she smiled down at Linda's eager face.

"No, how? Is it a story?" Linda was always ready for a story.

"Just a little story. You see, for many hundreds of years this kind of tree has been the favorite of the merchants, who are called banyas, for outdoor shops. They gather under these trees and spread out whatever they have to sell; then they can sit cross-legged on the ground in the shade and wait for customers. So they named the tree after the banyas."

"Ernie, I think it is time we are going. It's a shame to leave the gardens when there is still so much to see--but we can never see it all," said Lois regretfully as she looked at Jimmy asleep in Ernie's arms.

"Yes, we don't dare stay longer if we are to be ready for dinner. Maybe someday we can come back and see the rest." Ernie took a deep breath. "What a shame to be so near such a great source of knowledge about nature and not be able to really study it."

They found their taxi driver squatting under a tree, carrying on a relaxed conversation with several men while he waited patiently for their return. He opened the car door with a smile, and they were soon on their way back to the Mission House.

The next morning, when the freshly starched and white-clad bearer brought their tea trays, they learned that most of the shops were open and they could purchase the supplies they needed for their two-and-a-half-day train trip across India to Bombay. It was decided that Ernie would stay with the children while Lois and Kathryn went shopping, a job Ernie was happy to avoid. They would return by 11:00 a.m., the time the customs offices usually opened, give or take a half hour--and Ernie and Kathryn would try again to get their luggage released.

After a quick, cooling, pour-on bath, Lois dried herself with the Indian-milled cotton towel. A gentle breeze was blowing through the high window, wafting the sweet scent of jasmine into the room. She dressed hastily in a cotton blouse and skirt, ran a comb through her hair and picked up her purse and the list of things she needed to get.

Ernie looked concerned as he kissed her goodbye. "Mornings in Calcutta seem to be the time of day when the streets are the most free of political activities, but be careful. Just follow Kathryn's advice."

A few minutes later Kathryn and Lois were in a taxi, which had been called by the office, and heading toward a street where they could find leather goods, bedding rolls and luggage in general. Scantily clad men were pushing long, two wheeled carts of supplies; others were carrying great head loads. Another man had so many empty baskets tied together that they extended out from him on all sides, making him look like a giant basket with legs. Horse-drawn victorias were standing here and there, waiting for the day to advance and business to pick up.

When they arrived in the street of the luggage sellers, Lois and Kathryn told the taxi driver to wait while they went inside. It was early enough that some shopkeepers were just raising the huge, metal sliding doors that covered the whole fronts of their shops.

"Come. Come." invited the shopkeeper from the wooden step of the first shop where they stopped. "What you want? Come see. I have plenty." Smiling broadly, he stepped back into his shop to make room for them. Brown leather suitcases of several sizes were stacked along two walls all the way to the ceiling. Along the back wall was piled luggage made of other materials. Down the center of the shop was a long table heaped with rolls of canvas lashed with wide, strong, leather straps and sturdy buckles.

This must be what we are looking for, thought Lois as she followed Kathryn over to the table. Kathryn began pushing the rolls around, examining them carefully. Some were a tan color and others were a dull army green.

"May we see one of these open, please?" she asked, touching one of the large, tan ones.

"Oh, yes. You like this one?" He hastened to loosen the straps and spread out the six-foot-long envelope-like canvas. "This one very good--very cheap today--you my first customer. I give you good price."

Lois watched as Kathryn examined it again very carefully. It was stitched well, the edges bound throughout with soft leather. The straps were strong with no thin places and the buckles were not rusted, as sometimes happened when merchandise had been held over a monsoon.

Finally Kathryn looked at the merchant. "How much?" she asked.

The anxious expression on the shopkeeper's face disappeared and he smiled broadly. "For you--only twenty five rupees. Very cheap,"

"Oh, my!" exclaimed Kathryn. "That's too much." She hesitated. "We will give you ten rupees for one."

"No, no. My cost is more."

"We will buy two for ten rupees each," pursued Kathryn.

"Maybe, for my first customer, I give you special price--20 rupees for one."

"Your price is still too much for us. We will give fifteen rupees for one--you see, we need to buy five of them. But if that is below your cost, then we will look somewhere else," and Kathryn began pushing the bedding roll away from her, preparing to leave the shop.

"Wait. I give you at my cost price--eighteen rupees for one. You want five, no?" The shop-keeper was anxious to close the deal.

"All right, we will pay eighteen rupees for each one, but I want to choose five of your best."

Lois began to understand why shopping in India was going to be a very time-consuming job. Kathryn scrutinized each bedding roll warily, assuring Lois that just because one article was well made, didn't mean that the others would be.

After they had paid their bill and the merchant had cordially invited them back, declaring that they were among his favorite customers, Kathryn motioned to a ragged boy balancing a big, empty basket on his head, who was standing at the foot of the steps hoping to be called. He scrambled up the steps and quickly loaded their purchases into his basket. He followed Lois and Kathryn across the wide sidewalk to the waiting taxi and loaded them carefully into the boot, which had been unlocked by the driver. Kathryn tipped the boy and they pulled away from the curb.

Throughout the morning the taxi driver took them from one street to another where they could find the articles they needed; thin mattress pads to fit into the five bedding rolls, two rough, cotton sheets for each mattress pad, a small pillow and pillow case for each, mosquito nets, and a light, cotton blanket for each one just in case the air might grow chilly during the night. Lois couldn't see how that could possibly be, considering how hot it had been in Calcutta every night since they had arrived. They purchased flashlights, canteens, and white pith hats called topees with dark, green under-brims to cut the glare of the tropical sun. Finally, Lois insisted on buying a bottle of Lysol, determined to disinfect all surfaces that the children might touch inside the train car. Keeping things sanitary was a number one priority at all times, and this precaution along with plenty of soap and water should do very well.

Lois and Kathryn arrived back at Mission House with their purchases in time for the 11:00 o'clock meal. Ernie had already fed the children, who were delighted with their new topees. Linda wanted to wear hers all the time, but Jimmy liked best taking his off and beating on the top to hear the hollow sound it made. While Linda danced around the room in her new headgear, Jimmy pounded and squealed with delight.

"What's going on in here?" laughed Kathryn, stopping on her way to the dining room.

"Let's just say it's musical talent in the bud--very much in the bud," replied Ernie, holding his ears.

It took Ernie and Kathryn the whole afternoon to get through the red tape at the customs office; waiting on smalltime officials, checking over lists of luggage, sorting out the pieces that they felt they must have as soon as they reached their stations, and piling them to one side to be taken with them on the train across India, the rest to be shipped directly to Palghar where it hopefully would arrive within the next six weeks or two months. Finally by six o'clock everything was cleared except the final release, which they could pick up the next day at four in the afternoon, along with the luggage they would be taking with them.

That evening before dinner Ernie and Lois were sitting with the children on the stone bench under the gold mahor tree in the Mission House compound, enjoying the breath of cooler air that had come with the setting sun. A pair of common mynah birds ran about on the other side of the tree, carrying on a friendly conversation, nodding their heads and occasionally giving each other an affectionate peck. Their calls were a mixture of harsh gurglings and liquid notes. So self-confident were they that they ignored Linda who was scurrying here and there gathering up bean pods and stacking them on the bench beside Lois.

Several other people came into the garden to stroll among the flower beds. Kathryn and her missionary-nurse roommate, Janice Trent, came by and stopped to talk a minute.

"Kathryn has been telling me about some of the sightseeing you have been doing. There is so much of interest to see in Calcutta," Janice commented.

Lois moved Linda's pile of bean pods over. "Sit down a little while. It's really quite comfortable here," invited Lois. "There is so much here to see--and we are leaving the day after tomorrow; and, too, I have a concern about taking the children out so much in this terrible heat."

Janice nodded her head. "I'm sure you are right about that, but there's one sight you should see before you leave, and that is the early morning Hindu worship on the banks of the Ganges. If you would like, I could stay with the children and feed them while you three go there in the morning. I've finished the work I had to do for the hospital, and my train doesn't leave until tomorrow evening; anyway, I'd enjoy staying with Linda and Jimmy."

"Janice, that's an excellent suggestion," Kathryn agreed. "And it's mighty nice of you to offer to stay with the children. Ernie? Lois? What do you think? There's no one who could give the children better care than Janice. And I do think that you could learn a lot by seeing the early morning worshippers at the river."

Lois checked down a mental list of things that had to be done on their last day in Calcutta and decided that they would not be too rushed in the afternoon if they took the proposed trip to the river in the morning. They might never have such a wonderful opportunity again and she was excited at the prospect.

"What do you think, Ernie? I can manage what I have to do if you can." She felt excited.

"Sounds great. I wouldn't miss it." Ernie smiled. He was feeling more confident about moving about in the city, now that the Holi festival was drawing toward its close, although British troops and Indian troops were very much in evidence most everywhere.

It was decided that they would leave at 5:00 a.m. the next day, and Ernie went to arrange for a taxi.

They were pleased the next morning to find Padam Singh, their former Sikh taxi driver, waiting for them in the office, radiating self-confidence.

"Salaam," he smiled in greeting as he bowed with his hands together in front of him. "Where you want to go? I take you. I know about everything."

Upon being told that they wanted to see some Hindu temples and the early worshippers at the river, he exclaimed, "I know many places. I show you."

Even at that early hour there were many people on the streets: some were brushing their teeth, gums and tongue with neem twigs; others were squatting to relieve themselves. Lois noticed many women sitting on the cement walkway--their temporary homes by right of occupancy--nursing their babies or tending small fires under cooking pots. Some people were still curled up asleep on the hard street, sometimes with a thin piece of dirty cloth over their heads and faces.

As they neared the river, traffic in the street became heavier--people walking, a few with better dress riding in rickshaws, two-wheeled tongas, cart loads of merchandise, and cows wandering everywhere as if aware of their respected status.

Padam Singh parked the taxi on the left beside an empty tonga. The horse was lazily pulling some hay from a small pile that had been provided. Not far away lounged the driver, having a cup of hot tea while he waited patiently.

"I wait for you. Only walking people can go from here. The river is just there." He pointed down the street ahead of them.

"Here, boy." He motioned to a twelve-year-old boy who materialized from somewhere. "You show them all the river and show them Hindu temples." Padam Singh gave the boy a gentle shove toward the Americans. He beamed as though he had solved all their problems. "This boy my friend--he know much--he live here."

Padam Singh was right--the boy was very knowledgeable. With a deep desire to observe everything and to understand, Lois, Ernie and Kathryn followed the boy, mingling with the pilgrims who were on their way to bathe in the sacred Ganges, to worship and to have their sins washed away. The street terminated in a number of flights of steps that led down to the water. The entire bank of the river was steps with a wide level area between flights. On these levels "box wallas"--merchants who could carry everything they had to sell in a box on their backs--had spread out their merchandise. They sold things that the pilgrims might need for their worship: flowers, brass and pottery cups for pouring water on one's head, sacred turmeric, oil lamps made of clay, rice, and even small containers with tight lids that could be used for carrying away some of the sacred Ganges water to keep forever.

Ernie, Lois, Kathryn, and the boy went down one flight of steps and watched pilgrims going up and down, and bathing in the shallow water at the edge of the wide, muddy river. There was no doubt of their sincerity nor of their great yearning to know God. The boy pointed to an old man lying on the steps not far from them. He looked to be very sick. When Kathryn questioned the boy in Hindi, he told her that the man was from far away and his friends had brought him to the Ganges where he could bathe in the sacred river before he died. He had bathed the day before, now he was waiting to die. The boy pointed to the west a short distance where a small, rectangular structure about waist high had been built on the very edge of the water. Smoke was rising from it and a few people were gathered around it.

"That is the burning ghat," the boy informed Kathryn. "Many times a day there is fire. Sometimes people have to wait." He pointed to two wrapped objects lying on the steps nearby.

Lois shuddered. She felt repelled, for to her Western eyes the custom seemed heartless. "Why do they do this?" she cried.

"Why not?" asked Kathryn quickly. "The fact is that it is a very sensible custom for this country. India needs all the land to grow food for an ever-increasing population and it wouldn't be very wise to use it for burying the dead." There was no disputing her logic. "Unfortunately, sometimes the family has so little money that they can't buy enough wood to burn the body completely, so instead of scattering only ashes on the river, they push everything that remains into the water. That adds to the filth of this churning Hooghly mouth of the Ganges."

"Look out toward the middle of the stream. Do you see what looks like a log bobbing along?" Ernie pointed down river toward the east where after a moment the others were able to distinguish a long object that would appear and then disappear as the current moved toward the Bay. "It makes you wonder," Ernie said, "whether it's a log or--something else, doesn't it?"

It was nearly sunrise and yellow, orange, and red shafts of light were flooding the eastern sky. Silhouetted against that colorful curtain rose the domes and towers of hundreds of Hindu temples, ancient and mysterious, housing gurus and idols not only of the most popular gods of Hinduism, but those of hundreds of lesser gods and their cults. It made a beautiful scene--a world to be discovered--a people and a culture to learn to understand.

Lois turned and started an irregular course back up the flight of steps, moving aside for worshippers--some standing and praying, others sitting motionless as if they were a part of the landscape. The other three followed. "Could we go to see some of the temples now, Kathryn? I hope we will be allowed to go inside."

With their small, competent guide moving ahead of them, they walked through the streets of the temples, narrow and dark and crooked, the open drains running along the sides smelling of urine and gutter filth. The series of open doorways looked like shops getting ready for business, but more than half of them were entrances to temples, with large images of deities standing four or five feet tall in the dim recesses of the interiors, decorated with gold and silver, and laden with tinsel garlands that reflected an alien ray of light now and then.

Lois stepped across the drain to a doorway on her left that was painted a bright blue in an effort to see more clearly what was inside. A holy man wearing a knee-length cloth tied around his waist and a sacred cord across his chest, his hair long and straggly and his forehead marked with painted lines, was eating food with his fingers from a brass bowl. Scattered on the floor were grass mats, and to the back of the room was a doorway draped with a length of cotton cloth, perhaps masking living quarters for the holy man, thought Lois.

With an eye to business the guru set aside his eating bowl and picked up another bowl from in front of the image. Rising gracefully from his cross-legged position he stepped to the doorway and held out the bowl, saying something which Lois couldn't understand, but his meaning was clear. Lois shook her head slightly as she moved with the others on down the street.

Some of the doorways were food shops from which delicious smells of spicy foods reached them. Apparently many people lived in the back regions of these streets, for there were so many people and animals it was difficult to move forward. At one point a big Brahma bull came pushing through the narrow path. Lois flattened herself against the wall of a building as he swerved toward her, his big horns looking dangerous. His distended side brushed against her as he moved on by, eager to snatch morning handouts from devout shop keepers.

Just ahead Ernie, Kathryn, and their guide had stopped to talk to a man who stood on a wooden step that led into a temple dedicated to Krishna. His head was shaved and the cloth draped around his waist and through his legs forming a dhoti was shining white. In his hand he held a brass water bowl.

Lois heard him say in perfect English, "You are travelers from America. Are you too trying to reach God?" He addressed his question to Ernie, assuming that the man in the group spoke for everyone.

"We are Christians," Ernie answered. "We believe in one God, and we travel the way to Him shown us by Jesus Christ."

The Hindu nodded his head thoughtfully. "I have heard about Jesus Christ--he was a great prophet. I, too, am seeking to know God. I travel the way of Krishna. Yes, there is only one great God and his name is Om." Sincerity and devotion shown in his face. "May we meet again," he continued as he stepped down into the street, "and may you become one with Om." After delivering this blessing, he moved with other worshippers toward the river.

Their young guide looked after the Hindu admiringly. "He is very great man. He used to be very rich merchant, but now he is very poor. He gave his money to his family and now for many months he prays and does his worship by Mother Ganges. He is getting ready to die sometime and he wants to know God."

"Will he ever go back to his family?" asked Lois.

"No, he will not go back. He thinks only of Om."

They followed the boy on down the narrow street until they came to a more open area. Here visions of religious piety merged with those of political turmoil. The Kali Temple stood on one side occupying a much larger space than the one-room temples they had been seeing. As they stepped inside they saw a very large figure of the black goddess Kali, and to one side priests were sacrificing goats, and tossing the heads into a pile for the poor--the donors were retrieving the carcasses. Just outside the temple was a spiny tree where barren women were tying stones in quest of fruitfulness. Portraits of Mahatma Gandhi were in abundance with the inscription "Gandhi ki jai" (victory to Gandhi) or "Hindustan ki jai" (victory to India). Some places there were pictures of Mohammed Ali Jinnah with their inscriptions of "Pakistan zindabad!" ("Long live Pakistan!")

Reluctantly they realized that it was time for them to be getting back to the mission, for there were still things that had to be done in preparation for leaving the next day. Their guide took them a short cut through two other streets and miraculously they arrived back at their taxi. Padam Singh, who had been drowsing under a huge neem tree, smiled broadly to see them and opened the taxi doors. They thanked their young guide and tipped him generously for his knowledge and helpfulness.

Suddenly, as their taxi was about to pull out into the street, two crowded trucks swung down the road. In one a great Durga (fertility) image swayed and rocked against her lashings. In the other stood the lesser images of Laxshmi (wealth), Ganesha (elephant god), Hanuman (monkey god), and Saraswati (goddess of wisdom).

"What's happening, Mr. Singh? Where are they taking those images." Ernie watched curiously out his window as the trucks swerved to avoid three children.

"I think they go to the river to throw them in the water. It is the way they worship. Most days many people watch--today not many people for some say the Muslims are going to throw bombs to stop the worship. I think we go now--no?" and Padam Singh shook his head from side to side as the taxi moved forward.

The three passengers were quiet on their way back to the Methodist House, each wondering if India would be able to avert civil war, even if they did gain independence from the British.

> "THOU HAST MADE ME KNOWN TO FRIENDS WHOM I KNEW NOT.
> THOU HAST BROUGHT THE DISTANT NEAR AND MADE A BROTHER OF THE STRANGER."
> *Rabindranath Tagore*

Chapter 4

Off to Bombay

As the first sunlight struck the waxy, orange-red blossoms of the gold mahor tree in the Mission House garden, Lois lay relaxed on her cot, absent-mindedly watching the blades of the overhead fan move around. Mentally she checked over her list of last-minute things to be done before they were to leave for the train.

Yesterday, after they had returned from their trip to the Ganges River, she had secured the cook's help in procuring two large, earthen pots with lids, and preparing them for use. After being thoroughly washed they had stood all night with drinking water in them and the cook had promised that this morning he would empty them and refill them with fresh drinking water for their use on the way. The problem of clean baby bottles and boiled water for making formula had been solved by purchasing an aluminum teakettle which could be taken directly to the steam locomotive during one of the long, fifteen-minute station stops and filled with scalding hot water--all the comforts of home, thought Lois with a smile. It seemed that there was usually some way of solving difficult problems if one used a bit of ingenuity.

Ernie and Kathryn had been able to clear the last of the luggage late in the afternoon, and it was stacked now down by the office, waiting to be loaded shortly into their taxis.

The arrival of the morning trays interrupted her planning. Cook had added a bowl of cereal for each one of them, along with the usual tea, fruit and toast. What a considerate thing for him to do, thought Lois, as she jumped out of bed to begin a busy and exciting day.

An hour and a half later, after they had paid their bill and had received rather stiff good wishes for a pleasant journey from Mrs. Smythe, Cook came hurrying into the office with a large package wrapped in newspaper and tied with many strands of white thread.

"Here . . .for the little ones. . .clean food." He smiled broadly as he touched Jimmy's blond curls.

"Thank you so much, Cook ... for the food, but also for all the help you've given us. You have been a good friend." Lois remembered to fold her hands in front of her and bow in Indian fashion.

A few minutes later, squeezed into three taxis laden with several suitcases on the tops, they pulled through the iron gates for the last time and headed toward the train station.

It was still only a little after 9:00 a.m. as they rounded a very busy corner and came within sight of the railroad station--a large, impressive building constructed by the British to accommodate efficient movement of large groups of people such as troops. Activity was heavy even at that early hour, and as their taxis slowed down to pull into the designated space near the entrance, coolies came running hopefully from every side. Holding onto the sides of the taxis, they trotted along with the now creeping vehicles, shouting through the open windows, "Me, Madam Sahib! Me! Me, Sahib!" When the taxis stopped, Ernie managed to push his door open and step out. He placed his hand on the shoulder of one especially loud and fiery-eyed coolie, then holding up six fingers, he motioned for him to choose six more, which he did with great authority, yelling at the others to go away.

During this excitement the crowd had moved away from the other two taxis and Lois, with Jimmy's, and Kathryn, with Linda's hand firmly in hers were able to get out. Other people, too, were alighting from taxis, horse-drawn victorias and bullock-drawn carts; the amount of the luggage they were unloading and the way it was packed in bags or even four-cornered, thin cloths tied together by the corners, amazed Lois. The shrill voices of excited women, their bangles tinkling musically as they gave directions and managed children and baggage, mingled with the shouts of men and the wailing of a baby. Here and there among the people and vehicles unloading on the wide, dusty area in front of the station, she could see a few cows, even a goat or two waiting to grab banana peelings thrown down by people.

Vendors were moving about, selling food and trinkets, and near them a monkey man was beating on his drum, making a small, wizened-faced rhesus macaque dance about and hold out a cup for money.

The designated coolies unloaded the three taxis and Ernie paid the drivers while the head coolie divided up the pieces of baggage into seven piles. He supervised the loading of a trunk and at least one suitcase on each man's head, and then pushed high on their upraised arms any baggage with handles, as they used their arms to steady their head loads. Lois carried Jimmy and the big diaper bag, Kathryn carried several handbags and held Linda's hand, and Ernie carried a suitcase and managed the tickets and reservations.

As soon as the head coolie learned what train they were taking, he led the way through the station entrance, across a great waiting room, weaving his way through groups of people sitting or lying on the floor, to gate four; and like a great caravan crossing the desert, each camel swaying along carrying an incredibly enormous load, they all followed single file. They trailed through the gate, past a great, noisy, puffing engine and down a long line of brown, shuttered train cars, still dripping water from having been scrubbed out from their last run. The cars were marked first, second, or third class. On the outside of the reserved first class cars were posted the names of people who held the reservations.

Ernie located their reservation nine cars from the engine, a long way to have to go to get boiling water from the engine, but a good location for escaping the smoke and cinders that would come from the burning coal.

Ernie opened the door and climbed inside and then turned to help the coolie, who had followed him, set his head load on the floor. One by one the other coolies followed and were helped to unload. While the coolie in charge with short, authoritative commands supervised the stowing away of luggage under the three double decker berths, the placing of the two water pots under the fold-down table, and stacking the remaining pieces neatly at the end of the car, the women and children waited outside. The other coolies squatted patiently to one side, waiting for their leader to finish negotiations and pay them for their work.

As Lois and Kathryn with the children ascended the car steps, the coolie was opening the shutters outside the iron barred windows to allow more circulation of air. Using the colorless cloth he had formerly wound into a doughnut and placed on top of his head under the trunks, he energetically flipped off any dust that might be on the leather-upholstered benches and finally turned on the overhead fan. Then he turned expectantly toward the American Sahib.

Ernie had consulted with Kathryn about how much should be paid per piece of luggage. They had decided that four annas was the goal, but much bargaining had to be done before the coolies would feel happy with the final result, which must not be too much or too little.

Ernie started the exchange by offering two annas per package, while the coolie asked eight, no doubt adding on a couple of annas because his customer was an American. Then he offered four annas and the coolie eventually came down to six. After a time Ernie went to each coolie and handed him a rupee.

"That's enough." He turned away hoping that would conclude negotiations.

With a show of reluctance each coolie except the head coolie accepted his money, and winding around their hands the dirty, off-color cloths used for padding and balancing head loads, they climbed down from the car smiling. But the rupee paid to the head coolie, who squatted on his heels, relaxed as if he intended to make the entire journey with them to Bombay, lay on the floor in front of him like a worthless, untouchable object beneath his notice.

Realizing that this process might go on for some time yet, Lois dug out the bottle of Lysol and an old cloth from the bottom of the diaper bag and began washing off one of the leather covered berths, the window sills, the iron bars and the wall of the car. Very quickly one berth was ready for the children. Slipping off the children's shoes, the Shulls and Kathryn set the children down. Jimmy climbed up to the window and began pounding on the bars and squealing good-naturedly at the milling platform crowds outside. Linda sat quietly holding her doll, listening to the bargaining process, her blue eyes wide.

Eventually Ernie turned to the waiting coolie and said, as if he had just come to that conclusion, "All right. I'll give you just four annas more." He dug in his pocket for a four-anna piece and handed it to the coolie.

"Thank you, Sahib," smiled the coolie as he rose and walked to the door, pleased that already that morning he had earned the current daily wage and it was still early. Everyone seemed to be satisfied.

By the time that Lois and Kathryn had finished cleaning the benches and the little bathroom, and Ernie had gone down to the engine to get acquainted with the engineer and bring back some boiling water in the aluminum teakettle, it was nearing the time for the train to pull. The platform was filled with last-minute activity. Dozens of people were milling about, some waiting until the last minute to board and others lingering to say a final goodbye. Coolies pushing long, two-wheeled carts loaded with luggage, were moving rapidly down the long line of cars in search of a reservation number for a late passenger. As Lois watched out the window, a group of people hurried up to their car and tried to open the door, then banged on it with their fists demanding to be let in, but they had locked their doors just as the train guard had instructed them to do. With violent factions of both Muslims and Hindus attacking trains, this was the only safe way for Americans to travel. The train was not actually under guard, but there were a number of Indian army men in two of the cars, among them a few English officers. After a few minutes the pounding on their door stopped and the newcomers hurried along to try another car.

She noticed with interest another group of people moving toward the adjoining car. They seemed to be focused on a well-built man dressed in loose pajama pants, a collarless, loose sleeved shirt, and a Gandhi cap, all made of the patriotic homespun cloth. Around his neck were piled garlands of roses and gardenias. The man smiled as he held his hands folded in front of himself in an expression of gratitude for their good wishes. As the final signal was given and the train lurched into motion, he and his party stepped up into the car. People continued to wave a lingering farewell as the train moved out.

"I wonder who that could be," mused Lois. "No doubt someone very important. Did you recognize him, Kathryn?"

"No, not really." Kathryn had been watching from another window. "He is dressed like a prominent member of the Congress Party. Since that big incident when Gandhi encouraged people to burn cloth imported from England, the party has considered it patriotic to wear only khadi cloth because it is spun by hand in India and gives people work. He might be traveling to New Delhi for a political meeting. Congressmen now are spending all their time and effort to bring about swaraj--Indian independence."

As the train picked up speed, people, animals, and vendors whizzed by until they were only a blur. Lois felt herself begin to relax--two and a half days ahead of them with nothing to do but care for the children, keep the food and water clean, watch the people and the scenery, buy every newspaper they could get, discuss with others what might lie ahead for India, and their work in the Mission, and to try to stay cool in the scorching, hot season sun--for pre-monsoon weather is the most uncomfortable time of the year.

At the moment, however, the most pressing need was to feed the children, for it was already past Jimmy's feeding time and he had been most patient. Using some of the hot water in the teakettle that Ernie had brought from the engine, she mixed the formula and poured it into the bottle. With his teddy bear in one hand and his bottle in the other, Jimmy settled down on his berth quickly, and when the bottle was empty, he was asleep. Linda helped her mother open the package of food from the Mission House--jelly sandwiches, hard-boiled eggs, and oranges--and they all settled down to enjoy it.

Suddenly, as Lois was about to take a bite of her sandwich, she uttered an exclamation as she sat bolt upright staring at Ernie in dismay.

"Oh, no, how could we!" she wailed.

Ernie jumped to his feet and came over to her. "What, honey. What have we done?"

Kathryn looked anxious and Linda took hold of her mother's skirt.

Lois pulled Ernie down beside her and looked with consternation into his concerned eyes. "It isn't what we've done exactly--it's what we didn't do! We forgot to take all of our New York, rustproof safety pins out of those holey, old nets at the Methodist House! Oh, dear!"

Ernie stared at her for a moment, then burst out laughing as he pulled her into his arms pretending to comfort her for her great loss. "Is that all? I thought we had done something terrible like forgetting a piece of luggage or losing our passports," he teased. By this time Kathryn was laughing too.

Half in irritation Lois pushed him away, then she remarked with a grin, "Anyway, I'll bet you'll be sorry at some future date when I'm not able to hold things together because I don't have those safety pins."

"Don't worry," soothed Kathryn. "You can buy safety pins in Bombay--of course, they don't have very sharp points and they aren't rustproof, so just don't forget and leave a pin in cloth during the monsoon, but millions of Indian people seem to be getting along all right. Just tell yourself it will help you to find more indigenous ways of doing things."

The next two and a half days were miserable for everyone because of the intense heat which was like an inescapable, solid force pushing in on them from all sides. Those who could perspire freely were the most comfortable, but Lois wasn't one of them. She felt dizzy and saw black before her eyes if she sat up on her berth too quickly. With the setting of the sun came cooler evening breezes and the return of appetites and a renewed interest in the world outside their windows.

Although they had read everything they could and had thought themselves informed, nothing could have prepared them for the reality--the sheer immensity--of the dusty plains stretching away on either side of the track; the glimpses of villages unchanged for millennia, where life moved at the speed of a bullock cart, the endless crowds of people and animals traveling along the brown highways creating their own little clouds of dust with every step. Late in the afternoon they crossed from Bengal into the State of Bihar, and later that night into Orissa.

On that first day as the afternoon waned, Ernie jumped down from the upper berth where he had been sleeping with a little individual fan turned directly upon him, and opened one of the shutters by a lower berth. The train was just pulling into a station called Jamshedpur. Even before the train had stopped, a young man wearing a khaki-colored, short-sleeved shirt with brass buttons had jumped on the side of the car and was smiling through the window. "Garam Cha, Sahib?"

"Is it very hot?" Ernie asked

"Very hot," assured the vendor as he peered into the car. "How many you want?"

"Three cups then--no, make it four," Ernie ordered remembering that Linda was awake.

The cha walla, as Kathryn called him, disappeared instantly from their view, but he was back very quickly with four cups and saucers and a steaming kettle of tea. As he filled each cup he passed it through the bars of the window, and Ernie handed it to Lois who set it on their folding table at the end of the car. The boy held out his hand and Ernie dropped eight annas into it.

"Cha-a-a-a, Garam Cha-a-a-a," sang out the vendor as he moved on to the next car.

"You can depend on train-platform tea being nearly boiling hot," Kathryn commented as she poured some of the fragrant liquid over the side of the cup into the saucer, swished it around a bit and then dumped the still-steaming tea out the window, a procedure aimed at making the cup and saucer more sanitary. Picking up Linda's cup of tea, Lois followed Kathryn's example, then poured more tea into the saucer to cool it before she held it to Linda's lips. The little girl cautiously took a sip and then smiled, her face sweaty and smudged black with train cinders and her dress wet and clinging as she finished her cup of tea. Interestingly enough, after drinking the hot tea they all felt much cooler.

The usual frantic banging on the door had ceased and the cha walla had taken away the empty cups when a man dressed in white, a wide red band pinned with a big brass seal showing a number fastened across his chest and over one shoulder, a turban wrapped around his head with a stiffly starched, folded cloth fan attached on top stopped at their window and inquired, "You want dinner, Sahib?"

"He's with the dining car on the train," Kathryn explained, "and if we want food this evening, we had better order now. He is the official bearer." Turning to the man, she smiled. "What food can we get tonight?"

"Mutton curry, chicken curry, dal bhat, chapatti, poppard," he offered.

They decided to have chicken curry, chapattis and tea served at 7:30 in their car.

"I will bring!" he promised shaking his head from side to side as he moved on.

It was nearly 8:00 when the train pulled into the station of Rourkela in Orissa, and ten minutes later the bearer, balancing a huge, black tray on his hand and shoulder, smiled through the bars of the window.

"Dinner, Sahib," he announced as if he were inviting the family into a formal dining room with a crystal chandelier sparkling above the table.

Ernie hurried to open the door. He moved to help the man, but displaying the efficiency of long practice, the bearer slid the tray onto the table himself. Quickly he removed the silver lids from the bowls and salaaming respectfully he left the car.

The dinner received mixed reviews--Kathryn loved it, eating it as if it were macaroni and cheese, claiming that there was only a very pleasant stinging sensation in her mouth afterward; Ernie and Lois liked it, even though their mouths burned and tears rolled down their cheeks; Linda spit out the first taste, drank a whole glass of water and then would eat only the rice and the chapattis; Jimmy, of course, laughed throughout the whole meal while he enjoyed his canned carrots from America. *Some day,* thought Lois, *we'll all be eating spicy hot rice and curry just like Kathryn does.*

At Rourkela the train turned toward the west and south, moving all through the next day through Madhya Predesh. When the probable congressman in the next car left the train they didn't know, but in the morning when the bearer brought their cooked wheat cereal with brown sugar and boiled buffalo milk, they saw that the flower garlands that had been fastened on the outside of the car were gone and other passengers were loading in their luggage. At one stop during the night Lois had heard sharp military commands and the regular movement of many boots. Whether the troops were being replaced on the train or whether they were just being moved, she didn't know.

Toward evening of their second day on the train they entered the huge state of Maharashtra and when they looked out the window the next morning they saw mountains--the Western Ghats, Lois knew. The monkey god Hanuman and his tribe, according to mythology, had jumped from mountain top to mountain top when they traveled down to Ceylon to rescue the beautiful goddess Sita who had been kidnapped and was being held prisoner.

It was cooler traveling through the mountains. Here and there they could glimpse a spring forming a small waterfall over the rocks with lush green plants and brightly flowering trees forming an oasis in an otherwise brown landscape. As they descended to sea level nearing the five islands covered by the city of Bombay, the oppressive heat returned, leaving them panting for breath and wishing for a nice, cool shower.

Their train crossed over a high bridge connecting the mainland with Bombay. Watching out the window from the elevated tracks the train moved at a reduced speed. From high above the water, they could discern miniature people in toy boats, and along the edge of the inlet river tiny women squatting down to wash their clothes and then spread them out on the sandy beaches to dry. They caught a glimpse of a bouquet of flowers hurled from the next car as it fell down--down--down until it struck the water--an oblation to the god of the sea by a devout Parsee, Kathryn surmised.

As they moved down into the city itself, the view from the train window was depressing. While in the distance one could see high buildings and an interesting skyline, the area near the tracks was filled with thousands of society's rejects, people who had found discarded pieces of cardboard or tar paper or other junk and stacked it together in such a way that they could crawl under it for a bit of protection from the burning sun or the monsoon deluge which would, hopefully, arrive in early June. Even though Lois could understand why the few wealthy

Indians and the ruling British retreated whenever possible to their compounds and private swimming pools and clubs, distancing themselves from the clamor and poverty of the masses, these were the people among whom she and Ernie had come to work and her heart went out to them in their insurmountable misery.

As their train pulled into Victoria Station, which was the end of the line, Lois glanced at the stack of luggage including their re-rolled canvas bedding rolls and hoped that they could find enough coolies to move it to the next platform.

Kathryn had explained that the next step of their journey was going to be a bit difficult. They needed to transfer from Victory Station to Churchgate Street Station where they could get a train north along the Arabian Sea to their future location which was Palghar, a name that meant House of Lizards. In order to make that transfer, Kathryn thought that the simplest thing to do would be to take a local train, which they could get by crossing over a high pedestrian bridge to another set of tracks. Unfortunately she had underestimated the difficulty of getting that amount of luggage on a local train in the short time that it stops at any station.

As their train slowed to a stop in Victoria Station they were able to get seven coolies without difficulty. Loaded heavily, the coolies led the way through crowds of people up and over the pedestrian bridge. Ernie, carrying Jimmy, tried to stay with the coolies and the luggage, and at the same time keep an anxious eye on Lois and Kathryn with Linda between them as they struggled through the masses of hurrying people and up the long flight of metal steps, burning hot in the afternoon sun. By the time they reached the other side where they could catch a Churchgate Street train, the sweat was running down their faces and dripping off their chins as if someone had poured water on them.

They located their luggage stacked on the local platform near the tracks with each coolie standing near his head load ready to jump on to the train when Ernie gave them the signal, but finding space proved to be nearly hopeless. Each train as it pulled in was not only loaded inside the cars, but people were hanging on the outsides, clinging to the doorways and even riding on the tops. Lois was beginning to feel desperate for this was a bad place to have the children. Jimmy and Linda were tired and beginning to cry. Kathryn seemed nonplussed as train after train went through. Lois gave Linda a drink from the canteen, and sitting down on a suitcase she held Jimmy's water bottle for him.

The Americans were so obviously in distress that they began to attract attention. A few curious people stood by to watch with interest. Although it was nearly six o'clock, the heat rising from the platform was suffocating and Lois's concern for the children grew. After a time she glanced up to see a man, tall for an Indian, walking toward them poised and cool, his clean, loose clothing and his intelligent, black eyes marking him as an educated man before he even spoke a word.

"Sir, you look distressed. May I be of assistance? I am Ramchandra Desai of this city." he said with a courteous bow.

"Thank you, Mr. Desai, for your concern for strangers. We have managed to get ourselves into a difficult situation and don't know quite how to get out of it. Could you perhaps advise us?" There was a note of desperation in Ernie's voice as he explained about the embarrassing amount of luggage on a local train platform, and where they had come from and where they were hoping to go.

Mr. Desai listened carefully until he understood the situation, then he answered, "If you stay here you have very little chance of getting on one of these trains for hours, and all of you are already tired from the day. If I may suggest, why don't you take a private room for the night here in the station, have a good night's rest and in the morning have a good morning tea. The bearers will bring the food to your room. Then you can send a coolie outside the station to order taxis and coolies who will take you over to Churchgate Station in time to make the train for up country. If you are in agreement I will help you to make satisfactory arrangements."

The Americans were much relieved to follow Mr. Desai's suggestions. Giving the impression of one who was used to managing people and events, he soon had coolies to carry the luggage--the first ones had insisted on being paid and going to other jobs--and reservations for a room with a fan for the night.

When they were finally situated in their room and a dinner had been ordered from the station dining room, Mr. Desai turned to them as he paused at the swinging doors.

"I think you will do very well now on your own. You can lock these big doors when you wish to sleep. I will leave you now." And he smiled with his hands folded in front of him, showing no haste in spite of his own affairs having been postponed because of their predicament.

Ernie walked over to Mr. Desai and also folded his hands. "Mr. Desai, we can't tell you how grateful we are. You have been a true Samaritan, or--that is to say--I mean--"

"Yes, thank you, I know about your Samaritan. I have read some of your Bible. It reminds me of something our great poet Rabindranath Tagore wrote in his poem "Gitanjali." It is a prayer to the great god above all. 'Thou hast made me known to friends whom I knew not/ Thou hast brought the distant near and made a brother of the stranger.' Salaam. Peace be with you." With that he was gone, a Hindu good Samaritan to be sure. Never would they meet again, but they would never, never forget Mr. Desai.

Chapter 5

————— • —————

To Palghar

"Kathryn, come here quickly. What's this. . .and this ... and this?" Lois exclaimed as she leaned over Linda's bed and saw three small, black insects crawling on her sheets. Linda had started to fuss in her sleep and Lois had gone over to her bed to check on her.

Kathryn looked down at the offending little creatures and sighed, "Oh, dear! I was afraid we might run into some of these here. . .but I did check and didn't find any. Of course, they are very good at hiding."

"Well what are they, Kathryn? Don't tell me they are. . .surely they aren't. . . ." A shiver of revulsion crawled around Lois's neck and down her back; she had never seen a bedbug, but she knew them by reputation.

"Bedbugs." Kathryn finished her sentence. "I'm afraid so. It's almost impossible to travel and not run into them. But here, I think I have something that will help us. I picked up some tins of Gamexine powder in Calcutta. We can make a thin line of powder around the outer edge of each of our sheets and the bedbugs won't cross over that line."

They worked on the children's beds first, then their own. All that Lois could find she brushed to the floor and stamped on them with enthusiasm. Other than the trouble with bedbugs, the room proved to be very comfortable. There had been hot water for baths and the food, which arrived at 8:00 o'clock, was delicious. The long-bladed fan turning slowly above them kept a cool breeze moving and mosquitoes away.

Eventually Ernie returned from the ticket office with tickets for travel up country the next day leaving at 2:00 p.m. He had located a telegraph office and sent a wire to his brother Chalmer, letting him know when they would be arriving in the town of Palghar; their long six-weeks journey would soon be over. They were all glad, for they were anxious to move into the next phase of their preparation to do the work that had brought them to India.

When everyone else was in bed Ernie flipped out the light. The lamp from the hallway still shown through the open transom, casting the shadow of the moving fan across the entire ceiling. As Ernie lay down on his bed he asked, "What's this powder I feel on the cot?"

"It's Gamexine powder. Do you know we found bedbugs in here?" Lois exclaimed in disgust.

"Really--I wonder what kind they were," Ernie commented. "Did you save me one?" Lois thought she detected a tone of amusement in the dark.

"I certainly did not. For goodness sake, it doesn't matter what kind of bloodsucking creatures they are--they all bite, so if you meet one tonight kill it!"

"Yes, dear," Ernie chuckled, and after a few seconds he added softly, "after I identify it."

The following morning passed quickly. They all slept late—or as late as Jimmy playing on his bed would allow them to sleep—then they had morning tea and later a delicious meal of boiled milk, fluffy rice with a moderately-spiced dal to be poured on top, and chapattis with brown sugar syrup to dip them in. When it was nearing time for them to leave for Churchgate Station, Ernie had no difficulty in finding coolies to carry their luggage down to the area where taxis were waiting. As he watched Mr. Desai the night before, he had learned something about negotiating with these men, so in the end they were quite satisfied with the money they received.

The trip from Victoria Terminal to Churchgate Station took them through busy streets lined with many tall, ornate buildings revealing British influence. The names on buildings, businesses and banks reflected the cosmopolitan nature of Bombay--Bank of China, Assurance Company of New York, Trading Company of India, Burma and Ceylon--for Bombay was India's busiest seaport. Lois noticed sailors of a number of nationalities walking along the main streets and stopping at small street shops to buy souvenirs.

As they pulled up outside Churchgate Station coolies ran along beside the car urging Ernie, "Me, Sahib? Me, Sahib?" Ernie selected the ones he needed from the group, and after the usual lifting and grunting that accompanied the loading of luggage on heads and shoulders that seemed inadequate to carry such weight, they were soon moving across the station, its high-vaulted ceiling towering above the crowds of people below, and through the gate to number five platform where their train stood, still dripping from the thorough cleaning it had received after reaching the end of the line the night before. They found their reserved car with "Shull Party" posted on the outside and Ernie opened the door to let the coolies with their heavy loads climb up the steps. Taking turns assisting each other, the carriers lifted their burdens up to the floor of the car and then with a show of great concern stored each piece under a seat. They opened the shuttered windows, and then using the cloths that had been formerly rolled into "doughnuts" for padding on their heads, they wiped dust from all the berths and the little table at the end of the car. Feeling pleased at their own efficient service, they lined up in front of Ernie to be paid.

While Ernie bargained and Kathryn kept the children, Lois climbed into the car and washed off the window sills and the berths with the remaining Lysol which she still carried in the diaper bag, determined to make surfaces sanitary. The car seemed familiar since it was very much like the one they had traveled in from Calcutta to Bombay. Ernie ordered tea from the train dining car and they all settled down to enjoy the scenery of Maharashtra by the Arabian Sea as the monotonous rhythm of the turning wheels propelled their train northward toward Palghar, the House of Lizards.

Outside the train, across the baked earth over which they passed, the stifling, hot pre-monsoon air rose in visible heat waves, like a picture out of focus. Coconut and toddy palm trees kept their green umbrella tops in spite of the cracking, baked earth, and here and there an irrigated grove of trees displayed lush mangoes, oranges, or lemons. In spots near huts where waste water was drained, fast-growing papaya trees flourished, laden with large, green fruits.

Not far out of Bombay the train passed through huge fields divided into what appeared to be six-foot squares by mud walls eight or ten inches high, laid out like gargantuan game boards waiting for the Titans' next move. The squares were flooded to the top of the symmetrical walls with salt water from the sea, their surfaces like framed mirrors reflecting the deep azure of the sky, ready for the burning sun to evaporate the water and leave a thin covering of gray salt crystals over the surface. Salt was a highly valued commodity used by everyone; even the British exploited salt by levying the hated salt tax. How strange it was that such an ordinary thing as salt had become a political issue when the whole ocean was full of it, mused Lois.

"Kathryn, have you noticed how inconspicuous the soldiers have been in Bombay and along this railroad going north? What do you think that means? Could it be that there is less political activity on this side of India?" For a moment the picture of the mob outside their Mission House window in Calcutta flashed vividly across her mind and she heard again the mad shouting of the rioters and the death scream of the murdered Hindu.

"No, I don't think it's that--some of India's most prominent leaders come from the Bombay area--but Calcutta and the Punjab seem to have so many more radical groups and hate mongers. When they have that kind of leaders, the people seem to lose their heads." Kathryn shook her head regretfully. "I don't expect to find much political activity in the villages where we work."

Ernie who had been listening even though half asleep turned toward them. "Don't be too sure about all that; I read in the Bombay *Times of India* last night that there was a political demonstration in Bombay by several thousand people yesterday—marching, and carrying signs against the British like 'Quit India,' but also groups shouting against Jinnah and the Muslims. I don't think you can hope that all the violence is going to stay in the Punjab. I'm certain an efficient military service like the British-Indian Army has its units situated where they can materialize very quickly if, and wherever, the need arises."

Lois took a deep breath as she glanced uneasily at the children.

"I'm sure you are right," Kathryn agreed. "Anna Warstler, my fellow staff member in the Girls School where I am going to teach, writes that there is a British-Indian Army unit not far from their school in Ankeleshwar—and I have to admit that it gives me a feeling of security to know that they are so near."

"What are your plans about that, Kathryn? Are you going directly there on this train? My word and honor, how are we ever going to get along without you to guide us?" Lois squeezed Kathryn's hand.

Laughing confidently Kathryn assured her, "Oh, you'll be fine. Why after this week and a half of experience I think you are ready to handle most anything."

As the hours slipped by their anticipation of meeting family grew. Lois wondered what they would be like. Through their months of preparation, and then two years of waiting for visas, they had received numerous letters from Chalmer and Susan, revealing many things about themselves and their work, including the difficulties as well as their joys and hopes for the future. One learns things about people through letters that might not be learned through contact; her feeling of confidence in their ability to live and raise a family in this country had much of its basis in the example of Chalmer and Susan. All three of their children had been born here, Gordon and Lorita were now in college in the States, and eight-year-old Esther who was still at home. Esther would probably go away next year, 1000 miles across India, to Woodstock, a boarding school in the Himalayan Mountains, just fifty miles from Tibet. Lois didn't dare to think about that, for sending the children away to school would be, to her, the ultimate sacrifice. Just now she knew she couldn't do it, but she kept telling herself that Susan and the other missionaries were doing it--just how, she didn't know. Maybe her courage, her faith, and dedication were less than theirs. *Dear God, you certainly chose a person with a lot of flaws when you selected me,* she thought, *because right now I don't think I can ever do it! When I let myself think about it, I wonder how I have come to this point. But I don't need to think about it now--that's still three or four years away.*

Their dinner was served early at 6:30, after which the Shulls gathered together all their luggage and stacked it in readiness near the door. It seemed strange not to be including Kathryn's things with theirs.

Half an hour after the posted arrival time of 7:30 their train drew along beside the crowded Palghar platform. The air was cooler now although heat still rose from the cement underfoot. Ernie opened the car door and stood on the top step holding the iron handles at each side of the entrance, scanning the faces of the people milling about on the platform. Suddenly he shouted with excitement, "Hey, Chalmer!" And Lois, Kathryn and the children watching out the window saw him jump from the train while it was still moving and run to a man not quite as tall as he and several shades browner. His hair was dark and slightly grayed at the temples and he was wearing glasses. His khaki shirt and shorts hung loosely on his small frame as though he had lost weight lately. Knee-length khaki color sox fitted him snugly and, in Lois's opinion, made him look for all the world like a Britisher. The two men threw their arms around each other laughing and talking at the same time, clapping each other on the back, oblivious to all the curious people watching and wondering. Kathryn heard one bystander say to another, "I think a son has come home to his father." Not a surprising guess since there was twenty-three years difference in their ages.

A few minutes later when the men entered the car Lois met her brother-in-law for the first time. He threw his arms around her and kissed her, his sparkling brown eyes filled with welcome.

"I can't tell you what joy it is to have you here at last safe and sound, my dear. And this is Linda and Jimmy." He kissed each one. "It's good to have you back, Kathryn," he greeted her as he shook her hand. "The Committee has a temporary assignment for you . . . I'll tell you about it in a minute." He walked over to the door and motioned to four men standing not far away, who had obviously been waiting to be summoned.

"These are four Christian men who work at the Mission School. They are Walia . . ."

Walia, smiling broadly, folded his hands and bowed. "Sahib . . . Madam Sahib . . . Miss Sahib (meaning Kathryn) . . . Lahan Babi (little girl), Lahan Baba (little boy.)"

"And Devu . . . " Chalmer continued, " . . . and Ramesh . . . and this is Yohan." After each introduction each man followed Walia's example calling the newcomers by name.

Then speaking in Marathi, Chalmer asked the men to unload all the luggage and stack it temporarily on the platform; after that they could load it at their leisure into the Mission ox

44

cart waiting outside the station. By the time the Shulls' luggage was all out of the train there were still eight minutes left before the train departure. The station tea walla arrived with clean cups and boiling hot tea which Chalmer had ordered, and they sat down to visit for a few minutes and hear about Kathryn's added assignment.

Chalmer, who was chairman of the Committee, began by explaining the problem. "As you probably are aware, we have Ernie and Lois and the children, and also Dorothy Brown, a nurse out from Pennsylvania, who will be leaving in five days for Language School at Mahableshwar above Poona to stay until first exam time on June 10th just before the monsoon breaks. We want everyone to be back on the plains before that, because monsoon is heavy there, normally 300 inches. That's a matter of about three months. Besides, it will be more pleasant there since that is a low hill station in the Western Ghats."

"I have a feeling I know what you are leading up to," guessed Kathryn.

"The point is that if these three students are to get any studying done, they are going to need a house keeper . . . someone to do the buying and the managing of the household. They'd have a hard time telling the cook what to do since they can't speak the language yet. . . . The Committee wants you to go along and help them, Kathryn. . . It means you won't be able to start your teaching for a while."

"I do see what you mean . . . and since I've just returned and won't be really interrupting anything yet, I can understand that I'm the logical one. . . Besides, like you say, being in a hill station during this hot season will be like a vacation. Yes, I'll be glad to do it."

"We thought you would want to go on to Ankeleshwar with your luggage and do some repacking for your three months stay in Mahableshwar," Chalmer commented.

"That's true," Kathryn agreed; then turning to Lois and Ernie she laughed. "So . . . it isn't goodbye after all. I'll see you again in five days. I'll let you know what train I'll be on and you can join me. Has the Committee made arrangements for us to have a place to stay?" she asked as she turned to Chalmer.

"All taken care of," he assured her.

The tea walla arrived to pick up the empty cups just as the train whistle blew, and with one last hug for Kathryn, the Shulls descended to the platform. The train started to move and Kathryn waved to the children out the window.

Chapter 6

—◦·•·◦—

Language Teacher

Lois stood for a moment as the train disappeared trying to rid herself of a feeling of loss, now that Kathryn was gone. Nearby a rather noisy demonstration by men dressed in the typical Congress white khadi garments and caps was going on, accompanied by their shouts of, "Hindustan ki jai!" and, "Mahatma Gandhi ki jai!" Although Chalmer ignored the demonstrators as he led the new arrivals through the crowd, Lois wondered if, since the newcomers looked so much like the British, they might not also be personae non gratae. This, added to the fact that she couldn't understand what they were saying, made her feel very much an alien. She was excited about the future and vowed she would learn the language as fast as she could, for that was the only way she could know what people were really thinking and feeling.

Chalmer was friendly with a few people near the exit as they turned in their tickets to a man dressed in a dingy white railroad-servant uniform including a white topi, and they passed through the open gate made of slats of wood that had at some point been white, but now were dirty with big splotches of red beetlenut juice and filth smeared along the bottom. Once outside they found themselves on a dirt street surging with tongas, carts, and bicycles, but mostly with crowds of people buying and selling and "eating the air" as they said idiomatically.

"That's the Mission tonga there with Devu, a Mission employee, driving," Chalmer informed them, pointing to a two-wheeled cart with a canvas-roofed top and hitched to a pair of sleepy-eyed bullocks. Just go and climb in the back and I'll ride in the front with Devu. I'll just check on the luggage here in the cart to be sure everything is okay."

They discovered the tonga tilted steeply toward the back and had a backboard through the middle dividing the front seat from the back seat. Those sitting in the back must ride backward

46

bracing their feet against the curved footboard to avoid bouncing out. Ernie lifted Linda to the back seat, then took Jimmy until Lois climbed in and held Jimmy on her lap. Linda's knees hit the dividing board as she half knelt watching the bullocks as they swished their tails, temporarily disturbing the flies on their backs. When Ernie started to climb in the back, the tonga tilted so low toward the ground that Lois grabbed the side with one hand to avoid falling out. Ernie quickly stepped back to the ground.

"I think I had better wait for Chalmer to climb in the front before I try to sit in the back," he laughed. "I'm not sure the bullocks could keep their feet on the ground otherwise."

"Let's try it together," suggested Chalmer, who had heard Ernie's last remark. This time it worked much better and the bullock tonga moved out slowly with the bullock cart of luggage following.

The two miles from the station to the Mission were covered at a slow pace, but it was an exciting time for Lois, full of new impressions. Twilight was moving fast into darkness as it does so often in the tropics, and the flowering trees and plants seemed to release an added burst of perfume with the coming of night. Many people, talking and calling to each other as they passed like shadows so near them, heard but not distinctly seen, added to the dreamlike world of strange tree shapes silhouetted against the evening sky, and always dust--dust from the passing of many feet--hanging heavily in the air. A lorry loaded with people came up on them from behind. The impatient driver manually squeezed the air horn, blasting insistently to move the pedestrians out of the road. Devu urged the sluggish bullocks to the left as the bullock cart, rambling cows, and bicycles made way for the faster lorry. Behind the lorry rose clouds of dust making it difficult to breathe.

"Put your hands over your nose and mouth, Linda," warned Lois as she turned Jimmy's face into her shoulder. "The air will be clearer in a few seconds."

Before long Chalmer drew their attention to a fenced corner of a field on their left.

"This is the beginning of the Mission Boarding School property and this is a field that the students cultivate. The lights you see up ahead some distance from the road are lights from our bungalow and from the school. I think Susan and Esther along with the students and faculty are there awaiting your arrival. They won't stay long, for they know that you are tired, but they just want to say welcome." Chalmer chuckled, "I see Jimmy is already asleep."

They turned in through a gate where two school boys were holding lanterns to light their way, then moved on down a short lane to a gate leading into a low bungalow with a long, wide verandah, well lighted by kerosene lanterns. The tonga stopped at the bungalow gate, and after Ernie and Chalmer climbed out at the same time, they helped Linda and Lois to the ground.

Susan and Esther were waiting at the gate.

"Oh, Lois, I thought this day would never come," exclaimed Susan as she folded Lois into her arms and kissed her. "We can't tell you how happy we are that you are here. And Ernie . . .and Linda. . . and Jimmy . . ." She kissed each one, then taking Jimmy into her arms she said, "I'll take Jimmy. The rest of you come along--there are lots of folks here to meet you." Esther and Linda had already gone ahead to the verandah.

As they walked along the gravel path toward the bungalow Lois could see blooming flowers in cultivated beds outlined by red bricks, their corners forming a rickrack design. The verandah itself was crowded with people smiling expectantly as they sat close together on the cool, stone surface of the floor. At one end of the verandah had been placed three chairs. Leading from the verandah the big, wooden double doors stood open revealing an interior room furnished with a large straw mat covering most of the floor, a couple of small tables with oil lamps, and several chairs.

Chalmer led Linda, Lois, and Ernie to the chairs, then standing to one side he became the interpreter for everything that followed. At given signals different groups came to them and placed garlands of roses and gardenias around their necks until the mound of garlands almost covered their ears. Only Linda's eyes showed above the fragrant blossoms. As each garland was placed the giver folded his or her hands in greeting, bowed slightly, and smiled. One nice-looking young man with wavy, black hair and alert, sparkling eyes placed his garlands around their necks, then said in hesitant English, "Welcome to India."

"Ernie and Lois, this is Paul Master, our headmaster at the Palghar Mission Boarding School. Paul is a good teacher, and he knows some English, so I know you are going to enjoy learning to know him and his wife Hirabai better."

But the person who impressed both Ernie and Lois most that first evening was the man who gave a few words of welcome from the whole group. Taller than most Indian men, he was dressed in a white dhoti, a long piece of thin cloth draped around and through the legs in such a way as to form a kind of pant that cover the legs to the ankles, a long-sleeved loose white shirt and a gray suit coat. He wore sandals and his black, wavy hair, like his brother's, glistened in the lantern light. His voice was strong and he spoke with dignity.

After the children had sung a song of welcome and were leaving to go back to their hostels, Chalmer brought the speaker over to Ernie and Lois to introduce him.

"Parlak Bohnsle, I want you to meet my brother Ernest and his wife Lois."

"Salaam, Shull Sahib--Madam Sahib," he greeted them, folding his hands. "Your arrival brings us great joy."

"The Parlak is our minister in the Church here and is an outstanding district officer as well," Chalmer continued. "We all depend much upon his leadership."

The Parlak bowed again as he picked up a lantern and joined others on the stone path below the verandah.

Quickly the verandah cleared and grew dark as the students in each hostel group picked up their Petromax lantern and returned to their sleeping quarters. Susan had already taken Jimmy, Linda and Esther into the house, and Chalmer followed with Ernie and Lois.

The room they entered just off the verandah was a large, high-ceilinged room with a second set of great, wooden doors straight across from the ones through which they had entered, and leading out onto a second, even larger, latticed-in back verandah, which was obviously being used for many activities of family living. Beside each set of double doors a high, wide window fitted with vertical iron bars about three inches apart had been cut through the thick wall to allow for any crosscurrent of air that might give relief from the intense heat during the hot season. Each window was fitted with window shutters, now fastened open, that could be closed in the cool season or during high monsoon winds and rain.

Susan had added little American touches such as half curtains at the barred windows, drapes, doilies and table covers, pillows, and pictures on the whitewashed walls. It reminded Lois so much of home that she felt tears come to her eyes, and for a moment a feeling of homesickness swept over her.

"Come along out here," Susan was urging them. "I was sure you would be thirsty and hungry, so Sovenji (the cook) and I have prepared some sandwiches and fruit. Linda and Esther have already started and Jimmy is eating mashed-up banana." She led the way through to the back verandah where a dining area was arranged at one end, and, after being introduced to Sovenji, a small, agile man with a ready laugh and a blind left eye, they sat down to eat mangoes and peanut butter sandwiches while Esther talked fluently to Sovenji in Marathi, explaining about her cousins from America.

Suddenly Linda pointed excitedly to a picture hanging on the wall. "Look, Daddy, there's a snake behind that picture! What is it doing there?" She had an insatiable curiosity and wasn't happy until she received answers.

Lois caught her breath, and Ernie, who was sitting nearest the wall, turned in his chair to look. Chalmer glanced at the wall and began to chuckle. "No, Linda. That isn't a snake; that's a lizard and he lives behind that picture. You see, he comes out every night to catch mosquitoes and eat them. He is one of our best friends. And he has lots of relatives around here. I suspect there are some behind every picture. The more mosquitoes they eat, the less likely we are to get malaria from mosquito bites."

"The lizards lived around here long before we came," Susan explained. "The name of this village is Palghar--Pal, meaning lizard, and ghar, meaning house--so it means House of Lizards."

Jimmy, sitting in a wooden highchair that had been Esther's when she was a baby, had slid down in his chair, his head resting on the arm, fast asleep. Lois lifted him into her arms, carried him into the bathroom at the end of the verandah, washed the banana off his face, then got him ready for bed without waking him.

While Ernie gave Linda a quick bath and helped her put on her pajamas, Susan explained to Lois about the room arrangement and the beds that were already made up with mosquito nets ready to be lowered. The house was built in the shape of an "L." The room to the west next to the living room where they had entered was a bedroom for guests and the last room in the line was to be their room. Its wall space was taken up mostly by doors and windows—one set of double doors leading onto the back verandah, one set leading onto the front verandah, and one set leading to a small verandah at the end of the building that was completely surrounded by wooden lattice work. It was on this little side verandah where a bed had been placed for Linda to sleep. It caught any cool breeze that might be stirring at night, but during the day it grew unbearably hot. Besides all the doors there were two huge windows like the ones in the living room. In front of one window a desk had been placed for study and there was a large chest of drawers at the foot of three single beds.

To the east of the living room were Chalmer's and Susan's living quarters. They consisted of a big front office behind which was a large bedroom that opened onto the back verandah, then a bathroom, and finally a kitchen and a storeroom finishing out the arm of the "L."

Ernie brought Linda to her bed on the verandah and laid her down. A faint breeze came in through the lattice. From some distance away a jackal howled and Linda's sleepy eyes opened wide.

"Where will you sleep, Daddy," she asked holding on to his sleeve."

"Right there," he assured her pointing to the first bed in the bedroom. "It's just five giant steps from your bed, so you can talk to me any time you want to." He ran his hand through her damp curls as he kissed her good night.

Susan came bustling over. "Let me help you tuck in the net for the first time, because we don't want to leave any space where mosquitoes can get in. They're bad around here and malaria is one of our worst enemies." Together she and Ernie lowered the net and carefully tucked its muslin border securely under the newly fluffed mattress pad. By the time they were finished Linda was asleep, and Lois, following Susan's instructions, had Jimmy on his bed under his net.

The hour was growing late as Susan turned from the doorway to say, "With all your traveling, you may have forgotten that tomorrow is Sunday. We have services in the Church at 8:30 a.m., so we will have our morning tea at 7:30. We always have toast and conji cereal. Esther likes it, so I think your children will like it too. There is a pitcher of drinking water on your chest of drawers and some glasses turned upside-down on their saucers to keep any insects from falling into them. I think that's everything I need to tell you. . . . Be sure to call us if there is anything that you need." Impulsively she threw her arms around Lois and exclaimed, "Oh, I'm so glad you are here . . . and you have such a wonderful little family! It's going to be great working together! Goodnight, both of you." She stepped out through the curtained, swinging doors onto the back verandah, and they heard her move down to their living quarters at the far end.

Lois took her time preparing for bed. She washed the dust out of her hair and toweled it dry, then she stood on a board placed in a shallow, bowl-shaped cement bathing area soaping herself and pouring cool water over her body. *Would she ever get used to this intense, sultry heat,* she wondered? This hot season had been a long one, so the weather was certain to get better soon. Strange how things can look really gloomy and discouraging sometimes, and then something happens and the whole prospect changes; like her feeling such an alien in the crowd of demonstrators at the railroad station, but now that they had met so many friendly and interesting people here at the Mission School, she no longer felt like an unwanted foreigner, but more like a welcome neighbor. By the time she made it back to the bedroom Ernie was already putting down their bed nets.

"We're going to have to do something about this as soon as we can get to a cloth market," he said with determination.

"About what?" She turned the lantern standing on the floor down low. They were to leave it burning just in case the children might need something in the night.

"Why, about these bed nets. We're going to buy a big double net and then push our beds together so the double net will cover both of them. These two separate nets cut off what little breeze there might be. Besides, how can I talk to you through two thicknesses of netting?"

Lois laughed. "Why that shouldn't be a problem. I'd think sound would go through netting very nicely. . . However, it's always revealing to see your expression when you tell me things . . . Yes, I think we had better get a double net." Still laughing, she helped him finish tucking in the nets.

Lois awakened the next morning to the shrill, shrieking notes of a koel being chased by a pair of irate house crows. Ernie had once explained that this member of the cuckoo family often laid its eggs in the nests of other birds and then left them to be cared for by the new parents. This time, however, the koel was caught in the act. The raucous confrontation soon awakened the children and they began to stir. Glancing over at Ernie's bed she saw that it was empty. She knew that he would not be wasting these beautiful, early morning hours sleeping when he could be out watching a whole new world of birds and other animals with his binoculars. He came in from the front verandah just as she was finishing dressing the children and said he would take the children for a bird walk while she dressed.

Not knowing what to expect at the church, she put on a good dress and heeled shoes. She laid out a big-brimmed, orange and cream-colored straw hat that she had bought in Genoa, Italy to wear to church instead of her British cork topee, which had obviously been designed for utility only.

When, at exactly 7:30, Sovenji, wearing a clean white apron and a broad smile, picked up the brass elephant bell from its holder on the breakfast table and began to ring it, they all gathered without delay around the breakfast table on the back verandah. When they were seated, Chalmer at the head of the table picked up the Bible resting beside his plate and read the scripture reference for the morning from "The Upper Room" followed by a short devotional and a prayer. As Jimmy began to grow restless, Lois broke off a crust of bread from the tray not far from her and gave it to him to chew on.

The conji cereal was a hit with everyone. It was made of ground wheat from which the flour had been sifted; it had then been boiled until it was tender, making an excellent hot cereal served with brown sugar and rich buffalo milk. This was followed by hot toast with guava jelly and ripe, juicy mangoes.

By 8:15 they were all ready to leave for the church. They went out through the latticed door by the kitchen where sweet smelling gardenias were growing and crossed the back compound to the path leading to the school. Along the east side of the path a long line of little two- or three-room houses made of wooden frames, cow-dung and clay-mixture walls, and tile roofs had been built, each with some space for a small garden. The gardens were protected from stray animals by fences made with sticks driven into the ground.

On the west side of the path were cultivated fields which were obviously being irrigated during this hot season by the power of a high windmill and a very good well. Lois read on a little metal tag attached to one leg, "Made in Chicago."

As though their passing was a sign to leave for church, family after family joined them, barefooted, on the path, greeting them warmly and studying everything about them with friendly curiosity. Because Saturday had been a wash day, and no school, most people were freshly dressed. Nearly all the men were carrying Bibles. The women were carrying babies or small children on their hips.

It was an excited, happy group which arrived shortly at the steps of the church. Lois had imagined a small chapel, but she discovered services were always held in the largest room of the long line of school rooms, for there just wasn't enough money to build a church. There was a long verandah running along the front of the school building where many activities could take place. The walls of the school were made of five-by-eight foot, wavy, galvanized sheets; the doors were of wood, and the roof was tile.

The congregation sat on the floor on colorful, long grass mats--men on one side, women on the other--and in the back of the room were two long, exceedingly hard benches for honored guests. Esther and Linda sat on the floor and Lois wished she could join them, but she was not appropriately dressed for that.

Lois and Ernie found the service interesting even though they couldn't understand what was being said, except as Chalmer translated for them. The singing was enthusiastic and loud, everyone clapping their hands in rhythm. At one point the Parlak asked Ernie to say a few words which Chalmer translated into Marathi. Eventually Jimmy began to fuss, so Lois took him out onto the verandah and walked up and down with him. She gave him a bottle of water to drink and he dropped off to sleep.

That she was really in India still seemed like a dream to her, both thrilling and frightening. How peaceful and orderly everything seemed here at the Mission two miles outside of Palghar; yet on the other side of India, in Calcutta where they had been just three days before, and in most cities of the land, rioting and violent confrontations were happening every day. There had been demonstrations even on the Palghar station platform. Were the people here at this mission school involved in the general national unrest?

She thought of the great variety of people they had met since stepping on the docks in Calcutta--Mr. Desai, wealthy, cultured, and kind; the devil-may-care, tough-but-helpful Sikh taxi driver, the deeply devout Hindu worshippers bathing in the sacred Ganges, the hopeless, hungry people, living and scrounging forever on the streets, the political zealots pledged to bring India freedom or die in the attempt; the born beggars who would consider it a sin to cast their eyes toward any other occupation, and now these folks, living in poverty according to her standards, and singing the closing hymn of Christian faith. Lois was glad to be living in a place where they could help educate children and where their own children could be educated. As her reverie continued, she realized there was no way to describe a "typical" Indian--just as you couldn't describe a "typical" American. Lois sighed. The few books she had read about Indian society and its cast system were just not enough to keep her from feeling confused. She vowed to use every opportunity to learn as quickly as she could--and she certainly was going to buy a couple of saris and learn how to wear them so she could sit on the floor with the other ladies. She wondered why Susan always wore dresses.

Chalmer told Ernie and Lois that the Joint Council, made up of Indians and Americans, had agreed that Ernie and Lois should first of all go to a three months session of language school in Mahableshwar then return to Palghar for a full year of language school with a full time Marathi pandit. They would be joined at Palghar by an American nurse from Pennsylvania, Dorothy Brown, who would be arriving from America.

On Monday morning, as Lois tackled the job of unpacking, she realized she would soon be packing again in preparation for going to language school in, some three hundred miles away. She glanced out onto the front verandah of the Palghar mission bungalow to see how things were going with Dayabai, the new baby sitter, and the children. Aware of so many hazards, she was still not quite comfortable leaving their care in the hands of someone else whom she didn't really know. Susan had said, "We chose Dayabai to be your ayah (nanny)--she was really about the only one we had--and besides, her husband Sovenji is going with you as your cook, and it's always best to send families together when it can be arranged. It's nice that their little Shamu (short for Shamuel) is almost the same age as Jimmy. She can take care of both of them at the same time. She'll find Linda easy to care for."

Dayabai had come to work early Monday morning, carrying Shamu on her hip and very pleased to have this new job. She was amply built, very pleasing according to oriental standards, and she walked with an easy, swinging grace that reminded one of a gently flowing stream. Red and blue glass bangles on her wrists tinkled musically as she moved across the back verandah to where Lois was sorting clothes in preparation for the laundry. She wore small glass earrings and had her long, black hair rolled on the back of her head. Her sari was white cotton with a green border, and her green blouse stopped a couple of inches above her waistline, the last two buttons remaining open as a convenience to Shamu who was still nursing.

"Salaam, Madam Sahib, I am ready," she bowed.

Susan came hurrying over. "What would you think of having Dayabai play with the children on the front verandah this morning, Lois? I've had it newly scrubbed and I thought it would be as cool a place as anywhere."

"A good idea. I'll try to find some toys that are washable."

That had been an hour ago. Since then she and Susan had gotten Sitabai started doing the laundry with two wash tubs, a wash board, and a cake of Sunlight soap. What I wouldn't give for a washing machine and some electricity right now thought Lois.

Lois saw Linda and Esther with their dolls and Esther's doll cradle playing at one end of the verandah by the open window. They had tiny clay dishes and were pretending to make tea. Dayabai was sitting near Lois's door with the two babies who were playing with wooden blocks, and she was having a rough time preventing Jimmy from putting one in his mouth. Lois had particularly cautioned Dayabai, admonishing her absolutely not to let Jimmy put anything in his mouth including his fingers. In the meantime Shamu was blissfully chewing away on a block and enjoying it immensely.

Lois wished she could tell Dayabai that she realized that she was having a hard time and that she was doing a good job.

"Dayabai," she called. When Dayabai turned to her questioningly, Lois shook her head "yes," thinking she was showing approval.

Dayabai looked alarmed and then called loudly, "Shull Madam Sahib,"

Susan who was working in the office came hurrying out. "Here I am, Dayabai. What's the matter?"

"Something is wrong, but I don't understand," she answered anxiously.

"I'm sorry. Does she think I was criticizing her?"

Plague this language barrier, thought Lois.

"Nothing is wrong. I was just trying to tell her that I thought she was doing a good job. I shook my head 'yes,' but somehow she didn't know what I meant."

"No wonder," laughed Susan. "How did you shake your head? Up and down like we do in America? If you want Indian people to understand 'yes,' you should shake your head from left to right, like this." She demonstrated. In retrospect, Lois realized she might well have used the wrong gesture.

"Now what did you want to tell Dayabai?" Susan soon had things straightened out and Dayabai smiling shyly again.

Well, how about that! I'm finding out more things I don't know every day. Not only do we have to learn the spoken language and the written language, but also the language of gestures. I wonder how many more things I don't know that I don't know, but that I need to know right now, Lois thought.

The next three days were spent in planning, unpacking and repacking, sorting out the things they would need in language school located at the hill station of Mahableshwar, and carefully squirreling other things away to stay at Palghar until they returned and would need them. On Thursday they met their pandit for the first time. Mr. Chopede arrived from Dahanu Road with a small bedding roll and one black, tin suitcase, ready to accompany them to Mahableshwar. He was a friendly, congenial man, fluent in three Indian languages, as well as English, and understood something of a number of others. He wore western style slacks and sport shirt, and the sandals he slipped off his feet and left on the step as he came onto the verandah to meet them. Having sandals was itself a status symbol setting him above most people in the village.

"Salaam, Mr. Chopede," greeted Chalmer as he came hurrying out of the office. "I want to tell you how much the Mission appreciates your assuming this task of language teaching."

Mr. Chopede folded his hands in front of him and bowed respectfully. "Salaam, Shull Sahib. I'm pleased if I can be helpful." He followed Chalmer into the big, middle room where Ernie and Lois were packing some books.

"Ernie, Lois, I want you to meet your new language teacher, Mr. Chopede; Ernie Shull and his wife Lois."

Ernie and Lois moved forward with their hands folded in the traditional greeting. "We are very happy to meet you, Mr. Chopede. You are going to be an important person to us in the next months. We want to thank you for accepting us as students," smiled Ernie.

Mr. Chopede shook his head from side to side a few times, then explained seriously, "We will surely do our best, but I have never taught language to English-speaking people before, so no doubt in the language school we will all be learning together."

I like that, and I like Mr. Chopade, thought Lois as she accepted a cup of tea that Sovenji had prepared for them. *We may move rather slowly on language at first, but I'm sure our new pandit will be teaching us many other things that are just as important about culture and idioms and attitudes that none of us is aware of, as yet, and we certainly need all the help anyone can give us.*

"Who would ever guess that 'table' is masculine
or that 'moon' is feminine?"
Ernie

Chapter 7

———◆———

Language Study

The Shulls and their entourage took up residence in a cottage called Treetop which belonged to another mission, but which the Church of the Brethren had rented for the language study term.

Because rationing of kerosene, as well as rice, sugar and a few other essential commodities, was an unpleasant fact in postwar India, the household at Treetop had accepted the necessity of having only one oil lamp burning during study time. Candles in old-fashioned, wooden holders with loops on the sides were used to go from room to room after dark or for late kitchen work. The supplies must be made to last until the end of the month, and Kathryn measured out each day's quota carefully.

One evening in late May while the three language students were gathered around the same study table placed in the center of the room for the greatest convenience and access to light, Kathryn sat to one side knitting a sweater for her little niece back home. It was going to be red with the white figure of a skier on the front. As fellow student, Dorothy watched the aspiring linguists, Ernie and Lois, pouring over their books, she mused that things had gone really remarkably well since the Shulls' arrival in late March. The household had run smoothly, the students' schedules and studies had worked out well, and Sovenji and Dayabai were quite content. First year exams would be coming up in two weeks and, of course, the language students were a bit anxious about that. There hadn't been very much sickness--a bout or two with diarrhea, probably from the fresh strawberries rather than from dysentery--which Dorothy had treated very effectively. Lois yawned--it was nearly 10:00 o'clock, and everyone had to be ready for 7:00 a.m. breakfast.

Suddenly Ernie threw down his pencil and took a deep breath. "I've had it. I simply can't think with the verb at the end of the sentence--and all these adjective and noun agreements--and genders that don't make sense! Who would ever guess that 'table' is masculine or that 'moon' is feminine? I've always thought that the face on the moon is a man's face." He leaned back in his chair.

Lois began to laugh as she stood up to stretch her tired muscles. She shoved the green language book over under his nose. "Oh, stop groaning and pronounce these vocabulary words for me--and pronounce them like Pandit Desai does so I know what you are talking about." (Pandit Desai was their classroom teacher; Chopede was their tutor.) Experiencing the same feelings as Ernie, Lois, too, felt buried under grammar rules, exceptions, and idiomatic ways of saying things as she shoved a written list into his reluctant hands.

Dorothy laughed as she reached across the study table and grabbed the paper. "Here, let me. Ernie, you take every other word. Okay, Lois, 'purush'--."

Dorothy was a few months ahead of Lois and Ernie in her language study, since she had arrived in India earlier and had been studying under a good pandit at the Dahanu Mission Hospital while helping out a few hours each day at the dispensary. She was a tall woman with beautiful, dark brown hair and eyes bordered by soft, long lashes. As Lois listened to the words being pronounced she thought, *What a lovely voice Dorothy has, and what an attractive personality to go with it--just what a sick person needs in a nurse.* Linda and Jimmy had fallen in love with her. Working and living together in Treetop they had become quite close. To Linda they were Aunt Dorothy and Aunt Kathryn.

At the end of the list Dorothy handed the paper back to Lois. When they came to the end of the vocabulary list Lois began to gather together her papers and books. Dorothy said,"Let's call it a day," she said. "You'll do--both of you. One of these days it will all fall into place, as if a light has suddenly been turned on, as they say. Let's go to bed."

"Oh, wait a minute. I forgot to tell you that a letter came today from Susan and Chalmer. They say they are being transferred to Dahanu Road to work in the Church and the village schools out in that district, and that Miss Ella Ebert is being placed at Palghar to be principal of that school and to operate the accounts and oversee you language students. That will all be taking place this week and next so that when you arrive at Palghar everything will be ready for you to settle in. Here's the letter--take it and read it," suggested Kathryn holding out the letter to Ernie.

"Okay," said Ernie as he lit a candle for each of them to carry to their rooms. He blew out the table lamp then followed the others up the stairs. With each step he was saying to himself, "To mulga ahey--he is a boy--te mulgi ahey--she is a girl...."

The headquarters for the language school was located in an old English church standing on a little knoll back a way from the wide road leading from the house of Treetop to the village of Mahableshwar. It was constructed of red bricks and had lovely, traditional stained glass windows throughout. It had been built by the British in this 4,500 feet above sea level hill station to remind them of home when they were on vacation from the burning plains stretching over most of India.

Although nearly half the students attending the school were American, there were a number of other countries represented. There were several British, some Scotts, some Australians, some Canadians, and a few French. There were even two Spanish Fathers who took part in the school, but of course, never attended the Church services. Lois stood in awe of these two well-educated gentlemen, for they had taken a vow of service in India for life--they would never return to their homeland. She respected their great dedication, but wondered why this personal sacrifice was required of them when, it seemed to her, it was so unnecessary.

The students took turns leading the services on Sundays. Lois wondered as she listened to the various interpretations of the scriptures whether the Indian pandits, cooks, ayahs, and business people in attendance found it enlightening or confusing. One zealous, young firebrand from the US one Sunday morning declared with a shout, "My dearly beloved Friends, unless you preach to make your audience angry at what you say, you are not preaching the gospel; you are soft-peddling it! Where is your courage?"

Lois glanced across the aisle to where her Hindu pandit, Mr. Desai was sitting and saw a bemused, half-smile on his lips. He appeared philosophical and undisturbed. *A man like him would never be reached by such methods*, she thought.

At the lunch table that noon, where they were having buffalo meat curry and rice, Kathryn brought up the subject of the morning sermon and asked what everyone thought of it.

Dorothy laid her fork on the table. "I felt very uncomfortable with that. He seems to be trying to make us feel guilty."

Lois lifted a determined chin. "Well I, for one, think he is wrong! Making people angry is not the way to get anybody to listen to you. Why, I felt absolutely embarrassed this morning when I looked at our Indian friends attending the service. I felt as if I should apologize! Do you agree, Ernie?" She laid a small piece of bread on Jimmy's highchair tray.

"I don't believe the method the speaker this morning was advocating will be very effective. Besides, we come as friends to share what we have and to learn what we can. If we begin by making people angry we are shutting off our channel of communication, and when we think that we are the only ones who know things good enough to share, I think we are arrogant. But after saying that, I say again that the way Christ taught us is the highest ethic that has ever been revealed to man, and I want to spend my time here sharing it with the Indian people."

Kathryn smiled. "I agree with most of what you are saying; and I have something else to be thankful for, and that is that I don't have that young man in this group--I'm sure I'd find him difficult to work with." Kathryn began gathering up her pattern book and knitting things. "But, Ernie, and all of you, don't expect everyone in our own mission to agree with you on some points. Then, too, you may change your minds about some things such as methods after you are here a while and have more experience among the Indian people."

Ernie readily agreed. "I'm sure we will, I hope so anyway. Every experience we have--every person we meet--is an opportunity to grow mentally and spiritually. I pray like Solomon that we may have more understanding of the Indian people and their culture, for without that our ability to help them will be limited. And Kathryn, I'm looking forward to some exciting discussions about lots of things with our fellow missionaries. I'm sure they can teach us many things that we need to know."

Sovenji began carrying out the dishes and Kathryn rose to help him. It was study time for the others as soon as Linda and Jimmy could be settled for their afternoon naps. *These new students were going to add a new dimension to the Mission Conference body*, thought Kathryn, *new points of view that might not always be welcomed by everyone--not just differences in philosophy and methods of working, but differences in dress, social habits, and even vocabulary, for society in the States hasn't stood still while we've been abroad—it's changed too. Because of the impossibility of travel during the war, everyone on the field, except for me, has been in India at least seven years without a furlough, and that long isolation has had its effect on them, for sure.*

Chapter 8

—— ·❖· ——

Islam and Hinduism

The new students pushed themselves even harder in their language study the last two weeks, taking time out only to be with the children and to eat and to sleep. However, one day Ernie played tennis for an hour with an Australian friend, Darrell Cartmell, enjoying the exercise, the fellowship, and Darrell's delightful accent, and one Sunday afternoon they hired a pony walla to lead his pony with Linda and Jimmy on its back down a mountain trail to a lovely waterfall where they could have a picnic and recover a bit from their studies.

The twenty-five foot waterfall was at the edge of an open, grassy glen. It was fed by cold, mountain springs and splashed into a sparkling little pool at its base, its muted roar soothing and inviting, spraying a fine, rainbow mist over anyone who stood on its banks. From the pool wandered a little stream across the glen and on down the mountain, later to join bigger streams, and rivers, and finally to blend itself into the Arabian Sea.

They spread out their blankets near the pool and sat down to enjoy the natural beauty around them. The black and white pony cropped the grass in contentment and the pony walla sat nearby leaning against a tree. The quiet of their shady, secluded retreat was so relaxing that they felt their tension over language study disappearing like early morning fog when the sun finally rises. They watched a white-breasted kingfisher sitting motionless on a dead branch near the waterfall where he could survey the grassy bank as well as the pool, his shining turquoise back and large, red bill and legs glinting like polished armor in the sun. Suddenly he dived down into the pool and came up with a fish in his broad beak. He flew to another dead branch where, after banging it against the branch a few times, he proceeded to swallow it.

After the picnickers had eaten their lunch, sharing it with the pony walla, they took a stroll along the bank of the stream. Suddenly a breathtakingly beautiful, silvery-white bird with a blue-black, crested head and fifteen-inch-long ribbon tail feathers enhanced by white flag feathers on the ends, flew over their heads. Its darting flight as it caught insects on the wing displayed absolute perfection of grace in form and movement.

"Oh, how lovely! Look, Linda, do you see it?" exclaimed Lois excitedly as she pointed to a tree near them where the exotic bird had perched.

"It's a paradise flycatcher--my first one seen in the wild here at Mahableshwar. If paradise is the home of perfection, then that bird is surely aptly named--and completely beneficial, because it feeds entirely on insects," Ernie explained. They watched as it darted out from time to time after a juicy dragonfly. As if it were putting on an air show for their benefit, its fairy-like movements with long streamers undulating, seemed incongruous with the fact it was hunting.

Such a scenic spot could not remain theirs alone for very long. They heard a group of people approaching from down the mountain along the path over which they had come. When they appeared around the bend it was obvious that the man, two women, and three children were fairly well-to-do Muslims. Catching sight of the waterfalls, the excited children went dashing off to the pool to get a closer look and to feel the rainbow spray. One little girl stepped onto a large rock lying to one side of the falls, and laughing, whirled around to call the others, but the rock came loose, sending the little girl rolling down in the red dirt to the edge of the pool. She screamed and grabbed another rock to keep herself from sliding into the water. The man, who was apparently the father, and Ernie arrived at the pool at nearly the same time. They pulled the screaming little girl back from the edge and the father tried to quiet her. The two women came hurrying up, obviously very upset and talking loudly. The little girl was crying and holding her lacerated foot with two hands.

Everything that had been said by the Indians up to this point had not been understandable to Ernie. Suddenly the man turned to Ernie and asked in English in a worried voice, "Sahib, are you a doctor? Could you look at my little girl's foot?"

"I'm sorry, I'm not a doctor, but we have a nurse with us . . . Dorothy," called Ernie, "Would you come over and look at this cut foot, please, and bring your first aid kit?" Dorothy always carried a hand-woven shoulder bag in which she kept, along with other things, a few essential first aid supplies.

Upon examination Dorothy found that although the wound was bleeding, it was not a serious injury. She cleansed it with water and disinfectant, then wrapped it tightly with a white cotton bandage. The foot would be all right in a week or so, but there was no way that the little girl could walk back to her home.

Turning to the father, who had finally been able to quiet his family, Ernie folded his hands in front of him Indian fashion and introduced himself. "I'm Ernie Shull, American, and this is Sister Dorothy Brown. We are studying in the language school in Mahableshwar."

"Salaam, Shull Sahib. I am Mohammed Khan and these are members of my family. We live in Bombay and are here in Mahableshwar to vacation for a week. Thank you, Sister, for helping my little girl." Dorothy smiled and nodded her head.

"Khan Sahib, your little girl isn't going to be able to walk up the hill. I'm sure the pony we have can carry three such little people. Would you like for your little girl to ride up the hill with my children?" Ernie asked, not being sure what taboos there might be to such an arrangement.

However Mr. Khan accepted Ernie's offer gratefully, and soon they were packed up again and headed up the gentle incline toward Treetop.

As they walked along Ernie had a rare opportunity to get better acquainted with Mr. Khan, since the wall of differences which would normally exist had been partially broken down by the minor emergency they had just experienced.

"You must be a Christian, Shull Sahib, since you are in the language school--I'm glad--because it's much easier to associate with Christians than with Hindus," Mr. Khan glanced at Ernie to see how he would react.

Ernie was surprised that Mr. Khan would make such a frank statement. "What makes you feel that way, Khan Sahib. Is it the political situation in India today?"

"Not basically," said Mr. Khan. "The real reason is that Muslims and Christians all believe in the One True God, while the Hindus have thousands of gods and are an abomination in the sight of Allah. We are so different--the Hindus and the Muslims."

"I realize that is true," agreed Ernie. "But Muslims and Hindus have lived together--side by side, peacefully--for hundreds of years. Why is all this antagonism between the two communities happening now? I thought your common adversary was the British government."

Mr. Khan looked again in Ernie's direction as if he was wondering just how much he should say. "You are right. . . I belong to the Muslim League and our great leader is Mohammed Ali Jinnah. He is a great man, and he knows what the Hindus are up to. He believes that the British will be leaving before long, but that the Hindus, who are the majority in India, intend to take over the government—and then where will the Muslims be? When the British are gone we will lose all our rights—we will have no protection."

"But I thought the British were proposing a coalition government where Muslim interests would be represented," Ernie commented.

"Represented? What good would that do when we would be constantly outvoted? The truth is that we are two separate nations mingled together in India. Jinnah Sahib says now is the time for us to demand Pakistan--a nation of Muslims. India must be divided. There is no other way."

By the time they arrived at Treetop, Ernie had come to the conclusion that if a well-educated Muslim like Mr. Khan was a true representative of the Muslim people, then any hopes for a coalition government were nearly nonexistent.

At Treetop they said goodbye to their new acquaintances. After paying the pony walla, Ernie lifted Linda and Jimmy off the pony, and Mr. Khan and his family, with the little, injured girl on the pony continued on to where they were staying.

Five days later Lois, Ernie, and Dorothy spent a day sitting for their first semester Marathi exams in reading, writing, and conversation in the language, and were delighted to find they had passed. Mr. Chopede was returning with them to the plains at Palghar where they would spend the next nine months in full-time language study, expecting to return to the language school the following March for another period of concentrated language study. It was a long, hard road ahead of them with a small gate through which they must be able to pass to achieve the ability to communicate freely with the people around them. The next day, along with Sovenji, Dayabai, and baby Shamu, they left the cool mountain retreat and headed toward Palghar, their home for the next nine months.

Chapter 9

— ◆ —

Monsoon

The rains came early that year, the first steamy showers falling just three days after the language students arrived at the Palghar Mission School compound. Splotchy, dark clouds appeared and thunder sounded, growling like an enormous dog disturbed from its sleep. Huge raindrops began to fall and the school children rushed out into the compound, their arms stretched wide, their faces turned toward the sky, and their mouths open to catch a few welcome drops. The giant drops thudding into the deep dust of the roads and village paths were swallowed up, leaving no trace where they had penetrated. The long, zigzag cracks in the thirsty earth, some as wide as two or even three inches, large enough for a small foot to slip into them and be injured, remained unaffected by those first token showers which only hinted at the deluge yet to come. Steam rose from the baked earth when the sun came out between showers, reminding Lois of a picture she had once seen of the entrance to Hades. Each day there were more showers and less sun--more pleasant weather and less unbearable heat.

Kathryn had left them in Bombay to go to her new assignment at the girls' school in Ankeleshwar, and the eager students immediately settled into their assignment of full-time language study on the plains. They set up study tables at one end of the long, front verandah where they could take advantage of the limited light of the rainy season and any chance cool breeze, while at the other end they arranged an area for the children to play, supervised by the ayah. In some conversational classes the three students met together. Other hours were for individual instruction or personal study.

Miss Ella Ebert, a no-nonsense sixty-year-old lady originally from Kansas, with short, graying hair and a firm step, was in charge of the boarding school, their household, and their language school. She was kept very busy and spent much of her time at the school or in her office. She lived in the east end of the house where Chalmer and Susan had formerly had their rooms.

Miss Ebert had never married. Seemingly her work had been fulfilling and she enjoyed operating the boarding school, including the vocational aspects consisting of growing crops and caring for dairy animals, which she supervised through the agriculture teacher Umade and several farm helpers. The students had their daily assignments of work in the fields, the gardens, and the hostels--all a part of their school experience outside the classroom.

Although she seemed to like small children, Miss Ebert never appeared to have quite the rapport with them that she had with the older, school-age children. She smiled at Jimmy and Linda and talked to them sometimes as she was passing by, her clean cotton dress always fresh and neat, but she didn't show much awareness of their problems or what might be involved in their care. Linda followed her parents' example of continuing to call her "Miss Ebert" rather than "Aunt Ella," which would have been more personal.

Under her care the school ran efficiently and academic standards were maintained for both students and teachers. Lois watched Miss Ebert with great admiration as she directed not only the students and teachers, but the field employees, the house staff and, Lois discovered, six schools in various surrounding villages. Her duties included paying the teachers at the end of each month when they came to the Palghar compound for a counseling session. There they met with other teachers where they could share problems and seek solutions. Besides all these tasks, there were the various accounts that had to be kept and report sheets (without errors) to be sent to the Inter-Mission Business Office in Bombay. It was an awesome assignment for one individual.

Almost immediately after their arrival, a problem developed about the menus and Lois set about trying to solve it tactfully. Many of the dishes being served for every meal except breakfast were so highly spiced that they left a burning sensation in the mouth a half hour after eating. One taste of these vegetables or curries and the children grabbed for a water glass and refused to taste them again.

On the second day when their lunch had been hot pulse soup and rice, fried eggplant dipped in a highly spiced batter, chapattis, and papaya, Lois turned to Miss Ebert, who was sitting at the end of the table watching the children with amusement, and said, "I'm afraid, Miss Ebert, this is not going to work. The children can't eat this highly-spiced food. For the the sake of the children, could Sovenji cook some of the food without the hot spices?"

"Why, my land," she exclaimed with a knowing chuckle as she pushed her glasses up into

66

place. "They'll get used to the Indian food very soon, if they just continue to eat it every day. All the other missionary children love it just like the adults. It doesn't pay to pamper children. Besides Sovenji has too much to do to cook two menus. You'll see--they'll be just fine in a few days." Dismissing the subject with these words of wisdom she rose from the table. "Well, if you'll excuse me, I must get back to the school." She stopped at her office to pick up a book and then hurried out the back door toward the school.

Not trusting herself to say anything, Lois put a spoonful of rice on Linda's plate, then added a bit of sugar and milk. The children would get used to Indian food eventually, but it would have to be a gradual process as they grew older. In the meantime she would have to find another way of preparing food they could eat, preferably without offending an older missionary with experience and seniority.

Dorothy was disgusted. "Wouldn't you know that Miss Ebert would say something like that? Have you noticed that so often people who have never had children are the first ones to tell you how you should take care of yours?"

"Now Dorothy, keep a sweet tongue," laughed Ernie. "However, those are my sentiments exactly. Honey, why don't you give Jimmy one of those few tins of baby food from America that we still have--I'll go get it for you." He brought an opened tin of carrots to the table and Jimmy ate every bit of its contents.

At four o'clock when she had finished her last class for the day, Lois went to the kitchen to see what she could do about evening food for the children. Since Kathryn had been in charge at Treetop Lois had not found occasion to go to the kitchen while Sovenji was cooking. Now, as she entered the kitchen, he looked up in surprise. She walked over to the shelf where the clean, aluminum pans were lying upside-down and, choosing the smallest one she could find, she set it down on the table. She noticed that he was preparing vegetables to put into a curry. By using the few words she knew by this time she managed to convey to him that she wanted to cook vegetables for the children in the small pan. Then, with Sovenji's permission, taking a few vegetables, adding water and a pinch of salt into the pan, she set it on the big iron stove to cook.

" Sovenji, masalla nahi, (no spices") she emphasized shaking her head.

"Barra," he seemed to agree, although he appeared to be uncertain about this whole procedure.

She went back to the children to begin the ritual of evening baths, popping back into the kitchen every few minutes to check on the vegetables. Finally they were tender and she set them aside to stay warm until serving time.

Sovenji rang the elephant bell he used as a dinner bell ten minutes late. Miss Ebert went to the kitchen to find out what was causing the delay. When she came to her place at the table she was unsmiling as she remarked, "Because of your extra requests, Sovenji had just too much to do to have the meal ready on time. It makes him nervous to have someone else in his kitchen puttering around. I don't think we can expect him to do extra duty. If you want something done, just tell me and I'll try to arrange it."

"Miss Ebert, I was only trying to make sure that the children would have food without spices--food they can eat. If you will have Sovenji prepare the foods, then I will not find it necessary to cook in Sovenji's kitchen," Lois declared firmly.

"I'm sure it can be taken care of," she answered rather stiffly. And the subject was dismissed.

But that didn't take care of it. Sometimes there was unspiced food and sometimes through oversight there wasn't.

About a week later a message came from the import office in Bombay that their luggage had arrived from Calcutta and that Ernie should come to the warehouse to clear it. They talked over the food situation and Lois made a shopping list of tinned foods and packaged things such as crackers that could supplement the children's diet during the next couple of months, for they knew that they probably wouldn't get to Bombay very often.

It took Ernie two days to clear all the baggage and to do the food shopping. Although it was well packed, moving all those pieces during the heavy monsoon downpours was a difficult job. The Mission School carts and drivers met him at the train station and brought the delayed shipment the final lap to the bungalow. They set all the boxes, trunks and barrels on the back verandah where they could be unpacked piece by piece as time permitted. The food boxes, however, were unpacked immediately and the food kept in their rooms separate from the general household supplies.

When these foods began to appear at the table for the children Miss Ebert was chagrinned.

"Why, my land! What did you go and buy food supplies in Bombay for? After all, you pay into the general household accounts, so if you wanted something from Bombay you could have told me."

"Since I had to go to Bombay anyway to get this shipment of luggage, and since the children's needs are rather special and different from the general household, we thought perhaps we had better get them," Ernie explained. "I think these will make the transition from American food to Indian food over the next months much easier for the children."

After that, the unspiced food for Linda and Jimmy was prepared regularly by Sovenji in the kitchen and the household settled down to more congenial mealtimes together. The chiledren hardly seemed to notice the adjustments being made to their new situation and easily related to the children in the community. They often played in houses in the village and regularly invited their friends and parents to come to the Shulls' house.

Sunday afternoons were set aside for visiting, sometimes in the Indian homes and sometimes in the bungalow, for the community soon learned that all were welcome to drop in without a formal invitation. Carrying big, black umbrellas and wearing rubber sandals they made their way splashing through the heavy downpour--puddles of water and mud everywhere.

Chapter 10

——— •❖• ———

New Clothes and Wild Dogs

In the village there was no convenient store to pick up clothes for the kids. Lois liked to sew and this would be an opportunity to put her abilities to work. She pulled the little, blue dress from under the old White Company treadle sewing machine she had been using for the past hour and carefully clipped the threads where she had been mending a tear in the skirt. Lois remembered the day she had bought that machine in an old secondhand shop in Lena, Illinois where they had had a temporary pastorate. They had been waiting there for visas to be granted to enter India. The old White was shoved back in one corner of a big storage room, covered with dust and sticky with old oil, but it was just what she needed to bring to their village in India where there would be no electricity available. It had cleaned up well, and now it ran like a top--an object of admiration by the Indian ladies who were used to seeing the tailors in the bazaar sitting on the floor, operating hand-wheel machines--or more likely, running the wheel expertly with their toes while they guided the cloth beneath the needle with their hands. The sewing machine had been uncrated only a week, but by using most of her spare moments she had about caught up on the family mending.

Linda and Jimmy really needed more sun suits--they would be cooler and easier to wash and iron than any of the clothes she had brought for them from the States. She decided that she would ask Miss Ebert how she could get to the market on Saturday to look for some pretty, cotton cloths, which were plentiful in any Indian bazaar. She had brought along from the States a large number of basic paper patterns, advancing in sizes to fit the children as they would grow older.

Miss Ebert agreed to have Devu drive the bullocks and tonga to the bazaar on Saturday morning, and while Lois was buying the cloth and a few other things she needed, Devu could get some supplies for the school, thus justifying the use of school equipment.

Dorothy left on Friday evening to go to the Dahanu Hospital to help out during the weekend. So on Saturday morning, feeling as if they were going to a party, Lois took Linda with her to choose a pretty cotton cloth for sun suits. It was an exciting excursion for both of them. Linda knelt on the back seat of the tonga facing forward so she could watch Devu, who looked for all the world like an animated Roman driving his beautiful race horses around a track. Devu would give each bullock a flat-handed smack on the rump and then a poke with his nail-tipped bamboo stick to make the lethargic animals go a little faster--a useless maneuver since the bullocks' skin was so thick they seldom reacted to it. Devu would yell a string of unintelligible words at the bullocks and wave his stick in the air as if a whole stadium of people and nobles in their royal box were watching his exploits, then in exasperation he would reach over the footboard of the tonga, grab the bullocks' tails and twist them, which usually made the sluggish animals break into a lumbering trot--for a very few steps. This made Linda clap her hands and laugh.

In spite of the heavy rain, the road was crowded that morning, people carrying on their heads broad baskets filled with fresh vegetables, going in to market to sell to the daily shoppers. Others crouched under their huge, black umbrellas, holding with one hand their long, cotton clothing above their ankles to avoid the mud, on their way to the tiny shops to get their day's supplies. Carts, other tongas, a number of bicycles and now and then a large, lumbering lorry, its bulb horn blasting. would bully everything else off the road until it splashed by. Most people were sloshing along barefooted on the muddy road; a few were carrying sandals, clean and dry, to put on once they arrived at wherever they were going. Like a knight in the days of King Arthur holding his lance before him as he charged his opponent in a tournament before the court, Lois held an umbrella tilted to protect the space between the overhead hood of the tonga and the foot board. Some people didn't seem to mind having no protection from the rain; after, they would soon dry off once they could get inside. People were used to being wet during the rains.

The whole scene around them was infused with life and the ongoing business of the day, making their slow progress practically unnoticed. Eventually, however, they arrived in the town of Palghar, and peeping around the edge of the umbrella in spite of getting splattered in the face, Lois could see shops on both sides of the street. Devu pulled to one side and stopped the bullocks. He pointed with his stick to three shops directly beside the tonga and explained that they were cloth shops. Stepping down to the small step beside the footboard, Lois climbed out and then lifted Linda down beside her. Holding Linda's hand she hurried to the first shop which had a wide overhanging roof to partially protect the customers. The shopkeeper sat on a platform about waist-high to the customers, his legs crossed like a Buddha, where he could reach without rising many of the bolts of cloth in his store. Lois lifted Linda up and set her on the edge of the platform.

The shopkeeper was very gracious pulling down bolt after bolt of cloth and spreading them out carefully for Lois to examine. Finally Linda chose one with a white background and little elephants of many colors scattered over it. The shopkeeper wrapped the folded cloth in old newspaper and tied the package with many rounds of sewing thread, then handed it to Linda. She was delighted and insisted on carrying it herself.

The second shop was a bit larger and had one step up for customers to enter. Here they were completely protected from the rain. The shopkeeper asked them to sit on a cotton mattress at the back of the shop. Slipping off their shoes they stepped to the back and sat down cross-legged on the mattress. This proved to be time consuming since they were courteously given hot tea to drink before they could look at the cloth. The tea was piping hot and delicious, adding immensely to the adventure of their shopping fun; besides, it was good public relations for the shopkeeper, thought Lois.

Again they were shown a number of different patterns, and Linda and Lois together chose a cloth with tigers and palm trees in red and white.

"I'll carry this one," smiled Lois as she took the similarly-wrapped package from the shopkeeper. They slipped on their sandals and Lois helped Linda down the steps. They stood for a moment, staring through the rain to make sure Devu was back in his seat, then raising the umbrella they hurried to the tonga. After helping Linda climb in, Lois stepped up into the back, making the tonga tilt backward and rock precariously.

After they were situated with the umbrella protecting them, Devu let out a yell and gave each bullock a mighty shove with his stick. He braced a foot on the back end of each one and bestowed them a vigorous kick. One bullock started forward; the other bullock gave a snort and deliberately lay down in the mud as though he had suddenly decided to take an indefinite period of rest. The yoke tilted to a perilous angle, pulling the head of the standing bullock low and to one side. The tonga upended, and Lois found herself lying on her back on the back of the seat with her feet up in the air higher than her head in a most undignified position, the umbrella her only protection against sliding skirts. Linda had slipped around easily and was sitting comfortably against the seat back. Devu was beside himself, trying to get the stubborn bullock to stand up. This turned out to be high entertainment for the Saturday morning shopping crowds who gathered around to watch the show.

"Madam, could I be of service?" inquired an educated voice in English beside the tonga. Lois quickly looked out between the bars that supported the hood of the tonga and saw a man dressed in loose, white clothing, holding his dhoti up out of the mud with one hand and his umbrella in the other.

"Oh, thank you, sir. You certainly can if you can help me figure out a ladylike way to get out of here," she exclaimed gratefully.

"Here. Let me first take the little girl." He reached in and lifted Linda out of the tonga and stood her on the ground. "Now, Madam, if you will turn and stand on the seat back, then I will help you to brace yourself on the spokes of the wheel and climb down."

Ignoring the rain, Lois lowered the umbrella and whirled her legs around so she could stand up on the back of the seat. Then holding on to the top rim of the wheel she stepped onto one of the spokes; then she put her hand into the waiting hand of her rescuer and jumped to the ground. Lois looked up at him with gratitude as she reached for her umbrella.

"Thank you, sir, for helping me out of a most difficult situation." Then she thought about how ridiculous she must have looked and she began to laugh. "I'm sure it must have looked very funny to you."

The gentleman's black eyes twinkled and a corner of his mouth twitched, but he gave no other sign of amusement. "I'm glad no one was injured," he said.

"Do you live in this town? May I know your name, please?" she asked wondering who in this town might speak such good English. "My husband will want to thank you for your kindness."

"No, Madam, I live in Bombay where I am a professor at the University of Bombay, and I am here for a few days visiting my brother. My name is Ram Das. If I have been of service, it was my pleasure. Think nothing of it." A small youngster handed him the two packages of cloth which he in turn gave to Lois with a bow as he bid her good day.

In the meantime Devu had about exhausted what he knew to do to get the stubborn animal to stand up. It was ridiculous to have to stand around and await the pleasure of a bullock! Especially since she felt that everyone was staring at them. As she stood there in the rain thinking about the whole incident, she came to a definite conclusion--she intended to change her mode of dress! As soon as she could, she was determined to buy some saris and dress like the Indian women. Not only was their dress more beautiful, it was also more practical for this culture and she had a feeling that it could become a big step in her being accepted among the Indian women.

About that time along came a friend of Devu's who stopped to find out what was the difficulty. There followed an excited conversation with many gestures and much demonstration. Apparently Devu and his friend finally came to an agreement about what should be done. They walked over to the irritating, sleepy eyed bullock and each man grabbed a wheezing nostril, pressing down and shutting off the animal's air. Instantly the bullock got to its feet snorting and shaking itself. The people standing around began to laugh. Devu climbed onto the driver's seat ready to go. Lois waited a couple of minutes to be sure everything was again under control, then she helped Linda in and climbed in after her. As they drove down the street headed for home the people who had been watching waved in a friendly way. *I believe they enjoyed the diversion,* thought Lois. *That's more than I can say for myself--but it was kind of funny,* she chuckled.

The two packages of cloth lay on the floor boards, muddy and soaked through. She looked at them ruefully, thinking about how pretty and clean the cloth had been when they bought it. But maybe that wasn't so bad after all, because whatever cotton cloth she bought in India would have to be washed before she could cut out a garment anyway, since no cloth was sanitized. So what had really been lost by this whole morning's adventure--nothing at all except her dignity--and that was repairable. In fact, Ernie laughed with glee when she told him about it--displaying much more levity about the whole affair than the incident warranted, Lois was convinced.

By the end of August the rains were growing definitely lighter; there were periods every day without rain. The rice and cotton crops were growing tall and the whole world looked lush and green. There were even sprouts shooting up from some of the wooden fence posts, and the town market displayed a great variety of fresh fruits and vegetables, which made the people happy with the abundance of food.

"Daddy, could we go to the sea shore and play in the sand," asked Linda one day when she had grown tired of her daily routine of playing with just two other people.

Ernie looked up from his Marathi reading book. "I can't do it today, Linda, because I have to study. But you've given me an idea--how would you like to have a sand box right here in our compound where you could play in the sand whenever you wanted to?"

"Oh yes, Daddy, I want a sandbox. Could you come and make it for me now?" Linda's eyes sparkled with excitement as she held on to his shirt.

Ernie put his arm around her and held her tightly for a minute. "I'll tell you what I'll do. This afternoon I'll work on the box and you can watch me. Then Saturday you and I will go to the sea shore and get some bags of white sand to fill it. How is that?"

"Okay, Daddy, I'll help you make the sandbox." Satisfied with the promise of future fun, she went to find Dayabai and the two little boys.

By the time Saturday came Ernie had finished a sturdy, wooden frame about four feet square and had placed it inside the compound just outside the back verandah lattice, where someone working on the verandah could at the same time supervise the play in the sandbox.

Miss Ebert, always on guard to protect the Mission accounts, said that the school bullocks and cart couldn't be used for such a purpose; so Ernie sent a school boy to the village to bring back a horse tonga and driver. Armed with several gunny sacks and a shovel, they set off for the beach.

Traveling behind a horse instead of the lumbering bullocks they were used to, it seemed to them that they covered the mile to the beach very fast. The sea looked blue-gray with a few whitecaps breaking here and there as the waves washed up onto the wide stretch of very white sand. In the distance out on the Arabian Sea the black hull of a fishing vessel appeared to be almost stationary as it moved with its cargo slowly south toward Bombay. Farther down the beach a lorry was stopped and three men were shoveling up sand and throwing it into the back.

Ernie lifted Linda down from the tonga and she immediately sat down and began to run her fingers through the sand. Ernie took the bags and the shovel, and walking off a few paces, began to fill the bags. When he had filled the four bags he had brought along, he carried them over to the tonga and began to load them. The tonga driver, who had been squatting content-edly by the wheel, helped to place the bags so that they were balanced in his two-wheeled vehicle.

As Ernie brushed the sand off Linda's dress and legs, he glanced down the beach a little way and noticed five dogs were chasing a goat and had it surrounded; it was bleating pathetically. Obviously the dogs were about to attack and kill it. Ernie was sure that helpless goat belonged to some poor family who needed the milk very badly.

"Wait here," he said to Linda as he walked down the beach toward the dogs, picking up a femur of a cow which had apparently died there. The long leg bone was bleached white from many days in the tropical sun. It was lightweight, but it looked like a weapon.

"Hey! Hey!" he yelled as he trotted toward the dogs waving the bone in the air. Two of the dogs turned toward him. Before he realized what was happening, all five dogs had surrounded him, and the goat had scampered off into the brush. Suddenly he noticed that all five dogs were a uniform tawny color, not splotched and of varying colors like ordinary dogs, and that they all had the same kind of bushy tails. Instantly he realized the danger, for these must be the wild dogs of India! Like the well-coordinated team of hunters that they were, the dogs began to close in yapping and snarling. Ernie whirled round and round as he swung the bone, hitting a muzzle now and then as he spun his way slowly up the beach toward the tonga. He must first of all get Linda to safety. He yelled frantically for Linda to climb into the tonga. The excited tonga driver lifted her into the front seat and climbed in beside her holding the reins in readiness to flee.

As if it were not really happening, Ernie heard the men with the lorry shouting to him to get out of there because the dogs were killers, but not one of them made a move to help him fight them off. By maneuvering with the swinging bone, he was able to eventually get all five of the dogs on one side of him away from the tonga. Once his loose Indian pajama pant leg caught in the teeth of one of the dogs and Ernie heard it rip. Finally he was close enough to the tonga to make a mad dash, a final jump over the footboard as he twisted his body and landed with a hard bump, his back against the backboard. The dogs were at his heels and began jumping up at him as he swung the only weapon he had with as much force as he could muster. The instant Ernie landed in the tonga, the driver screamed at the horse and it started racing down the beach toward the road. After a few minutes, three of the dogs gave up the pursuit, but the last two chased the tonga for half a mile before they dropped off at the side of the road. Only then did Ernie become aware of Linda's frantic sobbing as she gripped the back of the seat and looked over at her daddy.

"It's all over now, honey," Ernie assured her as he lifted her over the back of the seat and held her tightly in his arms. "We're safe now and we are going home." By the time they reached the compound Linda's tears had stopped, but her little body would jerk every once in a while with a leftover dry sob. But this would not be the end of it--for several months after that, Linda would sometimes wake up in the night crying, frightened by nightmares.

Later that evening Ernie picked up Dr. S. H. Prater's book on Indian animals and looked up India's wild dog, the dhole. There he confirmed that ". . . the Indian wild dogs are of a uniform tawny color and have bushy tails." He also noted that in groups or packs they kill bears and tigers--a sobering thought.

The world of the language students remained very limited--study night and day, the family, the Sunday visiting, and the Christian School community. At times Lois felt very impatient with the long period needed just to prepare them for an assignment where they would be working directly with the Indian people. As they studied on the front verandah of the bungalow, they could look down the long lane toward the road where almost daily they would observe huge crowds of noisy, shouting demonstrators passing by on their way toward Palghar. They could even distinguish the words of some of the slogans. "Gandhi ji ki jai!" (roughly translated "Victory to The Honorable Gandhi!") was one of the favorites. It was like a world apart--as if they were seeing it performed on a stage and they, themselves, were not really a part of it. They followed carefully the accounts in the newspapers that arrived in Palghar from Bombay each day.

The tension between the Hindu and Muslim communities was growing more intense, although Lois wondered whether it could get more intense than the atmosphere in the city of Calcutta the night they had arrived in India.

In the early part of August, Jinnah, the most influential Muslim leader, convinced the Muslim League to advocate setting August sixteenth as a "direct action day," a time when all Muslims should demand a separate state of Pakistan. It was agreed among the Muslims in Calcutta that, on that day, the Muslim League would attack members of the Congress Party and loot Congress Party property. Eventually, Jinnah's demands were met and the Bengali government did decide to make that day, August sixteenth, a holiday; a day in India's history which would later be remembered as a day of horror.

The worst of the action seemed to be centered in Calcutta. Unprecedented mob violence plunged that great city into an orgy of bloodshed, murder, and terror. Hundreds of lives were lost, thousands were injured, and vast amounts of property destroyed. The Muslim League took out processions bent on looting, arson, and killing. The city was in the grip of goondas of both communities.

Lois read The Times of India newspaper account aloud to Dorothy and Ernie as they sat at their study table during their morning tea break.

"Dear God! This whole country is exploding!" cried Lois, thinking of all the helpless people caught up in the inexorable struggle for power and independence.

"You can be sure this rioting and murdering is not going to be confined to the east coast of India. This violence has already spread to Bombay and all the other big cities; yes, and the villages, too. Look how much political activity we see in Palghar and along this road coming from Jawar. We have to face the fact that this kind of violence could break out anywhere in India at any time. It's like waiting for the other shoe to drop." Ernie's face looked grim as he faced what these new developments might mean.

"It appears to me," commented Dorothy, "that up to this time the Christian community has stayed rather apart, seeming to feel that they are not involved in this struggle which is primarily between the Hindus and the Muslims. Certainly they must have a part in the new India. I wonder what it will be."

"Whatever else it turns out to be," Ernie said, "it must be to uphold the way of peace which Christ taught and which Gandhi preaches." But Ernie could not have foreseen the long, bloody road ahead, before India and her diverse people would eventually find a way to live beside each other in relative peace.

The Palghar Christian community itself was made up of a few more than two hundred people--one hundred thirty of them being boarding school students and staff, the others living in the surrounding areas. Lois learned to know all the people living on the school compound quite well, but the ones she knew best were Dayabai, Sovenji, and Sarabai who worked in the bungalow and who were always ready to answer her questions or talk over problems about the household or the children. Lois showed Dayabai how to use the sewing machine and how to mend Sovenji's clothes or Shamuel's tiny shirts, all the clothing little boys of his age usually wore. When Lois wanted to buy cotton saris to wear instead of dresses, it was Dayabai who helped her select them and showed her how to "nes" (drape) them and wear them comfortably. Miss Ebert, trying not to be too critical of new missionaries who had to have time to learn, let it be known that she didn't quite approve of this change in dress, and implied that this "going native" was not quite in keeping with her high standard. After all, one doesn't see the British women adopting the sari as their customary dress. They always uphold their "high" British standards!

In September, Miss Ebert traveled to Bombay and back to bring school supplies. While she was in Bombay she attended an afternoon tea where there were several British ladies. In telling Lois about it, she made it a point to comment, "And every one of those ladies looked so crisp and fresh in her lovely cotton frock!"

"I can imagine they did look nice," Lois agreed. "You know, Miss Ebert, I've been thinking about all you've said about wearing a sari, and why the British ladies wear frocks and why I am going to wear saris, and I've decided that the British want to be different. They want to be considered better than the Indian women; while I want to be accepted as one of them, and certainly never do I want to be considered better--or worse, for that matter. I love the Indian dress and I am going to strive to look as lovely in a sari as they do."

Toward the end of September, Dayabai told Lois that Sovenji's brother Babu was coming home for a month's vacation from teachers' training school, where he had been studying for two years, and that she would be cooking for another person. Miss Ebert was pleased with Babu's progress and his good grades, and she was looking forward to his graduation in May when he would be available to teach in one of the village schools. Teachers with two years training were very scarce, and the Mission was working extremely hard to upgrade the qualifications of their teaching staff.

Babu attended church with Sovenji and Dayabai on Sunday where, after the services, Lois and Ernie were introduced to him. Lois was immediately impressed with his friendly smile and his enthusiasm for teaching.

He'll make a great teacher, Lois thought, and no doubt a very intelligent one. No wonder Miss Ebert is so proud of him considering that he and his brother came from a very backward village, and he and his brother were the first ones from that village to become literate. We will have him over for tea one day.

About a week and a half later while Lois, Dorothy and Ernie were studying together on the front verandah, Dayabai had Linda, and Shamu and Jimmy were out in the back compound playing in the sand box, when Miss Ebert came out of her office door with one hand on her hip and her lips pressed together. She stopped by the study table eying Ernie steadily.

"Well, Ernie, I think here is a problem that you should handle. It's really more in your field than in mine. You are the Reverend around here and trained to deal with such problems. My field is primarily education."

Ernie registered surprise. He wondered what was coming, since up to this time any signs of Miss Ebert relinquishing authority, even in small matters, had been lacking.

"Parlak Bhonsle has just been to my office and laid the problem in my lap." Miss Ebert remained standing, although Mr. Chopade's vacant chair was just beside her. She seemed upset and perhaps angry as well. "I told the Parlak he should deal with it as the minister of the Church, but he insists that since Sovenji and Dayabai are in our employ, we are the ones to settle it. I must say! I never expected something like this to happen! Why, that family has been Christian for--."

"Wait a minute! Wait a minute!" interrupted Ernie, half rising from his chair and motioning for Miss Ebert to sit down. "Just relax a bit! Could you tell us what you are talking about? What's happened? What won't the Parlak do? Of course, I'll be glad to help in whatever way I can. Why are you so upset?"

Miss Ebert sank wearily down on the chair as she rubbed her forehead with her hand. "I had so many hopes for Babu--he has been such a fine young man." She hesitated. "Ernie, Babu is living with Sovenji and Dayabai with all the privileges and relationship of another husband to Dayabai! This must be stopped at once!"

"How do you know this?" asked Ernie. Surely Miss Ebert wouldn't listen to gossip.

"Oh, there's no doubt about it--the Parlak told me. Don't forget--he and his family live in the other half of the duplex cabin with Sovenji's family. There is only a bamboo matting wall plastered with clay and cow dung mixture dividing the two living quarters. The Parlak has known what was going on for several days, but he hesitated to do anything about it because we pay Sovenji's salary and because of the support for Babu to continue in school; therefore, it is his belief that we should handle the problem."

"And what is your opinion of what I should do," Ernie questioned thoughtfully closing his study book and pushing it away from him.

"Well, I don't know--I suppose you had better talk to the Parlak and get it stopped," she decided as she rose from the chair and started back toward her office. The language students heard her say as if to herself as she stepped through the door, "I just never thought...."

Ernie excused himself from the study table and went in search of Parlak Bhonsle. He and Lois had been wishing for some time that they could be doing more in the work of the Mission, rather than spending all their time studying, but this looked like a very thorny problem with which to start their increased involvement. He could depend upon the Parlak to give excellent advice. Ernie was convinced that the Parlak of the Church, Parlak Bhonsle, was the one with the cultural background and the Christian teaching best qualifying him to try to solve this problem. Ernie would like to prevail upon the Parlak to handle the situation and let him, as the employer, support him in whatever way he could. He met Parlak Bhonsle coming from the school.

"Salaam, Parlak Sahib. I was just coming to find you," greeted Ernie as he turned to walk with him.

"Salaam, Sahib. Yes, I think we need to talk. I was just going to walk to the other end of the compound to visit Gracebai for a few minutes. She has malaria and she has no one but her little granddaughter to take care of her. Perhaps you will walk with me while we talk." The Parlak was always very concerned about the sick and the elderly, and made sure that they had food and care.

"Parlak Bhonsle, Miss Ebert has just told me about the situation at Sovenji's house. I'll be very glad to help stop what is going on, but I need your advice about how to go about it so the least damage is done. Don't you think that it would really be better if you and the Church officers took the lead in this?" Ernie asked with sincerity.

The Parlak was silent for a minute, then he said something that was to become a pattern that they were to follow through their relationship of many years to come.

"Sahib, I don't really think so. The truth is that I need you, and, yes, I can see that you need me. Let's walk for a while under the palms and talk, and think, and pray about this; then, let's go together and talk it over with the Sovenji family." The Parlak smiled as he glanced over at

Ernie. "It was good of you to come so soon to talk about the problem, although it will probably take some time to solve. We, here in India, take more time to do things than you do in America." As they strolled along the path, Ernie learned many things. It was like going through a door and finding himself face to face with an alien culture. He discovered that among the people from whom Sovenji and Babu came, family relationships and hospitality were very important. A visitor to anyone's home was offered the best of everything, even the wife of the master of the house. In this case, Babu was Sovenji's brother, honored especially because he had become educated. Offering him the opportunity to sleep with Dayabai was the best of hospitality, a virtue in the culture from which they had come. True, they had become Christian five years before, but entirely eliminating customs which conflict with Christian teaching, sometimes takes a very long time.

Intellectually and objectively Ernie understood what the Parlak was telling him, but emotionally he found himself repulsed by such an idea of hospitality.

That night after the work of the evening meal was all finished, Ernie and the Parlak went to Sovenji's house to talk things over.

At first Babu and Sovenji couldn't see anything wrong with the arrangement, although they did agree that it wasn't exactly according to Christian teaching.

Dayabai sitting cross-legged on the floor with Shamu on her lap exclaimed in surprise, as though there was nothing else to be said on the matter, "But Sahib and Parlak Sahib, Babu is our brother!"

As Ernie listened, he caught a glimpse of what it must be like to have an entirely different value system where, like the Greeks of old, hospitality is one of the greatest virtues.

The Parlak and Ernie made some suggestions to which Sovenji and Babu readily agreed. Babu would leave the next morning to go back to school where he would remain until he graduated. In the meantime, Sovenji, being the older brother, would make marriage arrangements for Babu, to take place the end of May. Everyone seemed happy about this and Ernie and the Parlak were about to take their leave when Sovenji stopped them.

"Sahib, if we don't have a suitable wife for Babu in our Mission, you had better look for one in another mission."

"I!" exclaimed Ernie. "I?" He couldn't believe what he was hearing.

"That's right," agreed the Parlak with a smile. "The custom is that if the family is not able to find a suitable wife, the Mission executive or the person in charge of the station should make an arrangement for one--but I'm sure Miss Ebert will help and many people can make suggestions. It could be there is someone in our own boarding school."

"Parlak Sahib, I'll be no good at that! Why, I had a hard enough time finding my own wife without trying to figure out who would be the right wife for someone else!" objected Ernie with a startled expression.

The Parlak laughed. "Yes, I understand. Getting a wife is much easier in our country." As they walked along the path toward the bungalow, the Parlak tried to reassure Ernie. "Sahib, it's the way things are done here. You may find it hard to believe, but Babu will be much happier with a wife that you will select for him than if he had to make the selection for himself."

Ernie shook his head in bewilderment. He wondered how long it would take him to understand the people with whom he would be working. In the few months he had been in this country, he had come to love India. He vowed to do all he could to fight the poverty, illiteracy, disease and superstition that were standing in the way of progress in this land. One difficulty would be to be able to distinguish between those things that were non-Christian and those things that were purely cultural.

"I KNOW YOU AMERICANS ARE VERY STRANGE,
BUT I LIKE YOU ANY WAY."
Sagaram

Chapter 11

Dahanu Road

Christmas was one of the two most important seasons of the year for the Christians in India as it is in much of the rest of the world, and every Christian family did many special things to celebrate. One of the nicest customs, Lois discovered, was for a family to prepare a special food and take it as a gift to some of their neighbors, even though there was very little food in their own house.

As Lois went to the door many times on Christmas Eve to receive small offerings of sweet dishes, she was conscious of conflicting feelings churning inside, tempting her to tell the callers to take back the food and save it for their own children. How could these folks from their meager supply, bring a gift of food to the Shulls? For, in spite of the fact that their missionary allowance was not quite sufficient for maintenance--for their medical bills had been quite high since they had arrived in India--she realized that they still had much more than their Indian neighbors. She had been unaware enough in her thinking and planning before coming to India to see herself always in the role of the giver, sharing food, faith, knowledge, healing and a better way of life. She had not seen herself as receiver. *How simple and naive I have been,* Lois told herself, as she recognized the wonderful spirit of joy in sharing that prompted these acts of generosity by people who had so little. She smiled with new understanding as she accepted the gifts with heartfelt appreciation. On Christmas Day, after the services of the morning, all the Christians were invited to come to the bungalow for a Holiday Tea. Sovenji, Miss Ebert, and Lois, along with some help from Dayabai and Sarabai (Dorothy had gone to Dahanu to work in the hospital during the holidays) prepared karanjis (pastries filled with coconut, raisins,

83

nuts, and sugar) and bhajis (deep-fried batter filled with onions, potatoes, and spices) along with gallons of Indian tea, which they served to two hundred people, Christians, Hindus, and a few Muslims who came from Palghar, during the afternoon.

That evening after all the guests had gone, the Shulls and Miss Ebert had a little Christmas time together. Lois and Ernie had brought from America a doll for Linda and a new teddy bear for Jimmy. The children clasped the new toys tightly in their arms and refused to be separated from them even when they were being tucked into bed. Miss Ebert gave Linda a tiny ivory elephant and Jimmy a British-made "Dinky" truck. Lois and Ernie presented Miss Ebert with a new, white, American purse, which she would find very useful shortly, since she would soon be leaving on furlough; and Miss Ebert gave the Shulls a set of orange-and-cream-colored table mats woven by the girls in boarding school.

All these experiences, along with many letters from America bringing news about friends and family, made the holidays very exciting.

Toward the beginning of January Linda began to run a low fever, and a week later Jimmy's temperature shot up also. They tired easily and wanted to lie down or be carried around most of the time. Lois and Dorothy assumed the problem to be malaria which was common among both adults and children in India, but the fever didn't respond to the usual malaria treatment which was Aterbrin, a tablet so bitter that the children often vomited it. Five days after the onset of the disease, Dorothy decided that it was time to seek more expert help, so she traveled with Lois and Ernie to take the children by train north to Dahanu Road where they could be examined by the doctors at the Mission Hospital.

The journey with sick children was arduous, beginning with a jolting ride in the Mission bullock tonga to the Palghar railway station. They waited, sitting on the end of a bench by the ticket gate for an hour, before the train finally pulled in. It was late because it had been held up by a mob of political demonstrators in Bombay. They climbed into a third class car, stepping over loosely-woven, bamboo baskets of smelly, dried fish partially wrapped in burlap. The fish was on its way to the open-air bazaars of Bombay. They finally found places for Dorothy and Lois to sit on the wooden benches holding Linda and Jimmy. The train was so crowded with people, animals, and merchandise that Ernie had to stand for most of the journey. At the Dahanu Road station they engaged a horse tonga to take them out to the Mission compound.

The hospital was an attractive, two-story structure set back among Indian cork and neem trees; and extending from its front entrance to the busy highway running from Dahanu Road to Jawar was a cool, grass-covered lawn, interrupted here and there by brilliant red canna beds, catching the eye like unexpected rays of sunshine on a cloudy day. There was a wide, shaded verandah with large pillars connected by rounded arches stretching gracefully across the proscenium, and approached by a broad, palm-bordered, gravel driveway.

Their tonga turned into the hospital compound and moved along the driveway up to the hospital entrance. Dorothy, to whom this was familiar territory, took Jimmy in her arms, and after Ernie had paid the tonga driver, Dorothy led them into the hospital, past two semiprivate rooms, a large ward entrance and finally to the office. As they moved down the verandah they met a student nurse who smiled at them shyly.

"Salaam, Sister, Sahib, Madam Sahib," she greeted them. "Shall I tell Doctor that you are here?" She started to turn toward the office.

"Thank you, Lilabai. Is Doctor in the office? If so, we will be able to find her ourselves," Dorothy replied.

Lilabai moved her head from side to side. "Yes, she is just there by the office window."

Following the student's gesture, they passed on down the verandah.

Fortunately Dr. Barbara Nickey, the Chief Medical Officer, was there working on the records. She had to do this whenever she found a minute, for she, as well as Dr. Peter Paul, saw an average of a hundred patients a day. This didn't leave her much free time. Even her nights were usually interrupted, for the largest ward in the hospital was the maternity ward.

As the new arrivals walked into the office, Dr. Nickey looked up in surprise.

"Well! Welcome! Come in. Come in. What can I do for you? I assume there is something wrong or you wouldn't be here in the middle of the week," she observed abruptly as she moved toward them, glancing at each one in turn with her diagnostic eye. She was a small, fifty-two-year-old woman, scarcely five feet tall, a bit on the dumpy side; her iron-gray hair was pulled back severely and rolled in a knot on the back of her head. *For all the world like an elderly grandmother,* Lois thought. The Doctor's sharp, gray eyes looked at them keenly through her rimless glasses. She wore a white uniform, substantial, white shoes, and had a stethoscope hanging around her neck.

"Doctor, we have two youngsters who have been running low fevers of about one hundred to one-oh-one for about a week, and they don't respond to malaria medication. We thought we had better bring them to the hospital for you to check," explained Dorothy.

"Oh, well, in that case, I think the first thing to do is to examine them. I think this must be the Shulls' first visit to Dahanu Hospital," The doctor observed as she walked quickly toward the door. "Come along. We'll begin in here."

The next hour was spent in performing various examinations and tests. Dorothy helped the doctors as both Dr. Nickey and Dr. Peter Paul made their separate examinations, followed by a battery of lab tests. They found enlarged glands in the neck, underarm, and groin, as well as much-enlarged livers. But even after the results of all the lab tests were in, the doctors couldn't make a definite diagnosis.

Dr. Nickey decided that this was serious enough that they should keep the children in the hospital over night and call for consultation, Drs. Laura and Raymond Cottrell and Dr. Leonard Blickenstaff. This was not routine because these doctors were located in the Bulsar Mission Hospital, north about an hour's train trip along the Arabian Sea.

Dorothy and the Shulls stayed in Dr. Nickey's huge bungalow where they were very comfortable except that Lois couldn't sleep. She was afraid that this could be the onset of some terrible, life threatening disease. She was more worried because Dr. Nickey was unsure about the diagnosis. At that particular moment she wished heartily that they were all back in the States. How do you fight something when you don't even know what it is, and how do you tell how sick children really are? Lois wished that the illness were her own.

Lois was reminded of all the years of preparation that they had spent before coming to India; how she yearned to help the Indian people in every way she could. Growing up in an American middle-class family, she had enjoyed opportunities and privileges that had been provided for her—not something that she had earned. In her way of thinking, privilege and opportunity were not without obligation, they carried with them the responsibility to help others. But, if staying here meant sacrificing the health of the children, then she was ready to leave immediately. Besides, without their own health, they would not be an asset to any program.

The next day the three doctors from Bulsar arrived. It was a learned group that gathered around the examining table as the children were carefully checked three more times. Then, like a jury out for deliberations, they moved into the office. They soon emerged with their collective diagnosis which was that the children did, indeed, have their first case of malaria. With treatment, in a week or so, both children recovered but malaria was to strike the family dozens of times in the years to come with the typical and more serious symptoms of malaria including 104 or 105 degree fever, delerium, cold sweats and chills.

Later, as their language study continued back at Palghar, Lois glanced up toward the low, blue-tinted mountains in the east, and in a reverie, was visited by unbidden, shadowy thoughts, recollections of the Eby missionary children who had gone before, and who had not made it due to complications resulting from this killer disease—malaria.

Lois tried to cast these thoughts from her mind. Accidents and disease can be found anywhere. Ernie often reminded her that not even in the States could they have more personal, expert medical attention than what they had here on the mission field.

Lois brought her mind back to the Marathi translation lesson. Like many other mothers, perhaps she was just overly concerned. She believed that it was through God's guidance that they had come to serve in India—but so had the Ebys who lost several of their children because of disease. How could God ask anyone to make such a sacrifice?

During the first part of February, the annual meeting of the second district delegates of the Church was held at Palghar, and regardless of the fact that Ernie had been studying Marathi for only nine months, he was asked to be moderator and to chair all the business meetings. Lois was sorry that she wasn't given the opportunity to be in on any of these planning and evaluation sessions. She began to feel like an observer only, and that the important work of the Mission program was to be done by the men, and sometimes with the help of the "miss sahibs" (unmarried missionary ladies). With Mr. Chopade expertly offering vocabulary, Ernie managed to moderate the business sessions very well.

Ernie spent many long hours with the delegates in thoughtful and prayerful decision making. All present agreed that the nationalistic fervor, and the antagonism between the Hindus and Muslims, needed to be discussed by Christians. It had become apparent that the entire church program was in jeopardy and needed to be reevaluated in light of the national crisis and the unprecedented challenges of the escalating emergency. What should be the role of their church and what should be the role of Christians in general? The delegates were well aware that the Marathi District was only one of two Church of the Brethren districts in India. Furthermore, they knew there were many denominations of Christians working in different parts of India. Altogether Christians made up only two percent of the population of this diverse country. Still, they were the most educated group. The programs of the church, the schools, and the hospitals had to be made as effective and indigenous as possible. Even though the Christians were a small minority in a largely Hindu country, the Christians believed they had an important role to play in the building of a new secular nation. The Indian Church wanted to make a valued contribution.

As India seethed on the brink of civil war, Britain, in a last effort to keep the subcontinent from being divided, sent Lord Louis Mountbatten to India to supervise the negotiations between the Hindu Congress Party and the Muslim League in forming a responsible government that could assume power when Britain turned it over on the day of independence. Lord and Lady Mountbatten arrived on March 22, 1947. While the Congress and the League squabbled, the situation deteriorated even further. Riots broke out in Bombay, Amritsar, and Rawalpindi; thirteen deaths were reported in Lahore. The battle cries for a muslim nation separate from India, were being heard everywhere—"Pakistan zindabad!" ("Long live Pakistan!")

The new term of the language school began the second week in March, which was also the beginning of the hot season on the plains. The Shulls, accompanied by Mr. Chopede, Sovenji and Dayabai, were thankful to arrive in the comparatively cool weather of the Western Ghats and to concentrate again upon learning the language. They had had no trouble in travel except that the trains could not be counted on to be on time, and the streets and the stations seemed to be filled with shouting demonstrators.

Mahableshwar, in the mountains, was an isolated community and the political stress of the plains seemed quite removed from the language school. Therefore, the three months the language students spent in that atmosphere were quite refreshing. They missed Dorothy, who had taken her tests early and had decided to remain at the hospital where she could study with a private tutor and still work in the hospital many hours a day. They missed Kathryn also, for now they had to do all the managing, communicating and planning for the household. They were pleased at how much language they had learned in a year. By the end of the school session in June they were reading, writing, and speaking quite fluently in the Marathi language. When word came that their assignment on the plains had been changed, and that they had been transferred to Dahanu Road for the rest of their five-year term, they were delighted with the new responsibilities.

The executive committee of the Mission decided that there was not adequate housing on the Mission Hospital Compound for a family, so they purchased a property located a mile farther east along the Jawar road. It was a two-story cement house with a few acres of land that had been owned by Shri Deshmukh, a Parsee in the town of Dahanu. High on the front wall of the house was carved in curling English letters the name "Grace Villa." With a few changes and repairs, the Committee made the house ready for the Shulls to move into when they came back from language school. Their assignment was to spend half of their time in language study for another year, and half of their time in educational and evangelistic work.

On their way home from the mountains in the middle of June, Lois and the children spent a few days in the steaming, pre-monsoon heat of Bombay at Raj Mahal, the mission apartment supervised by Mary and Lynn Blickenstaff, enjoying the unaccustomed convenience of electric lights and the cooling, long-bladed ceiling fans. Ernie went ahead up country to see to the transfer of all their trunks, boxes, and barrels from Palghar to the new house in Dahanu Road.

The monsoons arrived and it was raining heavily the afternoon that Lois caught her first glimpse of the house and compound that were to be their home for the next four years until time for furlough. The tonga swung back and forth on its two wheels as the bullocks, sensing that home and feed were near, broke into a lumbering, jerky trot, causing the luggage and packages that were stored around Linda and Lois, with Jimmy on her lap, to jiggle and bounce.

Suddenly the bullocks swung to the right through a wide gate and into a fenced-in compound. There was a short driveway that circled around in front of the house. Disregarding the rain, Lois stuck her head outside the tonga hood and stared with excitement at their new home.

Linda squealed and pointed to the top of the house. "Look, Daddy, the roof has stair steps up there like Old King Cole's castle in my story book," Linda exclaimed as she sat on the crowded seat of the tonga. She pointed to the slanting, tiled roof rising from each side of the house to a peak at the top-center of the building where a cement facade resembling stair steps lead to a point in the center.

On the ground floor the main entrance to the house consisted of two sets of double doors, the outside doors made of expanded metal, a wire mesh stronger than chicken wire, protecting a second set of doors that were made of wood. As a shield against inclement monsoon weather, there was a small, arched, portico supported by pillars. The portico extended out over the two steps leading up to the threshold of the front door. On the right of the building and attached like an afterthought was a garage-like extension, open across the front. This added space had a cement floor and windows that opened into Ernie's office. This window was barred like the other windows of the house. Steps and a door, as well as a window, led from that space into the house. The top floor was completely fenced in by wide-meshed, expanded metal.

After the first glance, Lois's eyes caught a glimpse of a long building consisting of a series of rooms facing the main house, but marking a sharp contrast to the two-story building. This building was constructed low to the ground, no doubt with cow dung floors. The walls were made of corrugated metal sheets topped by Bangalore tile roofs. Over each doorway was attached a small portico made of the corrugated sheets, supported by small, uneven log posts. She wondered if these small rooms could be kept dry during such a downpour as they were having. These rooms were for the Mission helpers.

When the bullocks would have gone straight from the gate, past the house on the right, presumably toward a barn or shed at the back, Walia, the bullock driver for the Hospital, gave each one a shove with a bare foot and pulled them around to circle in front of the bungalow. He brought them to a stop by the roofed open space to the right.

There waiting to greet them, wearing broad smiles and calling happy salaams, were Sovenji and Dayabai, along with Ratnakar, the farmer, and Gungubai, his wife, who would be helping in the house. The men stepped forward to lift the children down and stand them among several big-eyed children in a dry space under the roof. With everyone helping, they made fast work of unloading the tonga.

Each person moved quickly to bring order out of chaos; Dayabai gathered up Jimmy and Linda to take them to wash their faces and hands, Sovenji went to prepare tea, Rutnaker helped Ernie move boxes and carry packages to the proper rooms, and Gungubai (named after the sacred Ganges River) went with Lois to help unpack clothing and supplies. Already it was beginning to feel like home; and the greatest blessing of all--their family would be living alone, which would simplify everything from cooking to child discipline.

The office just inside the door from the "garage" where they entered was small but adequate, Lois told herself, as she walked on through to the main room downstairs. That room stretched three-fourths the width of the house, and along the far wall an open, banisterless stair, obviously new, led to the second floor. Just behind the office and the main front room were three very dark rooms, the center one without any windows.

The biggest room to the back of the house was a small dining room, obviously added on, hot because its roof was made of uninsulated, corrugated metal sheets. Glancing down as she and Gungubai toured the house, Lois was grateful to note that the dining room had a cement floor like the rest of the house. To the left and down one step from the east end of the dining room was a tiny kitchen area, also added on. For counter space there was only a cement ledge and a small, metal-topped wooden table. But the arrangement for a stove was the most disappointing. A two-foot-wide, cement ledge was the only table surface. Its height came up to Lois's waist. In the surface of this cement table top two holes had been made. It had openings underneath at the front where pieces of wood or charcoal could be fed into the fire. Cooking pans could be set over these holes.

As Lois went from room to room with Gungubai, she kept telling herself, *This will be fine-- we'll manage with that--surely we can figure out how best to use that*--but when she thought about that kitchen, her heart sank. How could they ever manage with this cooking arrangement! Just thinking of all the time needed to boil the drinking water with these facilities was staggering. Wood was scarce and expensive, so they would have to use mostly charcoal, dirty and smoky. She knew that Sovenji was familiar with the use of this kind of cooking fire, but she wasn't! She resolved to find something else to cook on. Perhaps she could get two pump-up, kerosine stoves, called primuses. The trouble was that they weren't very substantial for they could tip over easily and burn someone. *Oh, dear! Never mind,* she thought. *I'll find a way to manage and keep their food and water supply sanitary.*

Leading from the dining room through a back, expanded metal, double door were four cement steps, protected from the weather by a portico supported by unfinished logs. A path wound from the steps through an open area thick with weeds. A short distance down this path was a wide, open well surrounded by a brick wall, and on top of the wall, a rope and pulley system had been devised for lowering a water bucket and drawing water with a minimum of effort. This arrangement was quite an improvement over the typical village well; the water supply in most villages came from a well that was usually just level with the ground, and as a woman filled her water pots, spilled water could run over her dirty feet and back into the water supply.

"It's a fine well, Madam Sahib. We are very lucky to have such clear, sweet water; and the arrangement for drawing water is the best. All the neighbors are quite envious. You know there is a deep well just outside the front gate to our compound--it also has good water but there is no arrangement for drawing the water except by the hand-over-hand system. I'm glad we have this arrangement for I am to be your water carrier," Gungubai laughed.

When Lois went to see the upstairs of their new house, she understood why Gungubai was so interested in the well arrangement. The bathroom was located upstairs, and all water used for bathing and cleaning on the second floor had to be carried up an outside wooden stairway built between the house and the line of rooms where Gungubai and Dayabai and their families lived. All water for drinking as well as for washing clothes and other household cleaning jobs upstairs and downstairs, had to be carried from the well. The water was stored in huge, waist-high, earthen pots that were three feet in diameter. The outside wooden stairway was used as well by the sweeper when he serviced the toilet stools twice a day. According to the age-old, Hindu custom, the people of the caste from which the sweepers came like all Hindus were born into their caste. Consequently, the sweeper could never do any kind of work except work designated for his caste. The family of Ravi, the Grace Villa sweeper, had been given living quarters on the medical compound where all members of the family worked most of the day. Ravi was given released time in the morning and again in the evening to walk out to the new mission compound where the Shulls now lived and do his work there.

Lois was delighted with the light and airy upstairs. Extending the full width of the bungalow across the front was a very wide verandah, protected on all sides by an exceptionally wide-meshed expanded metal screen. As Lois stepped from the stairwell around the protective banister she thought, *Here is the ideal place for the children to play. It's big enough to run or skip rope, and there is little danger of snakes; besides, the cement floor will make it possible to keep it clean; one could even learn to roller skate up here--that is, if one had the skates . . . I know! I'm go-*

ing to put my sewing machine up here. What a lovely place to sew! Turning right at the top of the stairs, Lois entered the larger of the two bedrooms. Directly across from that door was the door leading to the smaller room that would become the children's room. Through the walls of both bedrooms had been cut windows looking out onto the big verandah, an encouragement to the cooling breeze. These windows, as well as all the wide, outside windows in the house, had iron bars and swinging window panes.

With so many people to help with the work, it didn't take long to settle in. By the end of the week the Shulls had established an efficient schedule and things were running smoothly. Children's needs, study hours, office hours for Ernie, tea time in the late afternoon--usually for guests who happened in--and for Linda and Lois, the beginning of kindergarten instruction.

Lois had prepared herself for this responsibility with care. Long ago she had sent to the States for the Calvert Course of Instruction, recommended for children of government personnel or any other Americans who did not have access to schools.

Also that year, Susan and Chalmer, who had been transferred to the station of Ahwa in the jungle, had vacationed in a cottage near Woodstock School, a thousand miles away in the Himalayan Mountains. Esther was in school there, and eventually Linda would be attending also; therefore, when they came down from the hills they brought the books necessary for beginning students. By following these courses of study carefully, Lois was confident Linda would be as advanced as the rest of her age group, and she would be prepared to fit into the school program without difficulty when they were ready to place her into boarding. Since this was her first school-teaching experience, Lois wanted to be sure that she covered more than the material required.

Linda enjoyed doing her school work once she was started; but, like most children, she hated to stop playing with the other children on the compound and come in to work alone. Indu, Gungubai's daughter about Linda's age, became Linda's best friend. They would play by the hour on the big, upstairs verandah, oblivious to the pouring rain just beyond the expanded metal. Often Indu would stay to tea with Linda and Jimmy, though sometimes Gungubai would call her home.

It wasn't long before Lois became aware of a problem that had its source in the Indian social system. As she watched Linda and Indu play, it became evident that while Linda was unselfish with her toys, their play was entirely directed by Linda. Indu agreed happily to whatever Linda suggested.

Lois observed the same situation in two-and-one-half-year old Jimmy's play; if he asked for a toy that another child was holding, it was given to him immediately without question and without resentment, as if it were his right.

"Honey, we have a problem," declared Lois one day when she and Ernie were lingering at the table over their second cup of tea, and the children had gone to play. Ernie, whose mind was still partly taken up with a difficult situation in one of the village schools, smiled at his wife.

"Which one do you want to talk about. We have quite a variety to choose from." He could never resist an opportunity to tease her.

"I'm serious about this! I feel as if we are fighting the whole system. The problem is that the Indian children give in to our children constantly. Not only do they refuse to stand up for themselves, but they won't even express an adverse opinion. We have to change this or Linda and Jimmy will develop dictator mentalities!" Lois lifted the cozy off the teapot and poured Ernie another cup of tea.

Ernie grew serious. Now that it had been brought to his attention, he realized that he had seen evidence of this relationship among the children since they had moved to Dahanu.

"You're right; this is no doubt a problem we need to be aware of. We must try to encourage the Indian children to become more self-assertive, and help our children to recognize the equal rights of others."

Lois groaned. "That's a lesson that can't be learned in one night's homework. We'll probably be working on that lesson when the children are old enough to go away to college."

"Maybe it won't take that long. When our children get into Woodstock school with students from America, Britain, Australia, Formosa, and other countries, they will be competing on an equal basis. I have a feeling they will lose very quickly any sense of privilege they may have developed. Much as we dread the time when they will have to go away to school, in some ways it will be good for them."

Ernie pushed his chair back and stood up. "Ratnaker and I are working to build a chicken house a little way beyond the well. We're using some old lumber that I found in the bullock shed. Finding enough eggs to buy since we came here has been such a problem, that I thought we'd get a few chickens and try to have our own supply of eggs. We're planning to plant our own garden, too, just beyond our back walk, just as soon as the rains let up enough. If you need me, I'll be out by the bullock shed." He picked up a few tools from the office and went out the back door.

Just east of the Grace Villa compound was an extensive buffalo dairy operated by a large Hindu joint family. Every day the sluggish, lumbering buffaloes could be seen plodding along the roads or grazing in the fields in back of the diary compound. They were herded by some of the many small children in the family group. The role of the women in the extended family, was to distribute the milk before noon, milk which is so essential in the Indian diet. These women were always dressed in colorful, bright red or green saris with the ends draped over their heads, and their ears, noses, foreheads, arms, and ankles were laden with heavy native jewelry. They effortlessly balanced the large, brimming, brass pots, stacked three--even four--on each head. They had many regular customers; what milk was left they would sell in the bazaar of the large village of Dahanu. In spite of the heavy weight of the brass pots on their heads, the dairy ladies, like brightly costumed dancers, moved easily past Grace Villa like swaying willow branches. They carried on a lively conversation among themselves as they slipped past pedestrians, carts, and lorries swinging their hips but keeping their heads motionless as they moved down the crowded road.

One morning a few days after they had arrived, Lois and Ernie were studying at a desk that had been set up in the front room where they could get the most monsoon light, when someone walked up to the front doors and cleared his throat loudly as if he thought they were a long way off. Then, before Ernie could get to the door, the visitor called excitedly, "Sahib? Sahib? Are you there. Sahib?"

"Yes, I'm here. Salaam. Won't you come in?" Ernie invited swinging the doors wide.

A barefooted young man about eighteen or nineteen years old, wearing a mud-splashed white dhoti and a loose, long-sleeved shirt, accompanied by a broad smile, stepped inside and looked curiously around the room.

"Goodness, you have changed things since the Parsees lived here! You have a stairway and there are no beds in here. I like it!" he decided as he deliberately crossed his legs and sat in the middle of the floor.

Taken aback by the visitor's manner and not being quite sure how to proceed, Ernie moved a chair out from the wall.

"Won't you sit on a chair and then tell me what I can do for you this morning?" suggested Ernie.

"Oh, I don't want anything really. I just came over to look at you and your wife. I heard you were from America and I just wanted to see you. I'm Sagaram, your next door neighbor to the east. I run the dairy now that my father is too old to work much any more," the young man explained as he continued to look around.

"What!" exclaimed Lois in surprise. "You mean that you run that big buffalo dairy? Why, what about all the ladies I see from your family who carry those big loads of milk on their heads? Don't they help you run things?"

"Oh, no, they just do what I tell them to do--like milk the buffaloes, handle the milk, and carry it to the bazaar to sell it," he answered loftily. "I do all the managing and the running of the dairy. My father is too old and my brothers are dead. I have a man I hire to help with the work."

Lois stood up and moved toward the door to the dining room. "Mr. Sagaram, may I fix you a cup of tea while you are visiting?"

"No, No. Don't be offended. I stopped in for only a few minutes this time, but I'll come again and have tea with you in the afternoon. I just wanted to see how you look." He rose from his cross-legged position and moved toward the door.

"I'm glad you stopped in to get acquainted," said Ernie, swinging open the double doors for their guest.

"I'm glad, too, I stopped in," agreed Sagaram; and as he moved out the door, "I like you; yes, I'll come back." He picked up his big, black umbrella that he had leaned against the house, and opening it stepped out into the rain.

Lois turned to Ernie who was still standing in the middle of the floor with an unfocused look on his face. "Well! What do you make of all that—and him?" she asked with a challenge in her voice. "I feel as though we have just been invaded!"

Suddenly Ernie started to laugh. "We are so funny! I think by his surprise entrance, he took us by storm. I'm sure he is still a teenager; but he apparently has power in his family and in the family business. I think we can count on his being a most interesting neighbor, and certainly a very friendly one. We must make a visit to his home very soon."

A few days later Lois was awakened early in the morning by unusual noises. She listened, but at first she couldn't identify them. She heard the usual sound of rumbling bullock carts going by on the Jawar road with now and then a lorry blasting its bulb horn to get the carts to maneuver to one side. The noisy call of the koel came repeatedly from the tree beyond their window. Then she became aware of excited voices rising from outside the kitchen and dining room area below.

She shook Ernie awake before she slipped out from under the mosquito net, automatically glancing at the floor to make sure there were no unwanted "beasties" resting there before she put her feet on the floor.

"I'm sure there is something wrong downstairs outside the kitchen," she worried. "You had better get dressed and come down and try to help me figure out what to do."

As she hurriedly slipped her feet into sandals, she peeped into the children's room making sure they were still asleep. Something must be wrong with one of the Indian families. Lois heard Gungubai's voice cry out something about water, then Sovenji was shouting angrily, interrupted by a loud clamor which she couldn't identify. A hubbub of voices and noises followed.

By the time Lois reached the back door Ernie was beside her. They stepped out into the confusion together. For a second everyone stopped screaming.

In the following moment of quiet Sovenji stepped forward. "Sahib, when Dayabai and Gungubai went to draw water this morning, they found Sagaram swimming around in the well! He won't get out because he says he is a friend of yours," finished Sovenji indignantly. Seeking to substantiate his case, he turned to Lois, "Madam Sahib, you know he comes from the buffalo dairy and his feet are usually covered by buffalo dung."

"Oh, my word, Ernie! Get that man out of our drinking water," wailed Lois. "That well was so fine--it had exceptionally clear, clean water. Now look what we have!"

"Okay. Relax, honey. I'll go take care of it. The rest of you stay here," Ernie ordered as he walked off toward the well, determined to be reasonable with their neighbor, but firm.

As he approached the well, he heard splashing and scrubbing going on inside, attesting to the fact of Sagaram's great enjoyment of his morning ablution.

Ernie stared over the wall and down into the well as he watched Sagaram swimming about. Catching sight of Ernie, Sagaram grinned broadly and commented with a lilt in his voice. "Salaam, Sahib. It is beautiful morning, no?"

"Salaam, Sagaram. Yes, it is a beautiful morning, and a beautiful well with nice, clean water. Sagaram, you must get out of the well. We don't want you to swim or bathe in this water. You see, it's our drinking water and we want to keep it clean." Ernie was trying to be very reasonable but firm.

"Oh, Sahib, you don't feel worry; I am good Hindu, you know? I did worship this morning first thing, so I'm very clean." Sagaram plunged his face into the water again and came up spluttering.

"No, Sagaram, I'm talking about a different kind of clean--dirt carries germs which make people sick, so come out of the well and don't get into the water again." Ernie struggled to keep the irritation out of his voice, realizing that there was more at stake here than clean water.

Sagaram sighed. "Oh, very well, if you say it. But I will just finish my bath today, now I am here." He started rubbing his head vigorously, then stopped and looked up at Ernie with a big smile.

"It's all right, Sahib. I know you Americans are very strange, but I like you anyway; yes, I like you!" And he went on scrubbing for a few minutes, then began to climb out of the well.

Ernie turned away with a chuckle and walked the short distance back to the kitchen door where the rest of the compound folks were waiting.

"What happened?" asked Lois anxiously as Ernie approached the group.

"Everything is going to be okay. He will not swim in the well again," Ernie assured them.

"But what are we going to do about our drinking water? It's this or nothing--we don't have any other, as you are aware." Lois was sure that from now on she would think of Sagaram in the well every time she went to take a drink of water.

"Well, my dear," Ernie grinned and his blue eyes twinkled, "I guess for the foreseeable future we will be drinking strained, boiled bath water!"

As they went back upstairs to get the children up and prepare for the day, Ernie couldn't suppress a grin. With his arm around Lois's small waist, he explained in detail how he had discovered that there was a big, green frog, classification as yet undetermined, living in the well, and in time, it would, no doubt, help clean up Sagaram's bath water.

Lois gave Ernie a big pinch in the side. He could laugh, but in spite of his encouraging words about ecology, Lois was sure that it would be quite a while before she would be able to drink water without remembering Sagaram's morning bath.

Chapter 12

—◆—

Murder

Since arriving in Dahanu, Ernie's work had become increasingly time-consuming but also increasingly satisfying. Although the household routines set up mostly by Lois involving child-care, cooking, and cleaning were now going along easily, Lois felt more and more as if the real work of the church was seen as Ernie's job and that she was basically expected to play the role of homemaker. She loved the job, but eagerly accepted the invitation of the Dahanu church to be their representative at a Christian Life Conference to be held in Bombay. She wanted to become involved more directly in church life and felt her example of leadership would be appreciated by the women she was getting to know. Besides, the change of pace would be wonderful and Bombay was an exciting city.

Leaving the children was hard when the day finally arrived, but their aya had learned their ways, and Ernie would always be nearby. Now she found herself on her first solo rail trip in India. She pushed herself back on the third-class car bench of the train and watched seven or eight children and their mothers trying to fit into crowded spaces with their boxes and bundles. They all seemed to know each other or maybe they were all one extended family.

Just before the train pulled the door of the car opened and a lady alone climbed in. She was dressed in a shirt and slacks, and she was obviously Anglo-Indian and disliked very much riding in this car with the Muslim women and their children.

Lois looked at her curiously, wondering how she could be traveling alone, and where she might be going. Since there seemed to be no obvious place to sit, Lois scooted over a little closer toward the little girl beside her and motioned for the new passenger to try to squeeze in beside her. The woman smiled a sad little smile and squeezed in.

When the other passengers saw that the lady was definitely going to sit there, they began to squeeze together and more space appeared.

"Salaam," Lois greeted her. "Are you going to Bombay?" Lois was trying to show a friendly curiosity.

"Yes, I think so. I will go to Bombay to get away from Calcutta as far as I can! But now I see the same signs of violence and fighting coming between the Muslims and the Hindus as I saw in Calcutta! I just want to get away before I get caught in it again!" The woman shivered and began to cry. "It was awful! Awful!"

Lois was surprised at the woman's good English.

"What is your name, Madam? Are you in trouble? Is there something I can do to help you?"

The woman wiped her eyes on a cloth and asked, "Have you heard about what is happening in Calcutta?"

Lois had heard that there was rioting going on and much trouble, but she hadn't heard any details. "Not really," she answered.

The woman burst into tears. Lois wondered why she was crying. In fact, she wondered why she seemed to be traveling alone. The other passengers in the car ignored her. The woman wiped her eyes on her sleeve and tried to stop crying.

Lois leaned over toward her and spoke quietly to her. "Why are you so unhappy, Madam? Is there anything I can do to help you," she asked.

"No, nobody can help me now," she tried to turn away.

Why would she say that? Lois wondered. If she knew the trouble maybe she could refer her to someone who could help if she herself couldn't do anything.

"I'm sure there is someone who could help you if we just knew what your trouble is," Lois urged as she touched her shoulder.

"No! No—you don't understand! They killed her! They killed her! She's dead! They cut her with a machete while she was still alive! It was horrible! Horrible!" she wailed as she buried her face in her arms.

Lois gasped in shock and horror. "Who was killed? Who did these awful things? Where did it happen? Are the police doing something about it now? Why are you here by yourself?"

"She was my sister! Don't you see? It was over in Calcutta! We were together just outside of where we lived when a mob of men burst forth in the street in front of us and they were shouting angrily at her and waving their lathis (long sticks). Then they grabbed my sister and ripped off her sari. They cut her body and slashed off her breasts. Oh, my poor sister! My poor sister," she wailed shaking her head from side to side as she struggled to breathe. She seemed to Lois to be scarcely conscious of the world around her. No wonder, after going through the experiences she had suffered the last two days.

Lois tried to talk to the woman, but she didn't answer—just continued to wail and repeat her story over and over.

Most of the other women in the car didn't seem to understand the woman's English, only her Marathi phrases. They, too, tried to get more details of the story, but no one knew how to help her.

When the train pulled into the next station, the wailing woman made her way slowly to the door of the car and climbed down the steps, not realizing this was not Bombay. She didn't seem to know where she was or where she was going. Lois felt helpless. She was limited by language and contacts with people in the area who could help.

The feeling of animosity between the Hindus and the Muslims was growing in intensity every day. Even Gandhi, a man of peace, didn't seem to be able to temper the growing hatred. The Christian community in India numbered only a few thousand—too small to have much influence on the growing horror. She felt almost as if she had witnessed the savagery of the murder and it filled her mind most of the way to Bombay. The train stopped occasionally but Lois barely noticed. At one stop, however, some activity caught her attention and she turned to watch some Hindu men apparently preparing a ceremony before a Hanuman (monkey) god carved on a two-foot cement slab positioned in the shade under a mango tree. On the ground before the slab were various little things—bits of food, nuts, and a dead chicken. The travelers had gotten off the train and, using some leaves, orange powder, and oil, bowed with hands folded before marking the idol. They hurried back to the train as it pulled slowly away. She made a mental note about intending to find out as much as she could about the customs in her village of Dahanu when she returned—indeed in all of India. She was aware that the more she could learn about India, its people, and religious customs, the better missionary she could become. Yet on this day, the horror of man's inhumanity to man in the name or religion or simply because of perceived differences, left her sad and discouraged.

Chapter 13

───•·•───

August 15, 1947

"Quickly! Dorothy, move the soup tureen! Hazel, rescue the chapattis!" ordered Dr. Nickey in her usual brisk manner as she whisked the tray of browned lady's fingers out of the way of the sudden stream of rainwater descending from a new break in the tiles of the leaky roof.

"Got it!" exclaimed Dorothy triumphantly, lifting carefully the large, covered dish of hot oyster soup.

"Chapattis safe!" laughed Hazel Messer, the other American nurse stationed at Dahanu Hospital, and living with Dorothy and Dr. Nickey in this rambling, high-ceilinged bungalow, so much in need of a new roof.

Lois couldn't help but laugh as the three grabbed swiftly to save the dinner. Dr. Nickey was so short that she had to stand on her toes to reach the dishes on the second shelf of the dish cabinet.

"I'll have to move the table," Dr. Nickey decided. "But where to? Here! Look, here's a dry place--at least for now." Impatiently the doctor took hold of the table to lift it.

"Wait, Dr. Nickey! Don't try to lift that table," Ernie warned as he pushed her gently to one side. "Lahanu and I will move it--just show us where you want us to put it. Lahanu, will you please come here a minute?"

Lahanu was the excellent, good-natured cook for the ladies in the medical bungalow. The Shulls, who had been invited to take dinner with the three single missionaries, were always happy to taste the good dishes that Lahanu knew how to make. Like a squirrel having a store of nuts, he had an accumulation of knowledge about cooking acquired by working for several different missionary ladies through the years. He was past middle age, good-natured, and quite devoted to the American "miss-sahibs" in a leisurely sort of way.

Ernie and Lahanu carried the table to its new, dry location and the dishes of food were placed back on the table. They all had a good laugh about their "fresh water supply delivered directly to the table."

Dr. Nickey glanced ruefully at the water now running in a steady stream into the metal pan that Lahanu had placed directly under the brand new leak. The pan emitted a tinny, rapid "ping-ping-ping" which blended musically with the pouring rain outside the expanded metal fencing surrounding the open dining room area. They had had to use so many pans and containers to catch the leaks in so many of the rooms of the house that the cook was running out of vessels to catch the drips.

"Well, forever more! I don't know what we are supposed to do while the mission executive committee deliberates!" complained Dr. Nickey. "I put the request for roof repairs through to them at the beginning of the hot season. They don't need this much time to decide to plug up the leaks. I'm about to the end of my string!" She thought for a few minutes. "What I had better do, I think, is go ahead and have the roof fixed with my own money, and then the committee can reimburse me when they get around to considering it. There is no sense in our living like this."

Dr. Nickey was a woman of quick decisions, Lois realized, and no doubt Dr. Nickey was right, for she had run out of patience waiting for the Committee, who always had more demands on the funds available than they had money to spend. Once she had decided upon what action to take, Dr. Nickey was ready to move on to discussing more immediate considerations. Their lives were so busy and emergencies so frequent that "shop talk" in the interest of saving time was often the conversation around the dinner table. Lois and Ernie felt a part of these times, for often they knew the people involved, or the village from which the patients came.

"Hazel, how is that delivery case doing that came in at two o'clock this afternoon?" asked the doctor as she looked at the nurse over the top of her glasses.

"She's coming fine, Doctor--two fingers dilation an hour ago. Two of the nursing school seniors are watching her carefully. I'll go over and check on her as soon as we are finished here," promised Hazel.

Lois loved these Sunday evenings when, if there were no emergencies, they often tried to get together at either Grace Villa or the Medical Bungalow to eat together and spend some time just visiting. As they ate their meal, they shared news from the other mission stations and discussed the work in progress on their own compounds and in their community of Dahanu.

Always as an undercurrent was the feeling of political tension in the village and among the Christians living on the hospital and Grace Villa compounds, a tension amplified by the fact of their location on the main railroad artery between Bombay and the national capital of Delhi.

Keeping one ear to the ground for a possible summons from the hospital, they relaxed over a last cup of hot tea as they discussed the arrival of Lord Louis Mountbatten from Britain a year before to facilitate the transfer of government from the British Raj to an independent India. The Viceroy's stated goal was to help India remain one nation. However, as the missionaries read the Viceroy's statement in the Bombay Statesman, which always came a day late, even though Dahanu was on the direct railroad line from Bombay to Delhi, it became apparent that he had been forced to accept the reality of impending division. Mountbatten was now leaning toward the next best solution; the division of the subcontinent into two separate nations, Pakistan and India, to be accomplished peacefully and equitably, without bloodshed. Considering the anger in both communities, it was questionable whether it could be done. But the Americans gathered around the table in the Mission bungalow that Sunday afternoon were sure that if anybody could bring it about, Lord Mountbatten was the one. The day of division and the birth of two new nations was set for August 15, 1947, just a little over a month away.

What should be their plan of procedure, Lois wondered, *if violence between the Hindus and Muslims should break out in their village?* They discussed the possible need for more emergency help in the hospital, and how Lois and Ernie could best serve if this situation developed. So far, Christians were not being attacked by either of the other religious communities. But every day saw an influx of rabble rousers from Bombay and from Delhi, stirring up the crowds on the station platform and in the village.

"I think," Dr. Nickey declared, as if her subconscious had been working on the problem while the discussion had been carried on, "that if the situation deteriorates to a point of conflict, your family should move in to this compound where you would be safer than staying out there on the Jawar road at Grace Villa. We have plenty of room in this bungalow and several night watchmen."

Lois was startled. Mentally she dug in her heels as she prepared to object to any such plan that would move their family again into a house with someone else, no matter how nice those people might be. The trouble with Dr. Nickey was that she was so used to making fast decisions and having them carried out without question that she thought her authority extended to everyone. Well, this was one occasion when Lois intended to have something to say. Only if she was convinced that there was real danger to foreigners would she be willing to move to the medical compound. Apparently Ernie was thinking about the same thing when he turned to Dr. Nickey with a smile, receiving her decree as an invitation.

"Thanks, Doctor. If we find ourselves in a really dangerous situation, we will most gratefully accept your invitation. In the meantime we are getting well established where we are."

However, the Americans realized that Dahanu already was having its share of violence; there had been several murders in the village, and even the Hindu and Muslim shopkeepers, who had been friendly for years, were showing hatred toward each other and causing divisions in the community.

Their table conversation was interrupted by the approach of a student nurse gracefully ascending the verandah steps. She was wearing the uniform of a student nurse, which was a neatly draped, white sari and a royal blue blouse. She carried a large, dripping, black umbrella, and as she set it down on the cement water ran from it in a steady stream across the verandah. Hazel rose expectantly from her chair and started toward the door. "Did you come to call me, Mani?" she asked the student nurse.

"Yes, Sister," answered Mani with an apologetic smile. The student nurses were always smiling, it seemed, courteous, helpful, and so graceful. Hazel stopped only long enough to grab her own umbrella from the corner, then she and Mani went splashing toward the hospital.

Dr. Nickey looked very thoughtful. "This community is greatly blessed to have a Christian hospital here. Some folks appreciate it, like our Parsee (people of Persian ancestry) friends who own the big rose gardens and grow roses for sale in Bombay. But many people are still afraid of Westerners, and come to us only as a last resort, which is often too late."

"Dr. Nickey, I had an interesting caller this week," Ernie continued the conversation. "He is a quite well-educated man, a Brahman named Zoshi. Do you know him?"

"If you mean the Brahman teacher living out near the sea, then I have met him. How did he happen to come to your bungalow?" Dr. Nickey was curious, because Brahmans are very careful about caste, and people from the West are considered outcasts.

"It was a strange thing," Ernie continued. "He stopped at our house and I invited him in. Over a cup of tea he confessed that he would like very much to read some of my books, especially ones concerning Christian prayer, so I loaned him two very good ones. Later he returned those and took two more. Every time he comes we have a most stimulating conversation, sharing our spiritual experiences and philosophies. I just wondered if you had had a similar acquaintance with him."

"No, I've never had occasion to learn to know him that well, but I do know that he is very respected in the Hindu community and in this town; however, I understand the Muslims in Dahanu are very much afraid of his anti-Muslim sentiments, and suspect that he is working in a subtle way to get them out of the community. Some of the Parsees were telling me about it."

Lois remembered Mr. Zoshi's visits with pleasure, for he was a very interesting conversationalist. Sitting where she could look across the room toward the large, open double doors, she became aware of a slight movement outside on the wide, sheltered verandah. A woman had crept in unobserved out of the rain, and was now sitting there in the shadows, hunched over, waiting patiently to be observed. On the step beside her lay a primitive umbrella-cape woven of two layers of bamboo strips with a layer of large leaves sandwiched between. She could hang it like a basket over the top of her head, leaving her arms free to move. Seeing that someone had noticed her, the woman stood up, holding a baby in her arms, as she pulled the end of her nearly colorless sari up over her head in respect. The sari was wrapped around her tightly and extended down to her knees. Somewhere in the folds she had the baby wrapped. The woman's arms and legs had several grayish-white spots showing prominently.

"Dr. Nickey, there is a lady sitting on the step," Lois said, directing Dr. Nickey's attention to the verandah.

The doctor rose and walked to the edge of the porch, folding her hands and bowing slightly.

"Salaam, Bai. I am the doctor; what do you need? Are you looking for a relative in the hospital?" she asked.

"No, Dr. Mem-Sahib, I am the one who is sick. I know that I am going to die and I brought my baba to you so he will not die too. Take him, Dr. Mem-Sahib. He is nice baba." She pulled her sari back from over the little, brown body and held it out until she stood on a level with the woman. It took only one glance for her to diagnose the woman's condition as leprosy. Now the task was to persuade the woman to follow through on what needed to be done.

"Bai, you can get well again if you will come every day to the hospital where we can treat your disease. Come with me now and we will start treatment today." The doctor touched the lady lightly on the shoulder and started to move toward the hospital, but the woman became agitated and pulled away.

"No! No! Dr. Mem-Sahib, I cannot go to the hospital every day--my husband will not allow me. I must work. Please take my baba--keep him well!" She held out her baby once more toward the doctor. Because her baby was a boy, she thought surely the doctor would take him.

"What I can do, Bai, is make you well. I cannot take your baby, for we don't have any arrangement here for that. Your baby needs you, his mother. Come with me to the hospital and we will talk about it." Again Dr. Nickey turned toward the hospital.

The woman looked sadly at the doctor for a moment, then she seemed to wilt like a flower, all hope gone. She reluctantly covered her baby with her sari. As she picked up her basket umbrella and hooked it over her head, she turned toward the gate. "I must go," she said in a colorless voice. "My husband needs me." She opened the gate and quietly slipped through.

For a full minute the observers of this tragic drama sat, immobile, looking out onto the verandah, as if under a spell. Then Lois caught a quivering breath. "Why are we sitting here in shock? Isn't there something we can do for that poor woman? She is going to die when there is medicine in the hospital that could cure her. Could we go to her village--talk to her husband? Isn't there some way?" Lois felt impatient with her own helplessness and frustrated that no one else seemed to be able to do anything either.

Dr. Nickey's movements were weary as she climbed back up the steps and sat down dejectedly in her chair. "In spite of my thirty-some years in India and the many, many cases of leprosy just like this I have seen, I always ask myself the same question you are asking. Through the years I have learned that the fisher people, the group from which this woman comes, have their own culture, including many taboos. No doubt the woman's husband does demand that she stay with him and serve him as long as she can walk. Women are considered property and they must work. If I had insisted that she go with me today and start the outpatient treatment she needs, she would not have come in daily to continue the regimen, which is a long process. We can treat only those who are willing to cooperate."

Dorothy reached over to a side table and picked up her nursing cap. She fastened it securely. "I think I'll go over to the hospital and see if there is anything I need to do, Doctor," she said.

"And we must be going home," Lois answered as she lifted the sleeping Jimmy off her lap and put him on her shoulder.

Ernie took Linda's hand as he turned to Dorothy and Dr. Nickey. "These times together are enjoyable and important to us. Thanks for a delicious dinner. Plan to come out to Grace Villa next Sunday evening if you can." Ernie sorted out their umbrellas at the door and they hurried to the waiting tonga outside as Dr. Nickey and Dorothy headed for the hospital.

As the days went by Lois couldn't forget the poor fisher woman and resolved to continue searching for her role which she knew would have to begin with the people she worked with every day, and the people who came to the Mission.

A few days later Ernie was called to a two-day meeting in Bulsar, a town upcountry about an hour by rail, for an educational planning session. Lois didn't mind his going really, although it would have been nice to have gone along. Ernie had been given the assignment of supervising the village schools out from Dahanu, along with his half-time language study. Lois resented the fact that she had been given no assignment by the executive committee, except to be a mother. She couldn't help but get the impression that the men on the committee felt that men were more capable of making intelligent decisions than married women. It didn't really matter; she'd work on her own, beginning with her daily contacts. It seemed longer than two months since they had moved to Grace Villa, and she hadn't been anywhere else since, except to the Medical Compound. She had learned to know the large number of people on the hospital staff, the workers on the two Mission compounds and the Christians from the village who came to church; also, she discovered, the landed Parsee community was very friendly to the Christian community, and to the Americans especially. The influential landowner, Feroz Vakil, whose holdings lay just across the road from the Mission Compound, had, on several occasions that Lois knew about, been most helpful in community relations and legal matters, taking a personal interest in the welfare of the hospital. As Lois thought about the Parsees in relation to the political situation, she concluded that their community was in a similar position to that of the Christian community--finding themselves in the middle of, but not involved in, the dispute.

The morning Ernie left for Bulsar, Lois helped Linda with her lessons for two hours, then she assigned her an exercise to finish on her own before she could go to play with Indu.

Lois had been thinking for a long time of things that she could do to help ease the burden of the Indian women. They had so little to work with, and their position in society was so subordinate, that it was not surprising they seemed resigned to their hopeless situation of poverty, hard work, malnutrition, and disease.

As she sat in church the week before, she noticed again the ragged clothing most of the children and some of the adults were wearing. Granted, they didn't have the money to buy new clothing, but why didn't they mend the old ones? She talked about it to Sarabai, the wife of Dr. Peter Paul, the second doctor at the Dahanu mission hospital.

Sarabai smiled sadly. "You see, Madam Sahib, nobody knows how to fix a shirt or dress that is torn. They would like to make their children or their husbands look better, but they don't know how!"

Well! thought Lois. This is something that I can do something about. So she told Sarabai to tell any women she met who wanted to learn how to mend clothing to bring a torn garment and come to Grace Villa for a class and she would teach them.

Soon in the afternoon of the appointed day, a number of ladies from the community arrived. Lois folded her hands in greeting and invited them to come in. Shy but very curious about how the bungalow would look inside, they followed her up the stairs and onto the verandah with its broad open view. They sat down cross-legged on the cool cement floor and adjusted their saris comfortably with the end of the cloth draped respectfully over their heads.

There was a hot breeze blowing in, but no one seemed to mind. It was surprising that among the mostly Christian women, there were six Hindus, two Parsees, and three Muslims all easily distinguished by their typical dress.

Would they be able to get along together, she wondered apprehensively as she realized the make-up of the group? With the tense political situation between the Hindus and Muslims in their village as well as the country at large, could this project possibly work?

Obviously they didn't seem to mind sitting in the same room together. Although each group sat a little apart, they talked together and shared the news of the community. It was as if the Mission bungalow was neutral ground. As the women worked, some of the Hindus talked about the bad treatment they were receiving from several of the Muslim shop owners, some shops had even refused to sell them food. The women appeared uneasy and lowered their voices when they talked, almost as if they were looking over their shoulders. With new insight Lois recognized the fear in their voices--a fear they must constantly live with until this political situation could be eased.

Lois had estimated that perhaps seven or eight women would come, but counting the Christians, twenty three showed up! Gungubai, who had worked all week to learn how to sew two pieces of cloth together, helped distribute pieces of cloth, pins, needles, and thread to each lady. It took most of the afternoon for each member of the group to learn how to hold the cloth and push the needle and thread in and out to sew the two pieces together.

One of the ladies was very disappointed that she hadn't been able to finish mending a shirt with a sleeve that was torn almost off. She didn't realize that learning took so much time.

Most of the ladies had walked quite a distance in the rain to attend the sewing class, so toward late afternoon Lois and Sovenji served Indian tea with milk and plenty of sugar, the way the ladies liked it best. Upon Dr. Nickey's advice, Lois served nothing with the tea--an effort to avoid making Rice Christians, a term used for people who would convert for a small handout. This was an ever-present danger among people constantly hungry. She had learned that when people have practically nothing, the smallest thing--even a cup of tea--could be considered as an inducement. It would be so easy to pass out a few peanuts along with the tea--she, herself, would feel better about what she served--but she didn't dare; it would defeat the goal of helping the people become independent and self-sufficient. The hot tea made all the women feel better before they began their long walk home through the rain. Most of them were pleased with what they had learned and promised to come back the next week. They were pleased with themselves that they could be learning a skill that would be so helpful to their families.

Lois was sure she wouldn't be able to sleep much that night with Ernie gone. She wasn't exactly alone with the children, for the Ratnakar and Sovenji families were in the line rooms nearby; although, in true Indian fashion, they liked to go inside their rooms and pull the doors and windows tightly shut. She doubted that they would hear her even if she were to call them during the night. She would have to go out and knock on their doors to wake them up if she needed them.

She fed Linda and Jimmy, bathed them and, after reading them a story, tucked them under their mosquito nets in the room next to hers. She was glad there was no access to the children's room except through the master bedroom. These days the Jawar road in front of their house seemed always to be busy, even late at night, with noisy, shouting people. Sovenji had finished his work in the kitchen some time ago and gone home. Lois checked all the doors, making sure they were securely locked, then climbed the stairs again to her room. She placed the lighted lantern on the floor near the stairs where it would give a low light to the room, but wouldn't shine in her eyes. She lowered her mosquito net, then climbed under and tucked it securely beneath the mattress pad on all sides.

The concerns that Lois was sure would keep her awake seemed to drift away like clouds as she watched the long, dancing shadows cast by the excited lantern flame, puffed here and there by a strong breeze; then she slept without knowing it.

Suddenly, through the trailing wisps of her dreams, there was a loud, heavy thud that seemed to rock the house and shake the bed. Lois's eyes flew open and she lay tense, listening for what might have awakened her. Had she really heard a loud noise or had she only dreamed it? Collecting her wits, she quickly slid out from under the net and raced to the children's room to see if they were all right. Finding them sleeping and undisturbed, she quickly went through her own room and to the head of the stairs where she stopped to listen.

Strange rustling and movement seemed to come from the living room at the foot of the stairs. Adrenaline shot through her veins as fear gripped her. Swiftly she picked up the lantern, stepped back into her own room, and quietly locked the wooden doors, sliding the iron bar into place. This meant that temporarily she and the children were safe. If it was simply a case of robbery, which common sense told her it was likely to be, then the intruders might not chance coming up the stairs. She thought of screaming for help, but considering the tightly closed-in line rooms, she thought it unlikely that she would be heard.

Swiftly she made sure she had matches, then she blew out the lantern and listened intently. Because of the closed doors she could hear nothing in the house below, but as she strained her ears she heard through the barred window and the expanded metal of the verandah, the sound of heavy objects being dragged outside in the compound. Lois breathed a prayer as she listened intently, "Lord, I'm trying to think what I should do next! I'm not sure there is a Christian way to act in a situation like this except the common sense way. That means saving life. I think that if we stay here we are probably safe. What they can take downstairs is only material goods and certainly not worth risking my life for. If I scream, they might think it necessary to make me be quiet, so I think I had better stay right here until we are rescued. I know that you are with us, Lord, and therefore we are not alone."

The whisperings and movement seemed to have shifted across the compound and out toward the gate. Lois could detect no movement nor any moving lights close to the bungalow. "Lord, maybe they are leaving. They've probably gutted the downstairs, but what does it matter--we are safe."

The hours dragged slowly by. The cool, damp breeze, coming through the barred window where Lois sat on a trunk with her legs pulled up under her, made her shiver with a chill. She carefully pulled a sheet off the bed and wrapped it around herself. Maybe it wasn't the chilly breeze, maybe it was just a fear reaction to what had occurred, or what might have occurred. It was so easy in the silence of the night to remember the number of unsolved murders that had been taking place in their village of Dahanu. She gradually became aware of the silence and realized that she hadn't heard anything out in the compound for a long time--she wished that it would hurry and become light.

The next thing she knew she heard Sovenji unlocking the back door and sliding the bar open. She heard the steady sound of the rolling bullock carts making their way to the market, passing on the Jawar road outside the compound. Out in the chicken house that Ernie had just finished building, one of their new roosters crowed loudly. Quickly Lois grabbed her housecoat and hastened down stairs, apprehensive of what she would find. The sight that met her eyes was shocking.

The front door was standing wide open, and through the inner office door she saw that the outside office door to the west was also gapping open. Tying her housecoat as she ran, she hurried on to the office and, stopping short, stared in dismay. Desk and file drawers were hanging open and papers were scattered everywhere. Suddenly her eyes focused on an empty space just beside the door where a massive, wooden frame still stood, but the big, very heavy, practically immovable, black safe, which had been made in Chicago, USA, was gone! Why, that's impossible, thought Lois as she blinked and looked again.

"Sovenji! Sovenji!" she cried, dashing through the house to the kitchen, where the cook was using a piece of cardboard to fan the smoking charcoal to make it burst into flames. "Come and look what has happened! The bungalow has been broken into and robbed! Someone has stolen the safe from the office!"

Sovenji's mouth dropped open. "What, Mem-Sahib? Nobody can steal that heavy thing." He hurried into the office to check. "The safe is gone," Sovenji said incredulously.

Lois thought to herself, *That is probably the understatement of the year.*

At Sovenji's call Ratnakar and the other compound people came in to see the damage that had been done, and to declare that they hadn't heard a thing unusual during the night. How the safe could have been carried away remained a mystery. Almost immediately Sagaram from the buffalo dairy appeared, news in the village traveling as usual near the speed of light, and added the information that his family had heard unusual confusion in the road during the night, but they go to sleep early for they have to rise early to milk the buffalo.

At nine o'clock Ratnakar, driving the bullocks and tonga, went into Dahanu to meet Ernie's train. An hour later a worried Ernie climbed out of the tonga and rushed into the house, dropping his briefcase and bedding roll into the confusion on the floor.

As Lois came flying to meet him, he put his arms around her and said, "Darling, I'm so sorry I wasn't at home--and on a night when you needed me most! Are you sure that all of you are okay?"

"Of course we are," Lois assured him, fighting to keep back the tears. She didn't know what was the matter with her--she hadn't felt like crying at all up to this time, but the moment Ernie started to sympathize with her, she had to fight back the tears. Swallowing hard, she took Ernie's hand and led him to the office. "But the safe is gone," she exclaimed, "and the whole teachers' and evangelists' payroll was in there, wasn't it? What are we going to do?"

Ernie began gathering up some of the papers and the account books and placing them back on the desk. "Well, I have some good news about that! The safe is lying like a derelict in the ditch just outside the compound gate and apparently unopened. It appears to me that the handle is bent and twisted, as if someone tried to use an iron tool of some sort to open it, but the thieves were not able to break the lock, and since the safe is so heavy, they finally abandoned it. I'm amazed they could move it that far. The first thing we must do is notify the police in Dahanu."

It was the middle of the morning when the police arrived, proud to have been called onto the case by the American Sahib. They were filled with their own importance, determined to prove their authority and efficiency before the curious people who had gathered around, and incidentally to find the thieves if possible. Muddy footprints were discovered on the front of the safe still lying in the ditch, proving that one of the thieves had braced his foot on the safe door as he twisted the heavy, metal handle.

One of the officers came rushing to the bungalow door to talk to Lois. "The chief asks for your camera. He wants to take a picture of the footprint on the door of the safe, Mem-Sahib," said the officer.

Lois shook her head. "I have only a little box camera that doesn't take very clear pictures. I'm sure it would not do you any good."

"The Chief says he wants it anyway," the officer insisted, shifting nervously from one foot to the other. As Lois went to get the camera from where it was stored in a plastic, silica gel bag to keep it dry during the monsoon, she reflected with a smile that no doubt the Chief had read stories about investigations where Scotland Yard had taken pictures at the crime scene, and he was trying to follow procedures that would make his police department look professional. She found the camera packed in a trunk that she would rather not have opened during the monsoon, and took it to the officer waiting just inside the front door.

After some time the officer returned the camera and told Lois that the Chief would like to have a copy of the pictures as soon as she could get them developed. Lois couldn't suppress her laughter as she received the camera, probably mystifying the officer about the strange sense of humor of Americans.

Apparently the expense of developing the film is to be mine, Lois mused.

After the flurry of the first day's investigation, interest in the case seemed to disappear and no suspects were ever apprehended. They were shocked to hear later that during that same night the Brahman pandit, Mr. Zoshi, had been found murdered, and the police were preoccupied searching for the murderer. The Mission Executive Committee decided to place a permanent night watchman on duty at Grace Villa in light of the political situation and the much-traveled Jawar Road.

With the aid of eight hired men and the bullock team, the safe was finally brought back to the bungalow and embedded in cement to insure its permanence. When Ernie turned the key in the lock, the door opened smoothly and the contents, although shuffled around, were all accounted for.

Laxman, the new night watchman hired by the Committee, was a rather timid man and past middle age. He was hired mostly because he was a Christian who needed a job, Lois surmised, rather than for his ability to protect the property. She was sure that his main usefulness would be to report the crime the next day after it occurred. He took up his duties with a storm lantern for company, making his headquarters at night in the sheltered side porch just outside the office. At times he sang to keep himself company, and at other times he could be heard snoring, but periodically he took walks around the house and compound, theoretically to scare away any intruders. As to whether he was worth the money, Lois was skeptical, but Laxman was friendly, and his family needed the money. She gave him a bamboo mat to sit on, and with the heat from the lantern, he was quite comfortable, even during the rains. As the days of July progressed, work at the hospital grew heavier, although not as overwhelming as the conditions in the hospitals of the Punjab, where the results of the impending threat of partition were already being felt. There thousands of people were on the move. People who had never traveled outside their own villages had suddenly become refugees, fleeing from those areas where, almost overnight, they had become victims of radicals holding different religious beliefs.

Dahanu, which was, of course, located on the main railroad line running from Bombay to New Delhi, became a convenient point to eject ticketless travelers from the train; for hundreds of frenzied people in every province climbed on the railroad cars and rode as far as they could before being discovered, in a desperate effort to escape persecution. Fear became the great driving force, and men, women, and children with the belongings they could carry, were disgorged from the trains like refuse dumped from a lorry. Consequently, every open place in the village was filled with people, and the Dahanu Hospital had more patients than they could handle. Lois went in to help out three afternoons a week, visiting with the waiting patients, talking with family members, and also assisting Evabai, the very capable Bible woman (a position created by the Church which afforded her the opportunity to share her faith), who was always there to counsel, to witness to her own great faith, and to sympathize with the suffering. Although the patients wanted medicine, many were afraid of what was going to happen to them in the hospital, Lois discovered, and they needed words of assurance, and the feeling they gained by talking to her or Evabai that they had someone they could depend upon.

One busy afternoon a group of nine excited Muslim women came hurrying into the waiting area on the clinic verandah, chattering and swinging their arms, speaking in a language that Lois couldn't understand, although she would guess it was Hindi or Punjabi, North Indian languages. They were dressed in brightly colored, traditional, salwar-chamise a full-cut pajama pant, tight around the ankle, a dress top of three-quarters body length and split up the sides, and a piece of cloth worn as a stole with the ends hanging down the back. Lois smiled as she motioned for them to sit down and wait as several other patients who were ahead of them were doing; but the women grew more agitated, sounding like a flock of alarmed warblers, as they pushed one of their number, evidently the patient, forward for inspection.

Obviously, Lois decided, the first thing to do was to find someone who could understand Hindi or Punjabi, and then discover what was wrong with the patient. With this in mind, she hurried in to the desk where Robin, the accountant, was keeping books.

Robin shook his head when he heard about Lois's problem. "I don't think anyone on our staff speaks Hindi or Panjabi, those are North Indian languages, but I'll send Baulu quickly around to check." Baulu was back in a few minutes with the information that no one could understand either of the these languages, but Dr. Nickey said that the patient was to be brought back to the examination room and she would personally examine her and try to discover what the trouble was.

Lois made her way through the crowded verandah back to the Muslim women who still seemed to be talking all at once, their eyes flashing with excitement and something else that Lois couldn't name. "Come with me," she said taking the hand of the patient and starting to move down the hallway. They couldn't understand her language, but they understood her actions. Moving slowly, for the patient had some difficulty in walking, Lois led her to the examining room where Sister Dorothy Brown was on duty, and Lois explained the language difficulty. The other ten Muslim women crowded into the room also, shaking their heads with satisfaction now that they had finally reached medical help.

Dr. Nickey came hurrying in from the adjoining dispensary and began to wash her hands. "Sister, place the patient on the table," the doctor requested.

"Yes, Doctor," she answered as she touched the arm of the patient and motioned toward the table. The patient moved with difficulty over to the table. The nurse turned her with her back to the table and pushed gently on her chest and pointed to the pillow at one end. The patient tried to lie down, but she couldn't swing her feet up onto the table. Sister Dorothy quickly reached down to grasp her ankles and lift her feet.

"Oh, Doctor! Look at this!" exclaimed the nurse in surprise, as she swung the patient's feet up off the floor. Stepping forward to hold the patient's shoulders, Lois could see that one leg of the pajamas was hanging low and pulled taut across some weight caught inside.

"Well, what do you know!" exclaimed the doctor. "A baby! And sound asleep!" Lois glanced at the mother who was all smiles, now that the problem had been discovered. The women, standing around near her head were giggling and talking happily. One of them was gently rubbing the patient's head, apparently her way of showing her love and concern.

Under Dr. Nickey's excellent care the baby was rescued from its swinging hammock and it opened its eyes sleepily as it blinked toward the light. After tying off and cutting the cord, thus launching the baby on a life of his own, the doctor handed him to Sister Brown for his first bath. Eventually she delivered the placenta and the student nurses prepared the patient to be taken to her bed for rest.

In talking over the case later that evening, Lois and Dorothy couldn't stop laughing. "When

I remember how I tried to get the patient to sit down on the floor and wait while I tried to find someone who could understand what she was saying, I'm surprised she didn't become violent! I would have!" They nicknamed the baby "Swinger." Swinger and his retinue of women didn't stay very long; sometime during the night they all slipped away, probably to try to board another train heading north, hoping to travel as far as possible before being discovered again and ejected, for they were Muslims trying to make their way from India to the new Islamic country of Pakistan before the day of freedom from Britain.

As Independence Day, the day of partition, drew near, the hatred between the Hindus and the Muslims seemed to increase, bringing with it more killings, more burning of property, more displaced persons, more suffering and chaos. In spite of the planning being done by Lord Mountbatten along with the Congress and the Muslim League, the stupendous task of dividing equally everything from the fighting forces and the Civil Service Departments to office chairs and even rubber bands was so great that there was just not enough time. Besides, the main officers in all departments had been British, and now that they would be leaving, there was a great void being created, where inexperienced people would have to be appointed to take over.

Huge refugee camps were opened, the largest ones being in New Delhi, where violence often occurred. Mahatma Gandhi, who believed with all his soul in ahimsa (nonviolence) met with worshippers daily to pray for peace and brotherhood, but still the violence grew.

The Christians were deeply concerned for their nation, and for their Hindu and Muslim neighbors who were experiencing such trauma. Christian prayer meetings reflected the same theme as those of Gandhi, "Let there be peace and nonviolence."

Gandhi prayed a prayer that could be prayed by all communities in India, "Oh, Lord/ Lead us from darkness/ Into light."

But death was in the air.

One morning, as Ernie was preparing to leave by bullock tonga for the Christian elementary school at Kainard, and Lois was nearly ready to go into the hospital, Ratnakar came to the door. He didn't take time to clear his throat to let them know that he was there, he just began shouting, his voice quivering with fright.

"Sahib! Sahib! Madam Sahib! Come quickly! Something awful has happened. Oh, Lord, what should we do now." And he began to wring his hands. Ernie came hurrying from the office as Lois ran down the stairs past Dayabai and the children to the front door. *Has one of the Ratnakar children been in a terrible accident or possibly been bitten by a snake,* Lois wondered with a sickening feeling of apprehension?

As Ernie swung the screen door open, Ratnaker turned from the door and started down the drive toward the compound gate, shouting as he went, "Come quickly to the well outside the gate. You must hurry! Oh, what shall we do?"

Ernie and Lois ran down the drive, not knowing what to expect, but sure it must be something terrible to cause Ratnakar to be so frenzied. There was quite a crowd gathered around the well and the newcomers had to push their way through until they reached the wall that rimmed the well.

As Lois looked over the edge, she caught her breath in shock. There, floating face down with limp arms adrift slightly below the surface of the water was the body of a woman. By her dress, apparently she was a Hindu, but who she was or how or when she had fallen or been thrown into the well, no one seemed to know.

"Shall I go get some ropes to pull her out, Sahib?" asked Ratnaker, half turning, ready to run to the barn.

"No, Ratnakar, it's no use." Ernie stopped him. "She is dead. There is nothing that we can do to help her now. In fact, the first thing we must do is call the police. Take my bicycle and go as fast as you can to the police station and file the report of this death."

Lois watched Ratnakar go running toward the barn to get Ernie's bicycle. She turned again toward the well and looked at the grim spectacle of the unknown woman floating motionless near the surface of the water. Her clothes weren't torn. Nor were there any other signs of a struggle. She looked for any possible signs of a struggle between Hindu and Muslim groups, but there were none. *Had it been a family fight?* Lois looked at the people standing around the well. She saw only curiosity reflected on their faces. There was nothing that showed that anyone knew this woman or was grieving at her death. Since there was nothing that she could do to help in this situation, Lois sadly turned away from the well and returned to the bungalow. *The poor woman! She may have been a refugee. Did she have a husband? Children? Would they ever know what had happened to her?* While this woman was dying, she and Ernie had been sleeping peacefully. Somehow, it was all wrong, a part of the general madness that had taken control of this country. *How could it be stopped? Had rationality slipped completely from India's grasp? Was it too late?* Rumors flew fast. By evening Lois had heard many stories about the woman in the well; that she had been killed by a Muslim man and thrown in the well--that her husband had killed her because he wanted to marry someone else with a big dowry—that she had been so mistreated, beaten, and starved by her husband's family that she had thrown herself in the well and drowned. They would probably never know what had really happened.

Ernie stood guard through the morning. The police came, did a lot of questioning, and then removed the body from the well. They had a cover put over the well and declared it unusable for three months. Government people came late in the morning and poured chemicals into the water to start the purification process.

In the meantime, many people had no place to get water unless they walked great distances. Ernie decided that the best thing to do was to throw open the compound gate and gave permission for people to draw water from the Mission compound well for the next three months. They would have to work constantly to keep the water as sanitary as possible.

The police reported to Ernie later that no information about the woman was ever discovered. They shrugged their shoulders as they commented that she was probably a refugee anyway, or a runaway. During this turbulent time when death was a common, everyday affair, with many unsolved murders to deal with, the local police acted as if it was really a matter of little importance.

Chapter 14

— • —

Birth Pains of a Nation

Lois was personally affected by the drowning in the well. The impersonal, gruesome death of one individual, seemed to be representative of the low value placed on human life pervading the entire country. The month leading up to the day set for Indian Independence was a period of chaos and violent actions by various groups and individuals in communities all over India. Gatherings of people, especially on railway station platforms, became angry, disorderly crowds. Hundreds of people flooded onto the tracks, some sitting, some lying down, and refusing to move even in the face of oncoming trains. As a result of these mass actions, trains were always running late or not at all. A person needing to travel by rail had to go to the station, sit and wait for the next train going the right direction, and then try to find a place in an already overcrowded car, even though it might not be the one that was scheduled.

Because of the general political unrest, criminal elements in all communities, Muslim, Hindu, and also Christian, became bolder; robberies and muggings as well as murders, many of them unrelated to the political situation, were reported daily. Anarchy seemed to rule.

By the end of July the Medical Mission compound and the Grace Villa compound were finding necessary supplies running low, and it was obvious that someone must travel to Bombay to bring back medical supplies, school supplies, and provisions to fill many personal requests, as was always the case, from various people in the Christian community.

It was decided that Ernie should be the one to go, for he would be more likely to be able to hold his own in any emergency that might arise in the city or on the train. The tentative plan was that he would start from Dahanu before the sun was up, hopefully arrive in Bombay early that evening, stay over night with Lynn and Mary Blickenstaff at the apartment that the

Church of the Brethren maintained for mostly European and American travelers, do all the necessary shopping the next day and, if all went well, be able to take an early evening train out of Bombay, arriving back in Dahanu around 11:30 p.m. a total of two days later. Because most of the trains were made up in Bombay, travelers coming from there to Dahanu Road were more likely to be nearly on schedule than the ones coming from New Delhi in the North. As Ernie packed what he would need in Bombay in preparation to leave the next morning, he cautioned Lois not to worry about him if he was late in returning, for more than likely it would take an extra day to accomplish all the errands and to fill the long shopping lists.

Very early the next morning Ratnakar hitched the stolid bullocks to the tonga and drove Ernie and his black tin suitcase with a red rose painted on the side, to the station, arriving at six a.m. Crowded like the busiest day in the bazaar, the station platform was jammed with people waiting for a train. Some were sleeping on the ground, others were trying to get a turn washing at the one faucet on the platform provided for railway passengers. Many of the women were squatting on the ground, digging around in their parcels tied up in nondescript cloth, searching for food to give to crying children who were clinging fretfully to their mothers' saris. The four or five benches on the platform were occupied by sleeping people. Down on the tracks several hundred political demonstrators, mostly men dressed in khadi (loose, white clothing produced as a cottage industry) and wearing Gandhi caps, were milling about, shouting, "Jai Hind!" and, "Quit India!"

Ernie inquired at the ticket office as to when to expect the next train to Bombay. The busy ticket agent, looking very harassed, told him that no one could answer that question, but that there was a train standing on the platform up the line at Surat while the police were trying unsuccessfully to clear the tracks of over two hundred shouting, angry people. There was nothing to be done but wait.

Reflecting on one of his mother's favorite axioms that "patience is a virtue," Ernie made his way over to the tea stall where he purchased a cup of boiling hot tea; then upending his tin suitcase to use for a seat, he prepared to drink tea and relax while he waited stoically for matters to take their course.

Two hours later there was a stirring among the people as someone shouted, "Gadi ali! Gadi ali!" (The train is coming!) People began gathering together their bundles and children in anticipation of the mad rush to board an already overcrowded train. Ernie had an advantage, for he had only one small suitcase and his bedding roll. He picked them up and moved down beyond the platform to a position outside the station where the train was likely to have to stop because of the masses of demonstrators on the tracks.

The steam engine came puffing into sight, its whistle shrieking a warning, and moved very slowly toward the Dahanu Station. Still the demonstrators lying on the tracks did not move off. The train, with people hanging onto the outside of the cars and riding on top as well, was forced to stop down the tracks outside the station and wait until the police could clear the way.

Ernie hurried down the line to a third-class car where he observed a man climbing out and he quickly swung himself aboard. Once inside the car he was able to find enough space to shove his bedding role under a bench and, again upending his tin suitcase, sat down on it, where he waited another hour and a half before the train was finally able to move again toward Bombay. By the time they at last arrived in the city, it was well after midnight.

The Blickenstaffs weren't surprised to see Ernie; they were used to having people arrive at all hours. Mary explained that their rooms were all full and suggested that Ernie sleep the remainder of the night on the davenport. The next morning a couple would be leaving to catch a train departing Bombay at six o'clock, and then Ernie could have that room.

For the next two hectic days Ernie worked every minute to find and purchase all the supplies on his several lists. He had planned it so that his final purchases were in Crawford Market at a general food store called Cheap Jack's, whose owner was a good friend. The shop keeper agreed to box and rope all of his supplies for easier transport. By the time the supplies were all tied up there were five fair-sized boxes. Counting the boxes and adding his suitcase and bedding roll made seven pieces of luggage he would have to keep an eye on while traveling back to Dahanu. Ernie was glad that he would be boarding the train at its starting point instead of up the line somewhere. To facilitate matters he purchased a second-class ticket, knowing that there would be fewer people traveling second than third. He planned to stack the boxes at the end of the car near the door where they would be easy to unload when the train pulled into the Dahanu Road station.

Everything went according to plan. He was able to get to the station by five o'clock in the evening of his second day in Bombay, board his car and store his things conveniently near the door.

When the train left the station in Bombay, Ernie's car was about half filled. During the next five hours passengers boarded the train and then departed when they arrived at their destinations. The train was often delayed by shouting crowds, but as the hour grew late the numbers of passengers dwindled until by the time the train left the last station before Dahanu, Ernie found himself alone in the car.

The next station is mine, and we should arrive in another half hour, thought Ernie. He reached down under the bench and pulled out his canvas bedding roll, then stacked it with the boxes from Cheap Jack and his tin suitcase.

"Shull Sahib, open this door!" shouted an angry voice through the window of the moving train, startling Ernie who had been unaware of anyone clinging to the outside of the car. Ernie swung around quickly and recognized Martin, a trouble maker and a known thief from the Christian community in Dahanu. Martin's father, Habel, was a good worker for Dr. Nickey on the hospital compound, but Martin had turned against his father and the rest of his family. Ernie had been instrumental in having him arrested for stealing various items from the church and the hospital two months earlier. Martin's father had tried to restrain his son, but Martin was running with a bad crowd of young men in Dahanu.

Ernie hesitated, assessing the situation.

"Open the door, Sahib!" snarled Martin. "I'm going to get you for the way you turned me in. If not tonight, then some time when you don't know that I'm around. I heard that you had gone to Bombay and I knew that you would come back with valuables. As I think about it, I've decided that if you will open this door and give me the boxes, I won't get you with my knife. . . tonight!" Clinging to the window bar with one hand while the wind from the fast-moving train whipped his hair and his clothes, this teenage thief gripped a knife in his other hand flashing it threateningly just outside the window.

Ernie was not as much frightened as he was frustrated. Here was a young man who needed help, but so far no one had been able to reach him.

"Martin, I'm not going to open the door--you know that I have it locked. Why are you doing this kind of thing? You disgrace your father and your family," Ernie mentioned his family, reasoning that strong family ties might yet have some influence on this young man who was rapidly destroying himself. Ernie moved slowly over toward the emergency cord that was located in all Indian train cars directly above the door. Pulling the cord would automatically activate the brakes in all of the cars and bring the train to a slow stop. The guards and police would rush in to check on the trouble.

"Don't preach to me! You sound like my father and I'm tired of listening to him. The boxes, Sahib, the boxes if you don't want to feel my knife!" Martin moved along the car until he held onto the bars of the door, then he began to shake it. He reached one hand through the bars and up toward the loose-fitting lock above. Ernie grabbed a book he had been reading from the seat where he had dropped it and struck Martin's clutching fingers as they stretched toward the lock. With his other hand Ernie grabbed the handle of the emergency cord.

"Don't try it, Martin! I'll jerk the emergency cord and the guards will be on you in a minute!

Don't touch that handle!"

Martin withdrew his stinging fingers. The train was going too fast for him to let go, and if he tried to unlock the door the Sahib would pull the cord calling the guards. While Ernie stood tensely holding on to the emergency handle, Martin continued a steady stream of invectives. He spit through the window, declaring that some day he would get the Sahib--he would attack him when no one even knew he was around.

The train began to decrease its speed as it neared the Dahanu station, and long before it pulled onto the platform, Martin had dropped off the train and disappeared between the cars of a slowly approaching second train.

As the train slowed down Ernie opened the car door and stood in the open doorway. When the train finally pulled in it was very late at night. In spite of the late hour a number of coolies came running to help with the boxes and to earn a generous "bakshis" (tip). They loaded the boxes into a horse tonga. The tonga driver turned them toward the Jawar road and a half hour later Ernie was home.

Two weeks after Martin threatened Shull Sahib on the train, the police arrested him for murder. He was accused of brutally killing his young, pregnant wife by jumping on her stomach. A few days after Martin's "run-in" with the police he himself was murdered by his own gang and his body left by an open irrigation ditch half way between Palghar and Dahanu.

Martin's murder posed a dilemma for the congregations of these two Christian churches. He was the son of a Christian and therefore, in the eyes of the Hindus and the Muslims, he was a Christian; however, the Christian community knew what his character had been and they didn't want him buried in the Christian cemetery. Nevertheless, since Martin's roots had been in the Christian community, doing something with the body was clearly their responsibility. They turned to the District Elder, Parlak D. J. Bhonsle for help and guidance. He called together the leaders of the churches in emergency session where it was decided that Martin's body should be buried in the far corner of a forty acre field on the Palghar school compound. Their decision was carried out as quickly as possible, for Indian law dictated that a burial must occur within twenty four hours; it was hot weather and the body had already lain unattended for half a day.

The Christian community was torn between horror and outrage, but along with these emotions they were very sad for the wasted young life and for the grieving father who had, in reality, lost his son long before his murder. They closed ranks around Habel and his wife and tried to give them comfort the best that they could.

Even though the Martin case was a disgrace for the Christian community, some Hindus

and some Muslims recognized the relative safety in being a Christian during India's current political and social crisis, and began wearing crosses around their necks when they traveled on a train. In some cases it saved them from being murdered, but no one was really safe.

The daily newspapers coming from Bombay were full of confrontation on every level. The struggle between Jinna, leader among the Muslims on the one hand, and Nehru, leader of the Hindu Congress Party on the other, was growing even more intense, especially in the Punjab, as the lively discussions proceeded among themselves about which states should accede to the new Pakistan and which ones should stay in India.

Independence from Great Britain and the actual division into two separate states of Pakistan and India were really finalized a few minutes before midnight August 14, 1947, but August fifteenth was declared Independence Day from Great Britain. This unusual time was set because an astrologer had predicted that August fourteenth was an inauspicious day and should be avoided.

As soon as the bells began to ring at midnight declaring that India was actually independent, people took to the streets in great joy and celebration; however, before many hours had passed groups began to turn ugly. Marauding bands, some Muslim, others Hindu, set upon small villages and slaughtered people from the opposite community, often grossly mutilating their bodies. No group was spared--old people, children, women.

A long, dark red train coming from Panjab in the north, pulled slowly into the Delhi station. Strangely, there were no sounds of people and no signs of movement from any of the cars. Cautiously people waiting on the platform approached this eerie phenomenon and opened the car doors, hurrying from one car to another. In every car they found dead passengers, butchered and lying in pools of blood. The only living people on the train were the injured engineer and the fireman. The shock of this horrible atrocity spread like wildfire over the nation, but instead of bringing people to their senses and stopping the bloodshed, it seemed to spread the violence, driven by fear. The migration of people that had started earlier became a movement of millions, each person trying to reach the safety of being with others of like faith.

The village of Dahanu continued to be a crossroads for the Hindu and Muslim communities, Hindus going south and Muslims going north. But the exploding violence was even greater in the Punjab. Chalmer and Susan coming south from the American school of Woodstock in the Himalayan Mountains were horrified when coming through that area to have their train boarded by a band of Muslim men who dragged the Hindus in their car off onto the platform and slaughtered them there stacking their bodies. A few stations later the same thing happened in reverse, the Muslims being slaughtered.

Gandhi put his life on the line, fasting unto death to bring about peace in Calcutta. His efforts were successful in that area, but the situation in the country had gone too far to be stopped.

On January 26, 1948 India's new constitution was adopted and the day declared India's new Independence Day.

Two days later on January 28, 1948 Mahatma Gandhi was murdered, shot by a young Hindu at one of Gandhi's regular prayer services, and India was thrown into even greater chaos. Strangely enough, the Christian community remained relatively unharmed. Ernie and Parlak Bhonsale continued to visit the village schools and help the teachers as they taught not only the children, but the adults as well. They were working hard on programs of village sanitation and nutrition, and in the evenings the whole village would gather to hear teachings from the Bible. Once a month the teachers came to the Grace Villa bungalow for a conference and for talking with other teachers. They always went back to their villages with new ideas and renewed enthusiasm and dedication. Lois listened in on most of these meetings, but she was never a part of them--except to serve the tea.

By the beginning of February, Lois was sure she was pregnant. Nothing could have made her happier. Long ago she and Ernie had talked it over and decided that now was the time to have a third child, since they were stationed near a Mission hospital, and might not ever be again. They decided not to mention it to their Indian colleagues for a while until it became obvious.

One day soon after that, during an afternoon sewing class on the upstairs verandah, it became public knowledge.

"Madam Sahib, congratulations to you! We hear that you are going to have a baby!" smiled Premabai, the mother of five.

Lois was so surprised that she exclaimed, "Premabai! It's true that I am pregnant, but how could you have known? I've known it only about two weeks!" All the ladies began to laugh and look at each other.

"You tell her, Premabai. You started it," urged Ratanbai.

"Well, you see, Madam Sahib," explained Premabai, the sweeper told us!" The sweeper, since there was no running water, was responsible for cleaning the toilets twice a day. Lois was embarrassed and a little annoyed. It was obvious that it was useless to try to keep anything private. Living in this community was like living in the proverbial fish bowl--always under observation. It flashed through her mind that if everyone already knew about her pregnancy, she should accept it philosophically. Perhaps it was just as well.

"Since you already know about our wonderful news, let's celebrate today! Let's have our cup of tea early, and I think Sovenji found some peanuts in the bazaar this morning that we can have with the tea."

The women laughed and chattered as the party progressed. Never before had they seemed so happy and relaxed. Watching them, Lois realized that this was just an interlude from their lives of daily poverty and hardship. But regardless of what community they came from, Christian, Hindu, Muslim, or Parsee, they had all given birth. The women could identify easily with Lois on this occasion. Their shared experiences of pregnancy made Lois feel closer to the women than ever before. She felt their friendly sisterhood. So what did a little lost privacy matter? It mattered not at all.

Ernie and Lois continued in their half-time language study, but as the days went by the amount of work to be done grew greater, until it seemed that half time went to language study and seventy five percent of the time went to the job; not good math and not a comfortable way to live! Language school and second year exams would be coming up the last of May, uncomfortably soon; however, their pandit felt that they would be ready.

In the middle of national turmoil, many local communities settled into a comparatively calm routine. In the town of Dahanu was a shop that manufactured plaster-of-paris figures of the Ganpati god, known more universally over India as Ganesha. According to the Hindu Scriptures, Ganpati was the god of obstacles and Hindus starting any enterprise sought the help of this god to bring them success. The cult which worshiped Ganpati was found all over India. The image of Ganesha was a grotesque figure with a huge elephant head, an enormous stomach, and disproportional limbs. He was occasionally portrayed with a rat at his feet.

The story goes that the first time his mother, the goddess Durga, saw him, she reduced his head to ashes by the intensity of of her stare. The god Siva, his father, on learning this misfortune, and being sorely grieved at having a son without a head, sent his servants out to cut off the head of the first living creature they met and bring it back to him. An elephant happened to be the first creature they met. They cut off his head and brought it back to their master. Siva took it and fitted it on his son's neck, and since then Ganesha, or Ganpati, has been represented with an elephant's head.

These idols could be found everywhere--in temples, schools, public places, forts, highways, near wells, and on fountains and tanks. It was not surprising that the factory that produced these figures was very busy and successful. Lois asked their pandit, Mr. Chopade, if he thought it would be possible for them to see this god factory in production. She thought there might be taboos concerning Christians coming into the shop.

Pandit Chopade asked Mr. Patel, his Hindu friend who managed the factory, if he could show the Marathi students through.

"Of course!" he said. "I would be delighted!" The visit turned out to be a most revealing and thought-provoking tour.

The plaster-of-paris images were being produced in all sizes, and the cost varied from a few annas to many rupees. Wealthy families considered it a matter of social standing to purchase the larger idols. Mr. Patel explained that they had something new in the way of figures--they were placing other objects at the feet of the Ganpati, such as a car, or an airplane, along with the traditional rat. He explained that they were staying modern as well as traditional; that some pandits thought that the modern Ganesha figures were more effective in answering the prayers of the people. It was obvious that Mr. Patel was serious and believed implicitly in what he was saying.

That evening as Ernie, Pandit Chopade and Lois were having their language hour of conversation, Lois commented, "Mr. Chopade how can Mr. Patel really believe that those figures, which he is actually making himself, can have any power to answer prayer?"

Pandit Chopade rubbed his chin thoughtfully. "Very difficult question; yes, a very difficult question."

"But you do think he is sincere, don't you? He really does believe it, doesn't he?" Lois insisted. She felt confused as she struggled to understand Mr. Patel's thinking and point of view.

"Oh, he is sincere all right! He is my friend, and I know that he does his puja (worship) every day without fail," Pandit Chopade agreed. As he thought about it he chuckled. "Sometimes I think he is so faithful because he is afraid not to be. You see, if you truly think that Ganesha can withhold success from your business, you will be very careful not to offend him, I think."

Ernie pushed his chair back and walked over to the bungalow door. He watched for a minute the heavily loaded logging carts being pulled by teams of lumbering bullocks as they rolled slowly by. These ponderous burdens were like the heavy weight of superstition holding the people down where they were always fearful of offending one god or another and having to suffer for it.

"It's such a long way from believing that God is love, and that God is a friend and a guide," he said thoughtfully.

Not long after Gandhi's death, some people began talking about him as though he were a god, and it looked as if a cult might be developing. This would be a simple matter in the country of India where there were already millions of gods. A group of well-to-do business men in the large village of Dahanu built a temple dedicated to <u>all</u> religions. They pointed to one of the sayings of the Mahatma who had said, "All religions are equal--they are like leaves of the same tree."

"That's the genius of Hinduism," remarked Ernie one Sunday evening while they were having a late tea on the lawn in front of the bungalow. As was their custom, Dr. Nickey, Dorothy and fifteen of the student nurses had walked out to Grace Villa to spend a relaxed evening. "Hinduism accepts all other religions and philosophies, and then absorbs them so that they become minor parts of Hinduism! I didn't tell you, Lois," he continued, "but I was approached this week and asked to donate a Bible to be placed in one of the honored locations in the new temple, along with the Hindu's Bhagavad-Gita, the Muslim's Koran, and the Parsee's Zend-Avesta. I refused! I, as a Christian, could not agree that these other religions are equally true!"

Dr. Nickey bristled. "Well, I don't agree with you, Ernie. A delegation came to me also, asking for a Bible; and I gave them my best Bible! After all, it's putting the truth into the hands of people who have never read Christian scriptures, and it might help somebody whom we don't even know." She leaned back in her chair and took a sip of tea. "I was glad for an opportunity to share my Bible."

"I'm sure you did what you thought was right, Doctor; but the principle seems wrong to me. It's done now, however; so let's hope you are right, and that it will help someone who is searching for truth," Ernie concluded.

The Christians usually agreed on their goals and what they wanted to accomplish, but when it came to methods of working and how to help the Indian people, ideas differed sometimes radically. *That's where open mindedness comes in--and tolerance,* thought Lois. *After all, there might be a few rare occasions when a person with differing views might be right!*

Lois picked up the teapot and went around the group refilling hot tea, and Linda passed the plate of bhajis, an Indian dish for special occasions. As Lois poured Dorothy's tea, Dorothy remarked, "Lois, we lost a lady you knew today. She was from the village of Kainard where we have one of our schools. She has been to the clinic once or twice when you were there. Her name is Banibai. She wasn't a Christian, but her younger brothers and a sister are attending the school there."

"Oh, that's really sad, Dorothy! She was so young! What was the matter with her?" Lois remembered the lady, not much more than a girl, who had brought an older woman from her village to the clinic for treatment a few months earlier.

Dorothy hesitated. "Well, I hate to tell you about it, because it was so tragic.... Dr. Nickey?"

Dr. Nickey looked down at the teacup she was holding. "She was a delivery case and this was her first pregnancy. She started labor in the village at night and the family thought it was too far to try to get her here in time, so they called in the village midwife, the dai. Unfortunately the girl had a small pelvis, and because the labor was so long, the dai followed the ancient customs in her area and stuffed all sorts of foreign matter into the vagina--ashes, cow dung, cloves, etc.--and when the birth still didn't occur, she pressed her knees down on the girl's abdomen to force the baby out. The result was a ruptured uterus, and by the time they arrived here, the baby was dead and the mother had hemorrhaged so much that we lost her before we could try to help her."

"That's horrible!" Lois exclaimed setting the teapot down and coming over to stand by Dr. Nickey. "That's murder! Isn't there any law?"

Dr. Nickey answered sadly, "The law of custom, and the right of each caste to practice their ancient rites. Unfortunately this is not an isolated case. I get many cases that the dais have tried to deliver. But I'll tell you this," she continued. "Change is coming before too long, for already the new Indian Government is beginning to make some regulations for nursing schools and hospitals. Perhaps before many years they will get down to the village level and make some rules for those who practice medicine."

Maybe so, thought Lois, but considering the gigantic task of the new Indian government to deal with every aspect of the nation and its citizens, she guessed it would be a long, long time before there would be any help for ordinary village women. What had happened to Banibai was cruel and brutal, and the result of ignorance! No doubt it was happening to someone else at this very minute--and here she was, serving tea on a lovely Sunday afternoon. It felt like fiddling while Rome burned! She was filled with frustration at the Mission's inability to change things faster, and her own powerlessness to help more people.

"Because if the baby had been a girl,
we wouldn't have gotten any candy."
Lahanu

Chapter 15

❖

Ernie's Illness and The Birth of a Baby

By the end of April the Indian national scene was still one of confusion. Political demonstrations continued on the train stations and in the villages, Hindu placards seemed almost to scream the slogan "Hindustan ki jai!" Muslim people were still leaving their villages in India, becoming refugees and working their way north toward the new Pakistan and hopefully safety among like believers. Hindu refugees from the north were pouring down into India, crowding the trains inside, outside, and on top. Dealing with these uprooted people, and trying to protect the minority who still remained in the country were major problems for these two new, inexperienced governments. In both the Muslim Pakistan and the Hindu India there were radical elements who believed that the minority religion of either Hinduism or Islam must be stamped out, and as a result rivers flowed red.

At the end of April the Shull family again made the long trip up into the hills above Poona to Mahableshwar to study under the pandits at the language school and to prepare to take their final exams. They again took with them Sovenji and Dayabai to help them. The cool air was wonderful in the hills after the burning heat of the plains. For relaxation from study they walked in the evenings in wooded areas, and met many people from other parts of India, mostly well-to-do people who were on vacation. They enjoyed the fresh strawberries that Sovenji served every day.

Lois and Ernie took their exams the tenth of June, and their party left Mahableshwar two days later, hoping to arrive back at Dahanu before the monsoon broke. Mr. Chopade would no longer be a daily visitor, for their formal language study was over. They would miss their daily conversations with him, his advice, and counseling. He had taught them so many things about the culture, and the ways people in the East approach problems, things not found in their language books.

Since language study was now over, they were immediately assigned to full-time work. Ernie and Parlak Bhonsle cooperated very closely in improving the programs for the village schools. Half of their time went into adult education, encouraging the parents to send their children to school and to attend adult evening classes themselves, There they learned about cleanliness and child care, community responsibility in an independent India, and the love of God for everyone, including those of other religions. This was a difficult concept at this highly emotional period in Indian history.

The young Indian Church was alive and enthusiastic about sharing their faith. However, as was to be expected, there were certain difficulties and problems. The Church grew as people tried to radiate God's love by showing love and concern for people around them. It was difficult for new Christians, and for some others also, to completely disregard former caste status when dealing with people. For, after all, Christ taught that no one is to be considered higher or lower than another.

Lois pondered often the hold the concept of caste had on the Indian people. To ask them to stop seeing others by caste was almost like asking people not to think of an individual as a woman or man, but only as a person--a complete change of orientation.

Another challenge for the church was developing leadership. The people in the Christian community found themselves in a rather difficult situation where they seemed to want things both ways. Many were anxious to take over more of the responsibility for organization and finance, yet at the same time wanting any bad fallout from mistakes made to rest on the shoulders of the missionaries. The missionary personnel had been working for a long time to prepare Indian Christians to take over the responsibility and guidance of the Church, but in a few instances, a new leader had been too weak to stand against his own human frailties, and had been ruined in the process instead of becoming a strong leader.

One day in checking over the account books of station operations on the medical compound, Ernie found a number of strange entries. He went down to the bazaar and had a visit with several of the merchants with whom the Mission regularly did business and discovered that the prices paid for certain purchases was much less than the prices entered into the Mission account books. Johnbhai, who was in charge of the medical compound maintenance and its accounts, had worked for the Dahanu Mission for years. He was an intelligent, skilled manager and the medical personnel depended upon him and trusted him implicitly. The extent of the discrepancies amounted to a rather large sum of money, for the fraud had been going on for a number of years with the cooperation of the merchants.

During an interview with Ernie and Dr. Nickey the next day, Johnbhai admitted that he was taking a certain amount from each purchase, but he was convinced that with his responsibilities he was entitled to it, and besides, he insisted, this was the Indian way.

Johnbhai was allowed to keep his job, but the accounts had to be taken away, and the merchants in the village were notified that Johnbhai from now on could not do any of the purchasing for the Mission. The question remained, were they trying to push Indian nationals into positions of leadership and responsibility too rapidly before they were really ready and strong enough?

One day toward the last of August Ernie woke up not feeling very well. He ate breakfast with the family as they listened to the rain drumming softly on the tin roof of the dining room, but he couldn't keep his food down and rushed from the room. He decided to ignore the way he felt since the village masters were all coming in that day for a conference.

By the next day when he was no better he went in to the hospital to see Dr. Nickey or Dr. Peter Paul. After examining him and finding his skin quite yellow, Dr. Nickey decided that he must have yellow fever, although that disease was very rare in India.

The next three weeks were miserable. After the usual morning ritual of losing his breakfast he would drag through the day's work. One day about midmorning when Ernie was coming in late from feeding the chickens which they kept for a supply of eggs, he saw on the top back step a coiled cobra with its head raised and its hood spread, and just above it, opening the back screen door, was three-year-old Jimmy getting ready to come to his daddy.

Ernie grabbed a stick lying by the step and struck at the snake which slid off the step and over a few yards into the climbing beans in the vegetable garden. The beans were climbing on long arbors forming covered paths through the garden where the cobra could easily hide. Ernie knew that he had to get that snake, for it was a threat to everyone on the compound. He found a stronger stick and stepped carefully into the bean arbor.

He knew that most snakes will not bother people if they are left alone, but the cobra is different. It will fight. Ernie located it at the end of one of the arbors, with its hood spread and its body coiled ready to strike. He swung the heavy stick at the snake and was able to pin it down with the stick just behind the cobra's head and hood leaving the body to flop and coil around his arm. Ernie was about to step on its head when, because of the soft, rain-soaked, cultivated earth beneath, the snake slipped out from under the stick and made for cover. Ernie worked it slowly toward the end of the arbor, parrying its attempted strikes with his stick, until it left the arbor and was on solid ground. Then he again pinned its neck down with his stick and stepped on its head to finish it. That was one less deadly snake to hide in the tall grass and threaten the people who either wore sandals or didn't wear shoes at all.

By afternoon Ernie was feeling worse. They decided that something had to be done, so Lois asked Ratnakar to hitch up the bullocks and take Ernie in to the hospital. This time the two doctors together examined him and concluded that he had been suffering from infectious hepatitis for three weeks. They changed his medication and before many days passed he began to feel better.

Just a few days later, on September eleventh during the wee hours of the morning, Lois was awakened by Ernie's tossing and turning in his bed. Reaching over she felt his head and found him burning hot. *Oh no!* Lois thought. *Not sick again so soon!* Moving slowly because of the weight of they baby, she climbed out from under the mosquito net and went to get the thermometer, thankful that they had left the lantern burning low just in case the children needed something in the night.

She tried to wake Ernie, but he seemed dazed and only about half conscious. The thermometer read 104! She had to get that fever down! Taking a cloth and cool water from the big earthen water jar in the bathroom, she bathed his burning head and body, then alternated cool, wet cloths on his forehead and urged him to drink water. Morning came with pink rays of sunlight streaking around the clouds. The monsoon was nearly over and seeing such a beautiful morning made Lois feel better. As early as she could she sent Ratnaker with a note to Dr. Nickey, asking her to come to see Ernie as soon as she could.

Ernie's temperature dropped to 102, but by noon it was again up to 104 and he was delirious, jabbering nonsense, and singing hymns in the Marathi language mostly on key, but a bit wobbly on the high notes.

Dr. Nickey arrived by tonga about 4:00 in the afternoon. She looked grave as she saw his condition and said Ernie should be taken immediately to the hospital where there would be more facilities.

"He may have cerebral malaria, but I won't know until we have done further testing," she said.

Sovenji and Ratnaker held Ernie in the tonga and kept him from sliding to the floor. As the bullocks moved slowly forward, Dr. Nickey called to Lois on the step, "Lois, I don't think you and the children should stay here tonight with your baby due in two weeks. You might go into labor at any time. I'll have Dorothy come out and help you and the children bring what you need to stay with us in our bungalow until Ernie is well enough to come home." The tonga passed through the gate and out onto the road.

Lois took a deep breath and looked around her. Where to begin! There was no doubt that Ernie was seriously ill, and she didn't know how long they would have to stay on the medical compound. She decided to start by packing the clothing the children would need and a few toys to keep them happy. Linda was excited about the move, for she loved Aunt Dorothy and liked to be with her. She pulled her small suitcase out from under her bed and excitedly packed her own things.

When the packing was finished Lois looked around to see what else needed packing before she left the house for an indefinite period. Sovenji would take care of the last minute things and would close the house. She remembered that the upstairs verandah where the children usually played and where the women's sewing and mending classes met, needed mopping, and Gangubai hadn't had time to do it that morning with everything else that was going on, so she decided to do that before Dorothy came for them. She was just finishing her task when the medical compound tonga came into the compound and Dorothy got down. She was surprised to find Lois and the children ready. Gangubai was going with them to help with the children.

When they were all packed in with no room to spare, Lois relaxed against the seat of the tonga. She felt rather quivery inside, what with all the worry and the effort involved in their plans to leave for a few days.

An hour later they were established in a spacious, airy room in the medical bungalow. Ernie was lying on a bed by the front window where he could get the cool breeze and watch the families of other patients. From time to time technicians would come to do a battery of tests. Eventually the diagnosis was made—malignant malaria. Since Ernie's food had to come from the medical bungalow kitchen, it was decided that Ernie would remain there with the rest of the family instead of being placed in the hospital.

Linda chose the bed she wanted and laid her doll on the pillow. The other bed was out on a small, latticed-in verandah just outside the bathroom and would do temporarily for Lois and Jimmy until another bed could be moved in.

Dorothy and Hazel Messer, an American nurse who had just recently returned from a furlough in the States, had the room upstairs just above the Shull family. The nurses fixed up a bell arrangement that would call them just in case Ernie needed a nurse during the night.

Dorothy laughed as she put the bell on the table by Lois's bed, "Who knows? You might be needing this bell more than Ernie."

"I doubt it," Lois answered. "I'm supposed to have two more weeks before it is time for the baby."

"There will be a nurse in every hour to take Ernie's temperature, but if you need us you can just ring the bell. But come now; it's late and Lahanu has a meal ready for us."

The meal over, Lois bathed Jimmy and supervised Linda's bath, then put them into their beds. They were asleep before she had finished tucking in their mosquito nets.

Wearily she took her own bath, enjoying the feel of the cool water as she poured it over herself. She slipped a thin cotton nightgown over her head; then, after a last check on Ernie, and finding him still resting quietly she crawled under her net and stretched out beside Jimmy's comforting, little body. "Lord, be with us through the coming hours," she prayed. "Touch Ernie with your healing power, loving Father, and give me strength to bare what is ahead this night." She moaned as she tried to relax for she hadn't realized how tired she was until that moment. She was deeply concerned about Ernie's condition. He was sleeping quietly under his net. His fever must be down, she thought. Memory of the events of the last day passed slowly through her mind. She didn't remember when she had been so tired! It was comforting to realize that they were at a Christian hospital where Ernie would receive the best of loving care.

Lois relaxed as she felt a breath of cool breeze drift in through the lattice, soothing her like an evening blessing. Her thoughts were with Ernie lying in the bed so near to hers. She prayed that the malignant malaria he had would soon be healed. She couldn't even talk to him, because his fever was so high he was delirious. She was just drifting off to sleep when she was startled wide awake by a vicious thump inside her abdomen, more violent than a baby kick. She felt a gush of liquid and knew immediately that the baby had decided that this was the time to be born. She felt no pain and everything around her in the house was quiet. It seemed that the whole world was standing still waiting for the next glorious moments when this beautiful baby would be born. She put her arm around Jimmy, holding him lovingly, relishing the comfort of that quiet moment, storing up energy and strength for the difficult experience and labor ahead. The feeling of God's presence surrounded her, giving her strength and a sense of calm anticipation.

Reaching out from under the net Lois touched the bell on the table beside her bed and heard it ring softly upstairs in the sparsely furnished nurses' room. Almost immediately she felt the jar of four feet hitting the floor above her. Dorothy and Hazel hastily slipped into their uniforms and then came hurrying down the stairs

Lois heard their hastening feet on the stairs and called out, "Sorry, Girls, to disturb your sleep, but I think my baby has decided to be born." She smiled as she carefully put her feet on the floor and tucked the bed net securely under the mattress of Jimmy's bed.

"What sleep!" laughed Hazel as she took hold of one of Lois's arms and Dorothy took hold of the other as they assisted her from the medical bungalow over to the hospital.

Things happened rapidly after that. Lois was aware that they put her onto the delivery table. Pains came rapidly. Then she lost consciousness.

The first thing that she heard that made any sense was when the doctor said, "Shut off the Ergotamine! She's delivering."

Then some time later, she heard, "Why are you screaming, Lois?" That was Dr. Nickey's voice that clicked Lois into consciousness.

She could still hear the echoes of her own screams. "I don't know why! I didn't know I was screaming," she answered now fully conscious. "Sorry about that--the baby?"

"He's a beautiful boy with blond fuzz all over his head and a little pug nose!" declared Dorothy. "He's been exercising his lungs ever since he hit the air. No doubt he is going to be a preacher or a politician and run for Congress." She picked him up off the delivery table and took him over to give him his first bath. He had been born at twenty five minutes before midnight on the night of September eleventh.

Later Lois lay relaxed in a special room upstairs in the hospital with baby Daniel Lynn in a basket near her bed where she could reach over and touch him. She was filled with wonder at the miracle of God's creation. As she thought about the new baby she prayed that he would grow up to follow God's plan for his life. She also prayed that the Holy Spirit would lead her into following the will of God. She sought guidance in her own life, for sometimes she didn't know what was the right thing to do. She wished that God would speak a little more clearly sometimes. Even some handwriting on the wall might be helpful, she mused as she drifted into much needed sleep.

The next day was a day of celebration. Ernie's temperature had dropped to one hundred degrees, and Dr. Nickey allowed him out of bed long enough to come over to the hospital to visit Lois and to see his new son. Dorothy brought Linda and Jimmy over before breakfast to see the new baby in the family. Each one held him for a minute or two before he grew tired. People from the community came in to see the American baby with blond, fuzzy hair, so different from their own black-haired babies. One church lady laughingly pinched baby Danny's cheek and exclaimed, "Lardu! Lardu!" which is a round, delicious ball of candy.

After a day or two, when Ernie was getting his strength back, he bought some hard candy and passed it in the Christian community in celebration of Danny's birth.

"I'm glad you had a boy baby, Sahib," exclaimed Lahanu.

"Why is that?" Ernie asked.

"Because if the baby would have been a girl, we wouldn't have gotten any candy!" Lahanu declared.

Ernie explained that it didn't matter whether the baby was a boy or a girl, he would have passed around the candy, for boys and girls are equally loved but Lahanu and many in the community didn't quite believe that.

On the second day after Danny's birth Lois began to think about when they could go home to Grace Villa, but she encountered complications. She developed malaria, running a high fever, which stayed with her for ten days. Then because of weakened muscles she suffered a prolapsed uterus. It was not until Danny was twenty days old that they were able to return to their home at Grace Villa, and a week after that before Linda's home schooling could begin again.

Lois found that managing her family was taking most of her time. *Caring for a new baby is one of the joys of life,* she mused, but in spite of Lois's joy with her family she was baffled. For what was she doing to help anyone else? There were many times when she felt depressed and frustrated. She had to ask herself what she was doing to better the conditions of the people around her? How many people were better off because she had come to India? True, she had just finished language study, and she was a mother with a growing family, which took a lot of time, but she had come to India with a mission to help the Indian people find a loving God. She wanted to bring about some improvement in conditions, to teach children how to read and write, and help parents make their homes and villages sanitary. Until the people started practicing these basic principles, they could not be said to have improved. When she looked at the matted eyes and the distended abdomens of the children, swollen tight with starvation or some species of parasite, she felt angry at how difficult it seemed to be to improve basic health in the village. It seemed, to Lois, that sanitation had to precede other health concerns. Somehow, the Indian mothers must be convinced of the importance of keeping their children and their homes clean. But the Indian idea of cleanliness was so different.

Lois was very happy that she had been able to help out in the Mission Hospital sometimes when they were short of help. It seemed to her, as she thought about how little she seemed to be accomplishing, that there was so much to be done and she was doing so little. Was she just being impatient or was there something more that she could do?

Ernie didn't seem to feel her frustration. He was busy most of the time, and often had people waiting to see him. He worked with Parlak Bhonsle supervising the village schools in the district. Together they traveled by bullock cart into the surrounding communities to visit the local schools that had been established by the Mission. They observed the teachers in action and tried to help them with their problems. Each trip they brought materials for the teachers to work with and shared ideas and suggestions they thought might be helpful. These village teachers did a remarkably good job as a combination school teacher and social worker in spite of having so little to work with by American standards.

Usually out in the village, after school was dismissed and the children had gone home, Parlak Bhonsle and Ernie were invited by the teacher to come to his room and drink a cup of tea. It was obvious that the teacher and his wife were very lonely people, and they were so happy to have an opportunity to drink tea with visitors and to catch up on news of the outside world. It gave them a much needed boost of encouragement and renewed enthusiasm. News spread rapidly that the master had visitors, so in the evening after everyone had come home from working in the fields and had had their evening meals, the school bell would ring calling everyone to come to the school house for a meeting. Everybody loved to have an evening "sing," which was a combination worship and social time.

Ernie found his work very challenging and believed the educational program of the Mission to be good. He vowed that he would work even harder to get the villagers to send their girls along with the boys to school. Many villagers saw no need to educate girls. Besides girls were needed to work at home.

Chapter 16

———•·•———

Ahwa

The small, narrow-guage logging train chugged along slowly but steadily through the Indian jungle, whistling out a shrill blast whenever it approached a village. Lois leaned back relaxing against the leather cushion of their second-class car, while Ernie reclined half asleep on the bunk on the other side. How quickly a whole year of furlough back in the Sates had flown by. The year was supposed to have been a time of rest and renewal but in many ways had been hard work averaging more than 7 speaking engagements per week. In addition, there had been the question of Jimmy's health. Jimmy had contracted nephritis apparently from an infected mosquito bite, which left him with a baffling double beat in the heart. He went through endless tests in India and also in New York to try to positively identify the source of the double beat but it remained a mystery. The specialists wouldn't (or couldn't) say what this meant for the future of the Shulls' missionary career. Nevertheless, when it came time for a decision, the doctors said this strange phenomenon seemed to have no influence on Jimmjy's general phyhsical condition, so the Shulls were advised that Jimmy's health need not keep them from going back to India.

Linda, ten, and Jimmy, nearly seven, standing on their knees by an iron-barred window, held little towhead Danny, just three, up high enough to see the scenery outside, pointing out to him the interesting mammals and birds that they could glimpse as their train meandered along. If they would have had their choice of assignments of where to live and work during their second missionary term in this fascinating country, Lois and Ernie would have chosen to be placed right here in the Dangs, a beautiful jungle area in the Western Ghats, a range of low mountains, rising in some places to a height of 1,694 feet.

When they had received word while they were still in the United States that the Joint Council, a group made up of Indian Christian Church leaders and missionaries, had voted to station them in Ahwa, the capitol of the Dangs District, they were delighted. In addition to church duties there, they would be in charge of the rural boarding school in Ahwa and Ernie would oversee all the outlying district village schools.

This assignment wouldn't have been welcomed by some workers, for the Dangs Jungle was a hazardous place to live in some ways. The British, in the days when they ruled India, considered the Dangs to be a hardship station; the Indian Government followed the British policy and often, as a disciplinary measure, sent government officers to the Dangs. Malaria carrying mosquitoes were everywhere; various kinds of intestinal parasites contaminated the rivers; tigers and leopards roamed the jungle paths and even entered villages; poisonous snakes and pythons were a frequent danger. Besides the hazards of the jungle, access to the area was difficult. A narrow-guage logging train traveled once a day from the coast of the Arabian Sea seventy-five miles into the Dangs Area terminating twenty miles short of reaching the capitol village of Ahwa. Those last twenty miles had to be made on foot, by bullock cart, or by getting a ride in the single government jeep that sometimes came down to the rail line from the government headquarters. In spite of the so called "hardships," Lois and Ernie loved it here and completed not only a 6-year term here but a second term as well.

Lois was startled by two sharp blasts from the locomotive as it began to slow down and then ease into the station. It came to a screeching stop beside a big white station sign marked "Waghai," printed in three languages, Marathi, Gujarathi, and English. This was the end of the line for this little logging train. Lois was excited with anticipation. She stood in the doorway of the car beside Ernie, straining her eyes to see who would be on the platform to meet them, and the children were glued to the window.

"There's Chalmer," shouted Ernie waving his arms wildly in the air as he pointed down the length of two cars. "Hi, Brother," he yelled as he cupped his hands around his mouth trying to catch Chalmer's attention over the heads of the disembarking passengers.

Chalmer saw Ernie standing in the train car doorway, waving both arms in the air in greeting. What a wonderful moment--brother meeting brother in this deep jungle, halfway around the world from their native Indiana.

As soon as the train stopped the children rushed the door. "Uncle Chalmer! Uncle Chalmer! We're here!" Chalmer caught the children, lifting them down to the platform. It had been a year since they had seen each other.

"You are finally here, and I can't tell you how welcome you are. The people at Ahwa are so anxious to meet you, and of course, Susan can't wait! But first, I want you to meet the three Christian men who are with me to help us." He motioned toward the men who stood just behind him. They wore khaki shorts, long-tailed, loose shirts and broad smiles. As Chalmer mentioned their names, they stepped forward, folding their hands before them in greeting.

"Railu works for the mission, Hari works as a handyman and in the school gardens, and Jeva works with the bullocks and cares for them. These men have worked for the Mission and for the school for a number of years."

Ernie and Lois folded their hands with a slight bow in a return greeting as they were introduced.

"Let's first of all get the luggage off the train car, then we'll get the trunks and boxes out of the baggage car."

Railu, Jeva, and Hari took care of retrieving all the checked freight and reloading it. Ernie and Chalmer checked luggage receipts in the freight office, and made arrangements for receiving the trunks and boxes that were still lying in Bombay waiting to be shipped up country to Ahwa.

While they waited for all the luggage arrangements to be finished, Lois took the children over to sit on a bench in the shade under a banyon tree where they could watch a family of playful rhesus monkeys scampering around through the branches, grabbing the long, aerial tree roots and swinging gracefully like accomplished trapeze performers as they chased each other back and forth, around and around in an exciting game of tag. While the American children watched the monkeys play, a group of curious Indian village children watched the white faced American children sitting on the bench laughing at the monkeys.

One little monkey jumped down on the platform and, for a moment, sat motionlessly in front of Jimmy, Linda and Danny. Holding a nut tightly in his hand he cocked his head to one side and stared with solemn eyes into their faces. Sometimes he would snatch a bite of the morsel, then spread his mouth in a grin.

"Oh, Mom! Look at that! Isn't he cute? Mom, I want a monkey. Can we have a monkey for a pet? Please, Mom?"

"I doubt it, Jimmy. Monkeys take a lot of care. Besides, who would take care of it when you go away to Woodstock to school. You couldn't take it with you."

Jimmy looked disappointed for a minute, then his face cleared. "I guess it would be too hard to take care of. I guess I can go over to someone else's house and play with the monkey at his house," he reluctantly conceded.

Shuffling luggage papers and wearing pleased smiles, Chalmer and Ernie walked out of the railway office.

"Lois, it's all arranged and we are ready to go on to Ahwa. Bring the kids and the hand luggage outside the platform gates now."

The children ran toward Ernie and headed for the wooden gates. Lois picked up their packages and followed, wondering what sort of conveyance they would be riding in this time.

Railu was shoving the last big suitcase into a trailer fastened onto the back of a red Willys jeep, its sides wide open to the ever-present clouds of dust.

Chalmer chuckled. "Well, Ernie, you are the lucky ones! How do you like riding in style? The Foreign Mission Commission has decided that the Dangs area is in need of a jeep in order to carry on the work here more efficiently. So this jeep has been located here for you to use!"

"Wow!" exclaimed Ernie. Linda, Jimmy and Lois all began to talk at once.

"You mean no more bullocks and tonga?" squealed Linda.

"What wonderful news," exclaimed Lois, as her mind flashed back to their first term in India, to the many times they had traveled, riding in a two- or three-mile-an-hour tonga behind a pair of lumbering bullocks. What a wonderful blessing this jeep was going to be!

With the last piece of luggage loaded into the trailer the Indian men made a place for themselves to sit in the trailer and climbed in. Riding this way, they could steady some of the boxes. The children clambered up into the jeep, hoping to get the best seats so that they could see everything as the jeep climbed the low hills on the way toward Ahwa. By this time a crowd of curious people had gathered around to watch all the goings on, but especially to stare at the white children and hear them talk.

Finally Chalmer moved into the driver's seat and started the engine. As they pulled out onto the road he waved to many people and called greetings to others, for he was a frequent visitor to this village and knew most of the people who lived here.

"There are a number of Christian families living here in Waghai which is the end of the railroad line. They are very anxious to meet you, but I told them that we wouldn't have time to stop today, however, you would, no doubt, be coming to visit them soon. Until you have drunk tea together they won't feel as though they know you."

Traveling those last twenty miles up the hills was an adventure. Lois listened to Chalmer's comments along the way and watched the changing scenery with the rest of the family. A chital, so graceful like the other members of the deer family, sprang across the road in front of the car, its white spots flashing, making it difficult to distinguish from the light and shadow of its environment. Parrots squawked from the branches above them, disturbed by the noisy intrusion of the jeep into their lush environment.

Ernie and Lois were already aware that Chalmer and Susan were scheduled to leave India on furlough as soon as their replacements could arrive and take over the assignment. In fact, Chalmer explained that they were already packed, luggage marked, accounts balanced, and as soon as Ernie and Lois had received answers to any questions they might have, the older Shulls would like to be on their way home to America. Lois thought about their departure with mixed feelings, for when Chalmer and Susan left to go to Woodstock School to get their daughter Esther, they would be taking Linda with them and placing her in boarding school for the rest of the school year until December. *The necessity of sending children away for months without being able to see them is the most difficult thing that missionaries are required to do,* thought Lois for the millionth time. How could she let her go? She thought again of all the arguments for placing her into a Christian, American boarding school--the experience of being in the school environment with trained teachers was necessary for the best education of the child; all the missionary children for years have gone away to boarding school; the British actually send their children back to England to go to school; the children get experience associating with children from many other countries; it's like a small United Nations; the students are required to write a letter home once a week, and you get to know some of the thinking of your child that you wouldn't get to know otherwise.... All the logical reasoning in the world couldn't take away the heartbreak of this impending separation from Linda!

"Lois, since it is nearing dinner time and Susan and Gopal Mistri (the cook) will have the meal ready when we arrive at the Mission, I suggest we spend this evening visiting and resting, which will be good for the children. Ernie, tomorrow will be soon enough to visit the large number of Christians living in our village. We will look over the compound and visit the Ahwa boarding school in operation. We hope it works out so that we can leave Ahwa the day after tomorrow."

Lois shivered as she listened to Chalmer. "You mean to tell me that we can learn all we need to know in the next two days, Brother?" she exclaimed in shock. "Why, I have enough questions myself to take a week to answer."

Chalmer chuckled, "Now, Lois, you know that you will learn most of what you need to know just by starting and doing what needs to be done. It isn't as though you were new missionaries out from the States for the first time. You have had five years of experience in India. You'll find the opportunity to work with the people in this area a real challenge and a rewarding experience."

"Oh, I know we are going to love it here. It's just that I wish we had more of the answers and the know-how to meet every situation," she explained.

"Well, the truth is that if we had all the answers and all the knowledge, we'd be God, wouldn't we? No, God is gracious. He just wants us to do our best, and let Him take over from there."

Their excitement increased as they came to the edge of the village of Ahwa. They drove down the unpaved main road that ran past small buildings on each side, some of them obviously shops; others, huts where people were living, until they came to a little larger building in front of which stood a flag pole with the familiar orange, green, and white flag of India, its emblem of the wheel in the center, flying proudly in the breeze.

"This is the district government headquarters," Chalmer told them. "The one telephone we have in the district is here. The chief of police as well as the jail are located here, also. Another of the offices, important for our area, is the divisional forest office, for the teak wood and bamboo lumber in this jungle is worth a lot of money. The question of which state owns all this potential wealth is a very hot political issue in both state governments just now. Maharashtra and Gujarat both claim it. The Mission tries to avoid taking sides as much as we can, but all our classes are taught in Marathi and our state recognition for the school is by the State of Maharashtra.

"Since many of the Christians work for the forestry department, politics plays a part in decisions that are made whether we like it or not. You will meet all these officers in your daily contacts while you are carrying on the mission work."

Chalmer eased the jeep out into the stream of people who were wandering on the road through the bazaar shopping for food and staring at the foreigners who were an unusual sight in this out-of-the-way region.

"On our left, do you see our church?" Chalmer pointed out. Lois and Ernie had seen the church two years before, when they were visiting all the mission stations. It was an attractive, stone structure with three long porches, one on each side and one at the front of the building. These verandahs gave wonderful shade in the hot season and protection against the rains during the monsoon. A wire fence with a wide, double gate at the front set aside the compound area belonging to the church. Hanging from a bar over the gate was the message "Church of the Brethren, Ahwa, Dangs."

Chalmer drove slowly past the church compound. "The Mission property begins here," Chalmer pointed out. "You can see the Mission bungalow from here, ahead on our left, and on your right, the long school building. Just across from the bungalow, the low, small, bamboo-walled hut which is the girls' boarding hostel."

Susan was waiting for them on the front steps when they pulled up in front of the wide, deep verandah.

For a few minutes it seemed to Lois as though they were in America--the stone, one-storied bungalow with blooming flower beds, well-kept lawn, and Susan, wearing a dress and a big, welcoming smile, waving at them.

"Aunt Susan!" screamed the children as they rushed to give her a big hug. Susan hugged them as she gathered them all three into her arms.

"How wonderful it is to have you actually here! Just let me look at you! You've grown a lot since I saw you a year ago! But first, let's get you something to wash away the dust. Lois, how about something to drink? Do you want hot tea or cold lemonade? Come in with me!" She took them into the house where the table was set for tea.

"First, all of you, come and meet Gopal Mistri." The cook came into the dining room. He was wearing khaki shorts, a cotton printed shirt, a white apron looped around his neck and tied around his waist at the back. "Gopal, this is Shull Madam Sahib, Linda Kay, Jimmy, and Danny."

Gopal Mistri folded his hands in front of him and said, "Salaam ji! Madam Sahib, Linda Babi, Jimmy Baba, Danny Baba."

Linda and Jimmy folded their hands in a salaam and Danny imitated them.

"I have some hot cinnamon rolls if the children would like something to eat?" suggested Gopal Mistri.

Susan glanced at Lois, and Lois exclaimed, "Oh, they would love to have some rolls."

"Yes, let's have cinnamon rolls, hot tea, and lemonade. Then we'll have dinner in a couple of hours," suggested Susan.

Chalmer and Ernie came into the dining room and they all found places at the table. Gopal Mistri brought a basket of fresh, cinnamon-scented rolls to the table along with a pot of hot tea and a pitcher of cool lemonade.

It was fun having tea time in India again, Lois thought. Somehow, there was always something special about a tea break in such a hot climate.

Susan told them what she had been thinking about sleeping arrangements for the next couple of days. "As you probably remember, this bungalow has two inside bedrooms. There is also a wide latticed-in, verandah on the west side, and another about the same size on the south side. Chalmer and I are still in this first bedroom; there are two beds in the second bedroom and two beds set up on each of the verandahs. These can be changed around any way you wish."

"I want a verandah bed, Mom. May I have it?" asked Linda.

"Me, too! I want a verandah bed," Jimmy chimed in as he pushed back his chair and started toward the front verandah.

Everyone else moved toward the front verandah too where the luggage had been stacked which the workers had brought in as they unloaded the jeep.

The rest of the evening was used to get set up for the temporary living arrangement they would be using during the next two days until Chalmer and Susan would be moving out and leaving for the States.

Lois and Linda had done the packing so that Linda's things needed for boarding school could be easily pulled out at this time and made into a separate parcel. There were still some name tapes to be sewn on and a bedding roll with blankets, pillow, and bed net to be added to the stack.

The next morning soon after "tea," a time for breakfast, Chalmer and Susan took the new Shull Sahib's family around through the Christian part of the village to meet the people. Everyone seemed delighted to meet them and most folks insisted that they sit on the floor for a minute and drink a cup of tea! It was good hospitality to offer it and good hospitality to drink it. Where they were sure the people would understand, they told their hosts and hostesses that they had just drunk tea at home and didn't have room for any more.

It was a wonderful morning! The people were sorry to see the older Shull Sahib go, but they welcomed the new Shull Sahib and Madam Sahib, Linda Babi, Jimmy Baba, and Danny Baba, and they volunteered to help in any way they could. They loved seeing little children in the bungalow.

Susan took Lois to a tiny room built on one side of the office that had been converted into a dispensary. The room could be entered from either indoors or off of an outside porch. The indoor access was from Ernie's office. As soon as Susan opened the outside door, patients began to arrive. Three patients arrived that first morning and all three wanted cold medicine. Susan explained that they wanted eucalyptus ointment, a concoction she made up according to a recipe book left to her by a former missionary. The medicine consisted of vaseline and eucalyptus ointment. In a cupboard beside the door she showed Lois the book full of recipes for the treatment of many conditions."

"What's that?" asked Lois pointing to some shiny-looking metal tools."

Susan shrugged her shoulders. "Oh, you can do as you like about some of these cases. Those are tooth-pulling tools. Some missionaries a long time ago used them. I never did. But you can do as you like." Lois didn't like the idea. With the jeep stationed in Ahwa now she was sure they could get a patient out of the jungle unless it was during the monsoon when the rivers couldn't be forded.

Chalmer took Ernie through the classrooms in the nearby school. Classes were taught up to seventh standard. There was one boarding school residence for girls and two for boys. He showed him a separate building for food supplies needed at the boarding school hostels.

Long before Lois and Ernie had seen everything, the time came for Chalmer, Susan and Linda to leave. Ernie was driving out as far as Bulsar, seventy miles away, where Linda could get a train to New Delhi.

The morning they were to leave, the boarding school girls came over to the bungalow with colorful garlands which they placed around Linda's and Susan's neck. "Lindki (their approximation of Linda Kay) you come back soon," they told Linda.

As Lois tucked Linda into the back seat of the jeep she said, "Linda dear, we'll write to you at least once a week and probably more often, and you be sure to write to us. We love you so much. It's going to be hard to wait for your letters. Write whatever concerns you and we will help you. We'll be praying for you every day. If we have forgotten anything, just tell Aunt Susan and she'll get it for you."

A big crowd had gathered around the jeep. Ernie revved up the motor and the crowd moved back a step. "Salaam, Salaam, Salaam Ji!" Everyone was waving wildly. The jeep pulled forward, gathered speed, rolled down past the church, the government headquarters, and was out of sight.

Chapter 17

—— ◆ ——

Mass Wedding

Lois took a sip of hot tea having just come out of her reverie about Linda's recent departure for boarding school. A thousand miles separated Linda from her now, but problems in the Ahwa church needed attention. As she leaned back in her chair she realized how she loved breakfast time here in Ahwa, Dangs. She heard some of the children going by on their way to school to begin the day.

She wasn't really thinking about the school children just then, she was thinking about the problem of so many unmarried couples in the Christian community.

It wasn't a new problem for this area, for some of these couples had children already. The problem came about when couples simply didn't have enough money to pay for a marriage ceremony done according to custom, with a village tea and food and certain gifts involved.

How could they be married without mortgaging their whole futures, thereby having a huge debt hanging over their heads. The couples for a number of years had just been living together, not bothering with a wedding, for they didn't have the money for a customary ceremony.

"You seem very quiet this morning, honey. What are you thinking about?" asked Ernie taking a bite of toast. They liked toast made from the bread Gopal Mistri made twice a week from a recipe taught to him by Susan many years before.

"I was thinking about Wilson and the problems involved in finding him a wife. It is much more complicated because he is an orphan, isn't it?"

"Well, of course! He doesn't automatically have someone to make the arrangements for him. But the church elders are taking care of it. The Parlak has made a trip to Nasik to a mission school over there and has reached an understanding with some folks he knows for one of their girls and Wilson to be married. The only difficulty is that the expense of the wedding will have to come from here, and I'm not sure how we are going to manage that." Ernie shook his head.

Ernie, too, thought about the many other couples in the church who had never had a wedding ceremony. He knew many were living together, some of them for years, because they didn't have the money for a traditional ceremony.

Lois sighed and commented, "It's just too bad that, while the Church elders are trying to find an answer to Wilson's problem, they can't consider solving the problems of the other couples who are in a similar fix!" She thought a few minutes, then added, "It certainly would help if we could just get all these unmarried couples together and marry them all at one time. Then there would be expense for just one big village meal and have it done with."

Ernie stopped eating and stared at her. "What did you say?" he said.

"I don't know. . . I just said let's marry them all at once and be done with it. I was just being facetious . . . I'm not serious."

"But, honey, what if we were serious. If we could do that the cost of the wedding would be minimal. We could work out a ceremony in which each couple could take their separate vows, but the main service could be one in which they would all take part! Wow! I wonder if it could be done?"

For a week Ernie and Lois played around with the idea of one ceremony for all, joking about it, then half-way seriously proposing that Ernie should put the idea before Parlak Choudhari and get his reaction.

At first the Parlak shook his head and said it couldn't be done. It had never been done. It might not be legal if they changed anything. Changing things would not be acceptable in the community, etc. There seemed to be an unending chain of excuses.

A week later Ernie and Parlak Chaudhari were working in the office in the bungalow when Lois came in and invited them to come to the table for a cup of hot tea.

"Thank you, Madam Sahib," the Parlak accepted with a smile. The men came into the dining room and sat at the table while Lois poured each of them a cup of steaming tea. It didn't matter how hot the weather might be, hot tea was always cooling and refreshing.

"You know, Sahib, it might be possible for each of the unmarried couples to find a little money to contribute toward a village meal if they were all married at once. It does seem as though one wedding for all the unmarried couples might be a possibility. Will the government let us do that?"

"The best way to find that out is to ask them," said Ernie.

"Sahib, why don't you go over to the government offices and ask them if we can do this legally?" suggested Parlak Chaudhari.

Ernie dropped his hand on the Parlak's shoulder and said kindly but firmly, "No, Brother Chaudhari, why don't you go to the government offices and ask these questions? This is important because this is your church. You will be here long after we are gone. It is you who should make the request. You must be the leader to guide your people. I will go along with you if you wish, but only to stay in the background. Why don't you choose another elder to go along with you . Let's go tomorrow and find out how to proceed."

The next day, taking Gaiquad Master with them, Parlak Chaudhari and Ernie went over to the government offices to see the Collector who was the highest government officer in this tribal area of Dangs. The Collector welcomed them and assured them that there was no legal reason why a multiple marriage couldn't be performed at one time.

When the church members began to hear about the possibility of a marriage that would unite all the couples who wanted to take part in such a ceremony, they became enthusiastic. It was the first time they had heard of a way that could change the situation in which they found themselves. It would be wonderful to have all the church members who were living together legally married. They began to plan how to proceed.

The church building was too small to accommodate such a big occasion. They must first build a mandap, a small grass-roofed building, as a shelter from the sun. The walls would be mostly open with bamboo poles for a frame.

In the mean time the Parlak talked to each couple and their families, explaining to them their responsibility for becoming active Christian families and church members. Each couple agreed to give a small amount to help with the village meal. There was no trouble getting people to help do the work, for everybody wanted to help. It was exciting and fun. Lois was very surprised that all the grooms agreed that they would somehow manage to get a new wedding sari for their brides.

The day before the wedding six or seven ladies came to the bungalow carrying something made of cloth. They were laughing and having fun together. Lois left her desk where she had been working and went to the door to greet them. Sunderbai took the initiative.

"Madam Sahib, we came to see you because we have something special for you." Lois could tell that she was excited.

"You have? What is it?" she asked glancing from one to the others.

"Look!" exclaimed Sunderbai as she began to unroll the beautiful red sari with a wide gold border around the top and around the bottom. Across the end of the sari that is meant to hang over the left shoulder and down the back was a design made of gold thread.

"Oh! What a beautiful sari," Lois exclaimed catching her breath in delight. It was a cotton sari, not very expensive, but of fine thread.

"Madam Sahib, it is for you! You are to wear it to the weddings tomorrow. When Philip went to get the sari for Sitabai, his bride to be, he said that it wasn't right that you didn't have a new sari to wear also. So he bought this bride's sari for you too! Some of the other grooms helped a little too," explained Sunderbai.

Tears came to Lois's eyes. How could these people who had so little buy what was to them an expensive sari for her to wear to the wedding. Such a sign of love and affection touched her very deeply. She felt like saying no--that they should take it back and get any of a number of things that they needed so much instead of spending the little amount of money they had on her! Of course, she couldn't say that. It was a beautiful thing that they had done, and she would accept it with deep gratitude.

Folding her hands before her, Lois wiped away a tear as she said, "My heart is moved by your lovely gift. Thank you from the bottom of my heart. I will be proud to wear it to the weddings."

The next morning the ladies showed up early to help her dress. It was the custom to do this for the brides, but it was an act of affection that they would do this for Madam Sahib. What a fun time it was! They included the whole custom--from putting henna on Lois's palms and the bottoms of her feet to the draping of the sari over her head.

People began to gather around the mandap early. By early afternoon all was ready. The brides and grooms were meeting at the bungalow. When everyone had arrived, they began the short walk from the bungalow to the mandap where the Parlak was waiting. Lois and Ernie had gone early also to find their places on mats near the altar.

The couples came down the village path, each groom followed by his bride walking demurely behind him. They filed into the mandap and formed a long line from one side to the other, facing toward the altar. When they were all inside they sat down on the mats that had been provided for them. Every bride looked beautiful in her colorful sari, tinkling bangles and downcast eyes. Each groom looked pleased with himself but rather unsure of what he was doing. The grooms wore long-tailed shirts and colorful turbans with the ends hanging down their backs.

The Parlak stepped forward and motioned for Ernie to join him. Ernie rose from the mat and stepped up beside Parlak Chardhari.

The music began. The notes of the harmonium accompanied by the rhythm of the tablas filled the mandap and the paths throughout the village. The audience began to sing and clap their hands. Like a field of wheat in a light breeze the whole audience swayed with the rhythm of the music. Joy and happiness filled the air.

The Parlak reminded the audience that they were in the presence of God and that the vows they were about to take were holy; that they were beginning to build Christian homes and raise Christian families with the help of God. When it came time for the vows, the Parlak had the first couple step forward. First the groom and then the bride heard the vows and answered affirmatively. Each couple in turn did the same. When each couple had taken their vows the Parlak said in a firm voice as he went from couple to couple, "I pronounce you husband and wife."

Then all thirty-nine couples began to mix with the crowd and receive their congratulations.

Behind the mandap in the shade of the trees some of the villagers were tending the fires where the food was being prepared. The wonderful aroma of chicken curry, rice, chapattis, all with rich spices, and, of course, tea filled the air, making people so hungry they felt as if they couldn't wait.

Before long children began passing out huge banana leaves to everyone which they put down on the ground in front of them. Then followed two men to give each person a generous helping of rice. Two more people dished out the chicken curry over the rice, making sure each person got a piece of chicken with it.

As Lois sat waiting for her serving she was surprised to see that mysteriously some kind of container for tea appeared in front of each person.

"Where did all those tea containers come from?" Lois asked Ruthbai, the Parlak's wife, who was sitting beside her.

She laughed and pointed to the sari that Gangubai was wearing. "Do you see that Gangubai has something tied up in the end of her sari? Everybody brings her own tea cup. They know that when they are going somewhere and they might get tea, they had better bring their own cups if they want to drink tea."

After a while more tublas appeared. A big space was cleared and the Dangi dancing began. Most of it was done by lines of eight or ten men or women dancing together, or one person alone as the rhythm moved him or her. Rarely did she see mixed lines of man and women.

With the small amount the Dangi people had to eat, Lois wondered how they had enough energy to dance for so long without dropping. Everyone was so happy! She wondered if it was because they had had enough to eat for once. This occasion was possible because the Church would help out with the expense of the meal. Lois was anxious to see what the impact would be on the Church of having these couples married.

Toward evening Lois was sitting on a mat to one side of the dancing, tired after taking her turn three or four times in a ladies lineup dance, when someone whispered, "Here comes the Collector Sahib! I wonder what he wants!"

Lois and Ernie both rose from where they were sitting and went to greet the Collector, for having him call was an honor!

"Salaam, Collector Sahib! Welcome to our celebration," Ernie greeted him as he and Lois both folded their hands in greeting.

Three teacher's chairs from the school rooms appeared and the Collector, Ernie, and Lois sat down near the dancing. Next came three cups of hot tea for the Collector, Ernie, and Lois.

The Collector smiled as he accepted the cup of tea. "I thought I'd drop over and see how your big occasion was going," he explained. "You remember I heard you mention this as a possibility and it seemed like a good idea to me at the time. How do you feel about it now?" he asked. He seemed really to be interested.

Ernie appreciated this visit by the Collector. "I think it is working out quite well as far as we can tell at this stage. We will know as the months and years go by. The occasion is more appreciated now that you have stopped in for a while. Thank you so much. We are honored by your presence."

"No, no," objected the Collector courteously. "I was intrigued by your suggestion to begin with so I thought you wouldn't mind if I came to see."

He stayed a while visiting and watching the Dangi dancing; then he graciously took his leave. Having him come to call and observe was a good ending for the day.

The Sunday after the weddings the Church was full. Lois shared a mat with some of the boarding school girls and Ernie, Jimmy, and Danny sat with the men on the men's side of the church. The singing was accompanied by the harmonium and the tublas.

As they were walking the short distance from the church to the bungalow after the service Lois turned to Ernie and asked,"Did you see anything different about our school gardeners, Jiva and Hari today?" She was smiling.

Jimmy broke in before Ernie could answer. "I did, Mom. They were all dressed up."

"Yeah," Jimmy chimed in. "I didn't know they had so many clothes! Why, they both had on shorts! They never wear pants. What do you think, Mom? Why?"

"I guess they did!" Ernie agreed in surprise. "They were both married yesterday and I think they wanted to look as nice as they could."

"I think everybody noticed. The people were still congratulating the newly married couples and telling them how nice they looked," Lois observed as the Shulls stepped up on their verandah.

Standing by the door was a servant from one of the government offices. He was waiting to talk to the Mission Manager as soon as they arrived home. Ernie stopped in front of him and greeted him with folded hands. "Salaam, bhai (mister). What can I do for you?" Ernie asked.

The servant was dressed in loose, white pants and shirt, and across his chest was a wide, red ribbon with a brass seal pinned on it.

"Salaam, Sahib. The Chief Medical Officer, Dr. Davi, would like to speak with you this afternoon. He will come to you around 3:00, if you please."

"Yes, that will be fine. Please tell Dr. Davi Sahib that I will be glad to have him come this afternoon." The servant folded his hands once more and then left the bungalow.

"I wonder what he wants," mused Lois. "Something about the school, I'll bet."

But it turned out not to be about the school at all.

Dr. Davi came through the compound gate followed by his servant with the red ribbon across his chest.

Ernie met him at the edge of the verandah and invited him into the office and to sit on a comfortable wicker-bottomed chair. "It's a fine evening to walk," Ernie observed.

"It certainly is," Dr. Davi remarked. "It is nice to walk in your compound for you have flowers blooming so nicely. I always like the way the Mission Compound looks." He hesitated a moment, then explained why he had called.

"Mission Sahib, the government is running out of space for offices. I am one who is finding it difficult to have enough space. Your brother, Chalmer Shull, one time promised me that I could have a room in the other mission bungalow to use until such time as the government could build more space. I need that room now," he said.

A feeling of caution came over Ernie. "I can't give you that permission until I talk it over with the Mission authorities. I will let you know later after I receive word, " Ernie told the doctor.

A week later Ernie had word back from the Mission Committee. He could rent the room to the doctor with a written promise from him to vacate the premises in eight weeks.

One day after the government medical office had been set up in the other mission bungalow Lois went over to talk to Dr. Davi about a medical problem in the village. The doctor invited her to sit in a chair next to his desk while he sat in a swivel chair behind the desk.

As he was talking along Lois dropped a paper on the floor. It fluttered down between Lois's chair and the doctor's chair. Lois automatically leaned over to pick up the paper. But the Dr. held out his hand to stop her. "Ah! Ah! Ah!" he exclaimed, stopping her from doing such a menial thing as picking up a paper off the floor. Reaching over to the back of his desk the doctor tapped a bell with quick strokes. A servant came hurrying in from another room and when the doctor pointed to the paper lying on the floor the servant stooped over, picked up the paper and laid it on the desk in front of the doctor. Then their conference proceeded.

Lois was amused by this effort to avoid doing anything that was below one's dignity. What a waste of time and effort, she thought. And it was also asking someone else to do something that one could very well do for one's self. But that was just her American way of thinking, she mused. To someone in India prestige was a more important issue than saving time or doing what you can for yourself. She knew that if she was going to live and work with the Indian people she needed to understand what they thought and why they thought that way.

The Dangs jungle was a beautiful place to live and Ahwa was its capitol. It was a fairly level area surrounded by low hills. From the mission bungalow where Lois stood one evening looking toward the east she could see the hills where the Indian hero Shivaji had established his stronghold. The area was almost like a low hill station, a little cooler than Bulsar and the other mission stations located out along the coast of the Arabian Sea.

Gopal Mistri rang the evening dinner bell. Ernie left his desk and came strolling out onto the front verandah. "Dinner time, honey, and I'm hungry." said Ernie. They went in to the dining room table and sat down at the table.

As Ernie returned thanks for their food they were conscious of the many people in India as well as the rest of the world who were hungry. "I'm concerned about the vegetable content of the diet of the boarding school children, Ernie. I am afraid they are not getting enough green vegetables," said Lois.

"That's true, but getting green vegetables in this hot, dry season is hard. I'm planning on driving the jeep loaded with Dalvi Master and a trailer full of agriculture students out to the Mulchond garden in the morning for class and work. Of course we will bring back as much as we can find for the boarding children to eat. The children aren't particular. They are glad for most anything to eat. At home they would be hungry most of the time."

Here am I, thought Lois, *with a degree in home economics and I am having a hard time balancing the boarding school diet. I know we have to be careful eating green leaves from the jungle, for some of those plants are poisonous!* Of course, the safest thing to do was to eat only things that the school could grow. But they couldn't grow enough food for that. This was a constant problem.

"Let me take the cow dung off the baby's navel and I'll let you
keep the cow dung on the top of the baby's head."
Lois

Chapter 18

———◆———

First Delivery

Once back for their third term, a second 6-year term in Ahwa, there seemed to be an even larger work load consisting of adult and children's education, agriculture, church duties, their own family concerns, and medical work. In fact, when they arrived, after another year of furlough in the States, a line of patients was already waiting by the dispensary door. Lois began seeing patients the day after the Shulls arrived.

"Sahib! Sahib! I've caught a snake!" called a boy's excited voice from the office verandah. "What do you want me to do with it? It was just outside our door of the hostel!"

Ernie jumped up from his desk in the bungalow office and rushed out the door. A fourth standard school boy was gripping a foot-and a half long snake just behind its head with one hand and trying to hold the snake's flopping body and tail with the other to keep it from hitting him in the face.

"Hold it for just a minute until I get a tin to put it in," said Ernie after getting a glimpse of the little brown snake being held tightly in the thrilled small boy's hand. Shull Sahib had told the children that he needed snakes for a project to save snakebite victims and this fourth standard boy had caught the first specimen. Ernie hurried to a stack of containers he had formerly stashed away in a corner of the office, selected one the right size and hurried back to the verandah. Carefully he and the boy maneuvered the wiggling creature into the opening of the container and quickly pushed the lid down tightly shut.

"That's a nice specimen, Baba," Ernie complimented, " but do you remember I told you to call me when you found a snake and I would take care of it? I don't want you to get hurt."

"Arrae, Sahib, I've caught snakes before. I know how to do it."

Ernie smiled as he patted the excited boy on the shoulder. He didn't want to kill the boy's enthusiasm but he did want him to follow instructions and be careful. "As it happens, this snake is not a poisonous snake, but many of the snakes here in the Dangs are poisonous. You remember I wanted to catch poisonous snakes to send them to the Haphkin Institute in Bombay where experts will use them to make anti-snake venom to be injected into people who have been bitten by poisonous snakes and so be able to save many people's lives."

The boy smiled happily. He was pleased to do something that would help other people. It was nice to do something that pleased the Sahib too. He liked this man, especially since he knew so much about the jungle where they lived.

"I'll do it like you say, Sahib. I'll help you any time. Just tell me what to do."

"That's good, Baba. Thank you." As Baba ran out to the school path where some of the other boys were waiting Ernie thought, *Baba is a bright child. It is going to be great working with him.*

Lois, sitting at her desk in the office, watched the little drama with Baba, the snake, and Ernie take place, and thought what a great advantage it was for the school children as well as for Jimmy and Danny that Ernie had so much knowledge about wildlife and jungle living.

"Ernie, I spent two hours in the little school this morning observing, learning the names of the children, talking to parents outside the window who were listening, and trying to get the feel of what a job it is to teach when almost everything you use as tools has to be improvised," Lois said.

"What are you thinking of?" asked Ernie.

"Well, just for instance. Do you realize those kindergarten and first standard children don't even have slates to write on, let alone paper and pencil, and the 'blackboard' is only a wall painted black?"

"I know. The trouble is that the parents don't have enough money to buy slates, and the Mission policy is that parents should pay that much toward their children's education. Most parents have older school children also, and the older ones need slates more urgently than the little ones, they think!"

Lois nodded her head. "I understand the 'why,' I just wanted to tell you how we have figured out a way that we can get along! The teacher is pleased at how quickly the children are learning in spite of no slates!"

"Well?" Ernie asked. "How did you do it? I know you want me to ask you."

"Okay. You remember that every Saturday everyone pitches in to help and we make up a mixture of cow dung, clay, and water to the right consistency, then we spread a new cover on all the floors in all the school rooms and hostels. After that we let the newly surfaced floors dry. Sometimes we make pretty designs with our hands and fingers along the walls. Then we let it dry until it becomes a hard surface. Down at the little school house we make all the Marathi letters in the soft clay and cow dung mixture--then we let it dry to a hard surface. The next class period we send the students out to the jungle paths to gather little stones and bring them back to the classroom. By placing these stones in the hardened grooves the students learn the shape of the letters, and when they do get a chance to use a slate or the blackboard they will know how to make the shape of the letters."

"That sounds good, honey. I can see how that would really work--for a while, anyway." Ernie began to laugh. "I'd just never thought of making a pretty design using cow dung as a medium!"

One area in which the Mission policy cautioned missionaries as they tried to help in community life wherever they were stationed was to stay out of politics--the missionaries are in India to help to improve the community life of the villagers, not to take part in changing their form of government.

All this sounded good, but Lois remembered that she and Ernie hadn't been in the Dangs but a few days when political power and the different factions of moneyed interests, the desire to pull the rich lumber area of Dangs into a Gujarat State or Maharashtra State, the ever present problem of caste, and many other problems with political consequences became evident.

Lois was thinking about all these problems one night, wondering how to keep politics out of things like even whom to invite into your home, or where a person is invited to sit in relation to other people. She had just put the children to bed following a routine they had already established. After their baths they all ran to climb into Mom's and Dad's bed ready for their story. There was plenty of room this night because Ernie and Philip had gone in the jeep to try to shoot a rabbit or something else that they could use for meat.

Lois placed a Petromax lantern on the table just outside the mosquito net so she could see to read. When they came to the end of the book they had their prayer time together. Jimmy told about some of the new games he was learning to play with the school boys. He explained one game called seven tiles. One team would stack up seven stones and the other team would try to knock the stack down with a ball made of tightly wound rags. If the team succeeded, part of the same team would repeatedly kick the ball away while other team members would try to restack the stones and thus score points. Jimmy was delighted how they could have so much fun using only stones and rags!

When Lois tucked each of the boys in his bed, she carefully pushed the mosquito net under the mattress pad on all sides. She made sure there was not the slightest opening, or mosquitoes would be sure to find it--and this Dangs area was especially bad for malaria.

Lois placed ordinary lanterns, turned low, on the floor in the children's rooms, turned out the Petromax lantern and went into the next room which belonged to Ernie and her. She turned another lantern down low and placed it on the floor in her room. They kept lanterns burning for safety sake, for anyone who got up in the night needed to check for little creatures that might have crawled into a shoe, or for a snake behind a trunk.

Lois climbed into bed, tucked in her net, and closed her eyes. She thought she would stay awake until Ernie got home. But she was asleep in minutes.

Through semiconsciousness Lois heard someone clearing his throat, and when he didn't get any reaction he cleared his throat louder.

Lois remembered that clearing the throat is the way a Dangi knocks on the door; so apparently someone needed something. The first thing she thought of was that someone was sick and needed medicine.

"Who are you? What do you need?" Lois called as she slipped out from under her mosquito net, reached down to pick up each of her shoes and shake them out, just in case.

"I'm the one who is here. We need you to come," answered the unidentified voice.

"Is someone sick? Why do you need me to come? Is someone in pain? Did someone have an accident?" Lois didn't question whether she should go with this unidentified person or not; however she did need to find out what kind of equipment she would need to take with her.

"Bhou (brother), is someone sick?"

"Madam Sahib, it's my wife. She is about to have a baby and she needs your help." he explained patiently as though she should know what the problem was.

Lois caught her breath. Here it was, the situation that was never likely to happen, she had reasoned, ever since her midwifery classes back in Hartford School of Missions in Hartford, Connecticut. Across her mind flashed picture after picture of the many deliveries she and the class had observed while the doctor in charge lectured as he went through the process of delivery--the beautiful, sterile delivery room--the latest of equipment at hand to be used in case of need--specialists waiting in the wings to help if called upon.

That wonderful American delivery room seemed a long way removed from this Dangs jungle in the middle of the night.

"Bhou, I will come as soon as I can get dressed. Please sit on the verandah and wait for me." She peeped over the half-curtain that she had at the window to see if he had understood her. She saw that he had brought a lantern with him which he set on the step, then squatted comfortably to wait until she called him.

It took Lois three minutes to drape on her sari. Then, grabbing up a lantern of her own she went out the back door over to the cook's house and sent him to bring Gungubai, their aya. Lois told him to ask her to come and stay with the children until Ernie got home.

The delivery kit that she would need if she ever was called out on a delivery case had been ready to go since the day they had arrived in the jungle, therefore Lois didn't need to take precious time to pack required supplies. Dr. Standish, back in midwifery class in the States, had told the students just what to put in such a kit. She added a flashlight and two baby blankets made by the Manchester Church women. Had she forgotten anything? Yes! A note for Ernie just in case. Quickly she wrote down where she was going and why. She wrote that Gopal Mistri, the cook, knew where she was going and with whom. She placed the note on the table and anchored it with a brass candle stick.

When Gungubai arrived at the bungalow Lois gave her a few instructions, picked up her medical bag, and told Gungubai that she would probably be back in a couple of hours, then went out onto the verandah and pulled the heavy double doors shut behind her. The man waiting patiently on the verandah still squatted on the top step.

"I'm ready, bhou; let's go!" said Lois as she stepped back waiting for the man to go first and show her the way. Indian custom dictated that the man must always walk ten steps ahead of the woman. In this case Lois was glad for him to walk ahead of her carrying the lighted lantern which would help to keep leopards or tigers at a distance. She looked off into the deep shadows expecting to see two shining, fiery eyes of one of the big cats. Seeing Shull Madam Sahib come out the door, the waiting village man without a word picked up his lantern and started down the pathway into the dark and Lois followed about ten steps behind. She wanted to follow as closely behind him as custom said it was courteous to walk. She felt fairly safe as long as the man ahead of her had a lantern and she was carrying her own lantern. Even though she told herself this she felt some fear.

"Lord, walk with us on this mission of service," she prayed, "Help me to remember all the things I have been taught to do. Speak through me and guide me through this joyful experience."

The man led her through the winding pathways, where some huts had been built very close to the path, while others were built back among the trees. They went into the bazaar section of the village where all the huts were closed and big wooden shutters had been pulled down in front of the doorways where customers usually entered the shops. Just behind one of these shuttered huts was a round house made of bamboo stakes driven close together into the ground to make the walls, and then these walls were covered with a plaster made of cow dung and clay. The roof was made of bundles of grass laid carefully to shed the water during the rains.

The man walked over to the door of the hut, pulled the bamboo door open and stepped to one side motioning for Lois to enter.

Not knowing what to expect, she stooped and walked through the doorway. Inside it was so dark she couldn't see very much. On the floor was a metal wok-shaped pan holding smoldering charcoal which gave very little light. The man had kept the lantern he held with him. Lois thanked God that she had brought her own lantern or she wouldn't have had any light at all! Beyond the pan of smoldering charcoal a woman lay on the bare cow dung and clay floor. On the other side of the hut was a kind of cot made of four legs and a wooden frame around it. Over this frame hemp rope had been wound around and woven through to make a crude rope surface. On this makeshift cot a heavy lady was sitting cross-legged staring fixedly at Lois, seeming unsure of what to expect from this American.

Assuming, because of her size, that the woman on the cot was the one about to deliver, Lois walked over to her and asked, "Salaam, bai, are you having pains? How long since your last one?"

The woman on the bed sat up straighter and a look of anger came over her face. "What are you saying! I am not the one having a baby. She is!" and she pointed an indignant finger at the woman on the floor. "I am the mother-in-law!"

Here Lois was lost in custom again. In India, a mother-in-law holds very high status and must always be given the seat of honor. The expectant mother, lying on the floor, must remain there. Turning, Lois went over to the young mother lying so uncomfortably on the floor and knelt down beside her.

"Do you have pain?" she asked. The young woman gasped as she nodded and put her hand on her enlarged abdomen. Lois put her hand on the woman's abdomen and felt a contraction pull the muscles tight. The woman didn't scream, but her face twisted with pain.

As Lois timed the contractions she found that the pains were coming about every two minutes. She took some of the newspapers she had brought along and spread them beneath the patient. On her other side she arranged some newspapers to act as a table. Opening up her kit she laid out the things she would need. By this time the pains were coming more rapidly. When the water broke Lois was very glad that she had brought along plenty of newspapers.

What a thrill when she could see the top of the baby's head. The baby emerged fairly quickly after that. Lois held her hands to catch the baby as it progressed a little more with each pain.

As soon as the baby's face hit the air the baby made a small squeaking noise and caught its breath. Lois held the ankles and lifted it up, and the baby began to cry lustily.

Laying the tiny human being on the floor between the mother's legs, Lois took the small bottle of alcohol and pulled a string out of the liquid. Carefully she tied off the cord in two different places about two inches apart as they had been taught in Midwifery class and then cut the cord. With care she washed the baby with water that a little girl brought her, and then applied a sterile bandage to the raw navel.

Unfolding a white flannel North Manchester baby blanket from the town in Indiana where they spent furlough, she wrapped it snugly around the baby and laid it in the waiting arms of the new mother. By this time the baby was sleeping contentedly. In another ten minutes the afterbirth came and Lois placed it in more newspaper outside the door of the hut where a sweeper lady would come in a few minutes and take it away.

As soon as the mother-in-law back on the bed saw that the baby was a boy she started to laugh and call loudly to some people waiting outside the hut. The people outside began to shout and make a lot of noise. As far as Lois could tell they were all rejoicing that the baby was a boy.

The new mother touched Lois's hand. Then with a smile folded her hands in front of her face. The mother-in-law, smiling, said, "Thank you Madam Sahib. Thank you for bringing us a boy. I knew that if we called you, that you would bring us a boy baby!"

Oh dear! thought Lois, *I can't allow them to have a misunderstanding of how a boy baby came to be.*

"Bai (lady), I had nothing to do with your baby being a boy. That was brought about by God."

"Oh, I know! You wouldn't tell us, but we know. We know! And we thank you!"

Lois wasn't quite sure how she was going to help them to understand, but she would try. She finished taking care of the mother and baby, and then telling the mother-in-law she would be back the next day, she gathered her things together, said her courteous farewell salaams, took a look at the tiny new life snuggled beside its mother on the cow dung floor, and bending low as she went through the door, left the hut. The man who had brought her here waited for her outside, so following him ten steps behind she went toward home. As she went in her gate the sun was just coming over the horizon. She found Ernie asleep in bed. She stopped on the vine-sheltered little verandah by the back bathroom door and took off her sari, placing it in a bucket of water just in case she may have picked up some lice or bedbugs in the village hut. Then hurrying into the bedroom she slipped into her nightgown and tumbled into bed.

She slept for a full eight hours.

She regained consciousness with Ernie tickling her ear. "Are you going to sleep the day away?" he asked, laughing down at her. He was fully dressed and was sitting on the side of the bed. He had put up the net, and Lois could hear the boys playing in their room.

"Oh dear! Have I overslept? Why didn't you wake me up? I've got to go back to the village and check on the new boy in town!"

"Oh! So it was a boy, was it! I'll bet they were happy about that, weren't they?"

"They are very happy! But, Ernie, I'm in trouble. They are insisting that I selected a boy baby for them! They are giving me the credit for it being a boy, and when I tell them that I had nothing to do with the gender of the baby, they insist I am just being coy--that they know better. The mother-in-law is taking the credit for insisting on calling me instead of the village midwife. Now all the women are going to insist that I bring them boy babies. What am I going to do?"

"This is one time when time is on your side. The village women will learn the truth very soon. Come on. Get up and bathe. After you have some breakfast you will feel happier."

Lois had intended to be out and working by this time, so she made short work of the delicious breakfast that the cook had saved for her. Then, not knowing exactly what to expect, she picked up her delivery medical bag and headed for the village hut to check on the new baby. She was really feeling quite pleased that her first village delivery had been so successful. As Dr. Standish would have said, she had had a text book case for her first delivery. This was nearing the end of the rainy season, the morning shower was over and the sun was shining intermittently. Lush vegetation everywhere was a fresh green.

She stepped around the mud puddles and held the bottom of her sari up so it wouldn't get splashed as she walked down the village street, past a couple of shops with their front doors wide open, and stopped just outside the door of the new mother's hut. By daylight Lois could see that the family was a merchant family. She cleared her throat loudly and waited. A little girl came to the door and invited her in. Lois walked over to the cot where the mother-in-law was again sitting cross-legged. The lady folded her hands in salaam and thanked her for bringing them such a perfect boy. She clapped her hands and the girl came in answer. "Go and bring Madam Sahib a cup of tea," she ordered the girl, and the little girl hurried away.

"Thank you so much. A cup of tea will be very nice. I'm anxious to see the lovely little boy while I am here," said Lois. The white blanket was visible beside the mother on the floor. Lois rose and went to the mother, "How do you feel?" she asked.

"I feel fine, only I'm tired. I don't have pain today." Lois slipped her hands beneath the baby blanket and lifted the baby in her arms. It was such a tiny little tot. It must have weighed about four and a half pounds. Lois lifted the blanket off the baby's face and stared at the little head and gasped with shock. She thought she must be imagining things. On the top of the small head was a big glob of cow dung, partially dried. Some had gotten smeared on the white Manchester blanket.

Quickly she pulled the blanket back entirely and confirmed her worst fears. The lovely, sterile bandage that she had so carefully placed over the navel to protect the baby from infection was gone and in its place was another bigger glob of cow dung fresh and runny. Lois's fear was that cow dung would practically guarantee an infection.

"Oh, no! Our beautiful, clean baby! Do you know what you have done?" she wailed, turning to the mother-in-law. "You have opened the door to germs that make tetanus sickness and can kill the baby!"

"No, Madam Sahib. You don't know what you are talking about. Cows are sacred. Anything that comes from a cow is sacred. Cow dung is healing. We know about these things here in India. You are from America, what do you know?"

"Well, I know that this baby may die if you don't get that cow dung off the raw navel."

"You go away. We don't need you any more. We'll do it our way," said the woman in an angry voice.

"I won't go away until you take the cow dung off the navel. If you won't do as I say, I'll not come to help any of the ladies. What is the use for me to come if you are going to kill the baby later!" Lois was angry--angry at ignorance, angry at disease, and angry at custom. How could she help this baby?

Lois was still holding the baby. She stepped over to the cot and sat down on the cot. "Look at this beautiful baby boy," she said holding the baby toward the woman. "Let's make a bargain, you and I."

The woman's nose ring quivered.

"You let me take the cow dung off the baby's navel and I'll let you keep the cow dung on the top of the baby's head. Then we both win. I won't touch the top of the baby's head and you won't touch the white bandage on the baby's navel."

The woman thought for a moment then she began to smile. "Very well, we can do that. Then we both win, no?"

"Yes!" Lois agreed quickly, with breath of relief, "We will leave his head just as you have it, yes?"

The woman nodded.

"Now I will put a new bandage on his navel, like this."

Quickly they brought her some clean water. Carefully she cleaned the raw edges. Then using alcohol she sterilized the open wound several times. She prepared a new bandage and put it over the navel. When she was all finished she walked over and sat down beside the now-satisfied mother-in-law. "Could we drink that tea now, bai?" she suggested "It would be very kind of you." The little girl brought them hot tea and they drank happily together.

"Tonight I will stop by to see the lovely boy you have." She gathered her things together. Then folding her hands in salaam and smiling she went through the low door and toward home. She hoped that by telling the mother-in-law that she would be back again to see the baby, that the woman would not touch the sterile bandage that she had just applied and would not try to reapply her "jungle" medicine of cow dung on an open navel.

Chapter 19

—◦—

An Abandoned Baby and Children's Games

Lois and Ernie found themselves immersed in the life of the village. Day-to-day concerns and long term planning, advisory functions in the church and school, and medical and agricultural work for the boarding school all took many hours out of each day. Their family time was limited and was usually involved with the people of the community. All three children, Linda, Jimmy, and Danny found that usually their own fun times came when they were playing with friends in the neighborhood.

This day it was very quiet in the deep jungle which surrounded Ahwa. The usual sounds that were common were missing. No monkeys were chattering at each other or scolding. No parrots were squawking. There was no splashing of a long crocodile tail or the panicked call of a doomed bird about to be pulled under. There was no sound at all--only a startling silence.

Hari, the handyman and gardener, who had worked for the Mission for many years, stood by a tall full fir tree and listened. He usually didn't go this deep into the jungle when he was looking for firewood, but the wood supply in his hut was low and the area near the village had been stripped clean. He needed some larger branches to drag back home. Besides, he liked the smell of the burning evergreen wood in his hut.

He listened. There was a sound like a tiny kitten. *That's strange,* he thought. *There are no house cats in the deep jungle.* He moved toward the sound which took him toward the river. There was the sound again, and as he focused on the spot where the sound seemed to have come from, he saw two shining eyes staring at him. They were wide apart--much too wide to be a kitten--and they didn't blink. It must be a fairly large animal staring at him. He went closer to the river bank and saw something moving. It appeared to be a bundle in a cloth, and as he pulled the cloth back there was another, louder "meow" from inside the bundle. He was completely surprised to see that the bundle was a baby. As he wondered what to do, Hari heard steps retreating from the bank. Someone was running away. He picked up the baby and then remembered those two eyes staring at him from the undergrowth. He shuddered with the realization that it was possibly a tiger that had the scent of prey. Without thinking, he lifted the baby, held it close, and began moving slowly away. If those eyes really were a tiger's eyes, he wanted to get away as quickly as possible. Without stopping to listen, he turned and began to run. If the tiger was looking for food, the baby would make a tender morsel. He ran without a thought for his own safety or what would happen to the baby if he fell. He had to get away from there.

Soon he reached the edge of the village and quickly ducked into his hut. When he showed his wife the baby, she was shocked. "What are you going to do with it?" she asked, thinking of her own hungry children.

"Why, I'm going to give it to Madam Sahib and she will give it to somebody," Hari said. Since his wife did not protest, Hari took the baby and set off for the Shulls' bungalow. He had the impression that Shull Sahib would know how to solve this problem.

Linda, who was home in Ahwa for the annual 3-month winter vacation from Woodstock, awakened early that morning with someone clearing his throat loudly on the verandah. She went to answer the door but had to go through the boys' room and her parents' room on the way. When she arrived in the living room she found a man standing just outside the big double doors that led onto the verandah. The man urgently cleared his throat again. Linda reached high on the doors and pulled down the sliding latch. When the doors swung open, there stood Hari, awkwardly holding a baby.

"If you want medicine for the baby, you will have to wait for my mother to open the dispensary. She hasn't had breakfast yet," Linda said.

"I know," agreed Hari, as he bounced the hungry baby up and down to keep it from crying. It had begun to fuss. He stepped forward and Linda automatically held out her arms. Hari laid the baby in Linda's arms.

"No! No!" Linda hastened to say as she tried to give the baby back to Hari, but he refused to take it and tried to further explain.

"I can't take the baby! I don't know how it got there, but I found it by the river and have brought it here to Madam Sahib because I thought she would know what to do with it. Sometimes mothers, if they have no milk, abandon their baby to the wild animals or hope someone might find it, but we can't care for it and we have no goat which could give the baby milk. Someone just threw this baby away, but I knew Shull Madam Sahib would know what to do."

Linda couldn't believe what Hari was saying. Was she not understanding his Marathi completely? No one could leave a baby by the river for the animals—or could they?

"Mother, Mother," she called. "I think Hari says that he found a baby by the river! Someone threw it away, he says! Could that be?"

Linda was still holding the baby when Lois appeared. "Well, Mother, what are you going to do? There is no milk supply. Couldn't we give it some of the milk powder that comes out from the States?"

"Linda, you don't realize how many problems are involved in trying to feed a tiny baby with this relief milk. It arrives ready to be mixed with water but the water has to be boiled first and the utensils must be sterilized. I know this baby is hungry, though, and can't wait much longer," Lois said, with growing frustration in her voice.

"I don't care, Mother, I'm going to feed that baby right now! That baby is starving and I can give it some milk. How do I do it, Mother?" Linda asked, not fully accepting the problems her mother had mentioned.

Linda stood holding the baby expectantly. After a moment's hesitation, Lois turned and went to the kitchen to get some powdered milk. She knew she would have to dilute it considerably, since the baby was so weak.

Hari was satisfied that the baby would be taken care of by Shull Madam Sahib, so he moved to the verandah steps, down into the compound and out the front gate.

Linda followed her mother to the kitchen where Gopal Mistri was putting the finishing touches on breakfast.

Using some bottles and nipples left over from when Danny was a baby, Lois prepared a half-bottle of weakened milk and walked toward Linda who was sitting on the back step with the baby in her lap. Linda took the bottle her mother had prepared and offered it to the baby while Lois went to look for something to use as a diaper.

The baby took one suck on the nipple, acted startled, then went on sucking until the bottle was empty. Soon the baby was asleep.

Once the baby was fed and sleeping, Linda noticed that it badly needed a bath. "This baby is filthy, Mom. If you give me a cloth and some soap, I'll give it a bath."

From that time on, the responsibility of the baby seemed to be Linda's. Lois did the mixing of the milk and regularly talked to Dr. Cunningham at the Mission Hospital at Bulsar on the only phone in the village. When she told the doctor of the abandoned baby, he offered detailed instructions about diet and baby care. In the mean time Lois and Ernie were looking for a family which might like to care for a baby girl and raise her as their own.

This went on for three weeks. Finally, Ernie found a family who already had five children including a new baby and who agreed to raise another little girl. It was important that the mother have enough milk for both babies. As the time approached to give up the baby, Linda found it very difficult. She hated to give her up, but she realized that she would soon be leaving for Woodstock where she would be in boarding school. There was no choice but to say goodbye and give the baby to its new family.

Even though Linda and Jimmy would soon be leaving for nine months of boarding school, seven-year-old Danny would stay with his parents on the plains for another year at least. Danny had many friends and entered into almost all of the boyhood activities of the village. One day a friend, Chandrakant, grabbed Danny by the arm as he ran down the road in front of the compound. He said, "Danny, why don't you go in your house and get some hard pieces of water. You know, out of your mother's refrigerator? I love to hold them in my hand and watch them turn to water again."

"Okay," agreed Danny who thought it was fun to see the Indian children's amazement when they watched ice cubes melt. "Then let's catch some lizards and have some fun with them," Danny proposed. Not waiting for Chandrakant to agree, Danny dropped the bamboo stick he was carrying and hurried into the house.

Lois was helping Gopal Mistri with the process of preparing drinking water. It involved first pouring the water through a cloth which was used as a strainer to get it ready for boiling. Once boiled, it would then be put into large earthen pots where it would cool nicely. The water seemed to get extra cool by sweating through the pots. "Mother, you don't care if I give the kids some ice, do you?" Danny asked.

"No, I don't care. Just don't make a mess. Hold it over the sink," she cautioned.

Danny broke out a tray of ice cubes from the kerosene refrigerator and then hurried back out to Chandrakant to have fun with the ice cubes.

In the torrid Indian sun beating down on the compound, the ice cubes quickly melted to little puddles of water, and the game was over.

"Come on, guys. Let's see if we can find any lizards. I'll bet I can catch a lizard that will run faster than yours!" By this time, a third boy joined the search. The most likely place to find them was on the side of the fence posts which lined the gravel road. There they would wait for some careless insect to come flying or crawling by. The lizard would flip out its tongue as fast as lightning and swallow the captured insect whole.

The game was that each of the boys would find a bamboo stick four or five feet long and tie a string in a noose onto the end of the stick. Carefully then, the boy would sneak up on a lizard and slip the noose over the lizard's head. Almost always the cooperative lizard would instinctively freeze when it sensed danger. It was easy to give the noose a quick jerk and the lizard was caught. Once snared, if the boys chose to, the lizard could be led around all day on its leash. But it was more fun to race them. At the sound of a whistle each boy holding a lizard on a string would give the string plenty of slack, and the lizards, sensing freedom, would bolt for the bushes. The one which arrived there first won the race. The problem was that, in this game, there were often some distractions along the way.

Danny and Chandrakant went out to the road and, sure enough, three lizards were clinging to the side of separate posts waiting in ambush for their prey. As the boys approached, the lizards slowly moved around the posts away from the boys as if to hide and then froze in position. Each boy slipped his noose over the head of a lizard and yanked the string taught. One jerked free but two large lizards were caught. They frantically thrashed about for a few moments and then stopped moving completely.

"Great," shouted Danny as he held his lizard string in his hand. "Here's a nice, smooth place for them to race." A few other boys stopped along the road to watch the action. They looked the lizards over and decided which one to cheer for in the race.

The boys set the lizards on the ground and held the strings taught waiting for the starting signal. Someone whistled and the boys, still holding the leashes, gave the strings some slack. The lizards raced toward the bushes and freedom. A few feet from the starting line, however, Danny's lizard stopped suddenly. In a flash, it flipped its tongue out and caught a fly. It hesitated only long enough to swallow and again headed for the bushes.

Meanwhile, Chandrakant's lizard came to a pile of cow dung and stopped to examine some interesting insects there. Chandrakant picked up his lizard in disgust. "Come on Danny, let's take our lizards somewhere else. This is not a good place," he said.

So Danny picked up his lizard and they went to find a better place to race or just walk their lizards on their leashes.

"Hey Danny, look here. A couple of old bidi butts someone threw away. Let's make some tobacco water with these and feed it to the lizards. It's always a lot of fun to watch the lizards do crazy things when they drink tobacco water," said Chandrakant as he stooped over and picked up two discarded native cigarette butts. He handed one to Danny. The boys carefully unwrapped the leaves on the outside of the cigarettes and dumped the tobacco onto a banana leaf and then began mixing the tobacco with a little water to get a solution ready to force-feed the lizards.

The boys held the lizards by the back of their necks and squeezed, forcing the lizards to open their jaws. Once enough of the tobacco juice had been fed with an eye dropper, they were turned loose because the boys knew they could not run away. The lizards lost control and began spinning in delirious circles. After a few minutes, the effect of the nicotine wore off and the lizards returned to more normal behavior. Soon they were ready for another dose. For Danny and Chandrakant, the lizards seemed like toys. It apparently never occurred to either boy that this was in any way harmful to the lizards. Danny left Chandrakant and went running onto the verandah to show the lizard to Jimmy and Linda.

Jimmy looked at the lizard Danny held, "Yes, it's a big one, Danny, but why don't you let it go now? You can always catch another one and its supper time?"

"Okay, if you will help me catch another one."

"Okay. Come to the table now."

"IT'S OUR WAGON, BUT MANAJI CAN HAVE IT TO RIDE IN
BECAUSE WE CAN WALK AND HE CAN'T."
Danny

Chapter 20

——•——

Manaji, The Wagon, and A Trip to Bombay

It was dinner time, but Ernie was busy in his office. A crippled boy named Manaji and his parents had arrived at the Mission and Ernie was interviewing them. It was their desire that Manaji live in the hostel with the other boys and attend classes in the school.

Linda, Jimmy, and Danny watched Manaji as he crawled from the office out toward the road, and they wondered how he could go to school. How could he crawl everywhere during the monsoon, through the cold, mud, and puddles?

Ernie came in a few minutes later and went to the head of the table.

"Linda, would you like to say 'grace?'"

Linda bowed her head and began with an often repeated prayer, "God is great, God is good, and we thank him for our food." Then she began to ad lib, ". . . and God, please bless all of the boarding school kids, especially Manaji, because, God, he can't walk. Amen."

Lois and Ernie were pleased with the way the school year was rolling along in an orderly fashion since their return from a furlough in the United States. They were surprised at how quickly they had been able to fit back into the ongoing program of the school with scarcely a disrupting ripple.

As the food dishes were being passed at the table Ernie told them about the couple with the crippled son, Manaji. The question was whether or not the school could take care of such a handicapped child in boarding.

Ernie explained that because Manaji could not walk he had to crawl everywhere. His hips and shoulders were strong, but his elbows were stiff making eating a difficult task, and his knees and lower legs were useless. By twisting his body he could use one hand to put food on the inside of the opposite elbow. By stretching his neck he could then put the food into his mouth. This was a difficult maneuver, but he had become quite adept at it. The boy was very anxious to go to school. Ernie told that Manaji had a beautiful singing voice and was determined to learn in school, so upon the recommendation of the headmaster Manaji had been accepted into school. Without this opportunity to learn to read and to study the boy had no future. The Mission school was his only hope. Everyone would work very hard to see that Manaji succeeded if there were any way at all.

The next morning as the Shull children were playing on the front verandah Manaji came crawling by on the road that ran just in front of the bungalow.

"Good Morning, Linda Babi! Good Morning, Jimmy Baba! Good Morning, Danny Baba!" called Manaji, in a voice filled with happiness. He was crawling along and would occasionally swing his body around and sit as he made his way toward the tin-roofed building where the class rooms were. Joy seemed to bubble over in the tone of his voice.

The children stopped playing and watched quietly until Manaji was nearly to the school, then Jimmy observed, "You know what Manaji ought to have? He ought to have a little red wagon like ours. You know, like the one we brought back from America! It's the one Danny loves to be pulled around in! Remember? One like that would be great for him!

"Yeah," agreed Linda thoughtfully. "Maybe we could push him in our wagon sometimes, but that might cause trouble."

Manaji reached the school verandah, sat and rested a minute, then crawled through the open doorway to begin his first day of formal education.

As Manaji disappeared from their sight Jimmy commented, "Maybe we should just give him our wagon. Then he won't have to crawl in the dust and mud. After all, we all three can walk. Manaji can't!"

Linda thought about it a little while, then asked Danny, "What about it, Danny. Would you like to give the wagon to Manaji so he wouldn't have to crawl to school?"

Little Danny thought about it a for a while, then said, "It's our wagon, but Manaji can have it to ride in because we can walk and he can't!"

"Come on, you two! Let's go talk to Mom and Dad about this. Let's see what they think." And the children started toward the office. There they talked over the suggestion. Lois and Ernie made sure the children understood that if they decided to give Manaji the wagon, the wagon would be his alone. They would have no claim on it. After thinking it all through again the children decided that that was what they wanted to do. From that time on the wagon belonged to Manaji.

The next morning it was one happy little Manaji who received a little red wagon with the possibility that he wouldn't have to crawl everywhere he needed to go in every kind of weather.

Manaji's transportation problem was but one of many for the school community. Another was finding enough qualified teachers for the upcoming term. Two teachers were needed for the higher standards.

By the end of the school term, the school still had two vacancies on the teaching staff and there was just one month until the next grading period would begin.

A neighboring mission recommended two young women who were just graduating with two years teachers' training and high marks. Ernie interviewed them and found them quite competent, so he hired them. They were to arrive the day before the school was to start.

Lois was very careful about living arrangements for the girls. Just behind the Shulls' bungalow was a small two room cabin, in one of which was Gopal Mistri, the Shulls' cook. The other room was empty. Lois thought this would be an excellent place for the two new women teachers to live. They would be close enough to the cook that they could call for help if they needed anything.

When the teachers arrived and saw their quarters they were very pleased. School started and all seemed to be going well.

One day during the second week of school Lois was visiting a Christian family down in the village when the mother said, "Madam Sahib, is Philip working for the school now?"

Philip was a deacon in the Church and felt some responsibility to help staff the school. He was a good helper, always ready to lend a hand, sometimes even when a hand wasn't needed. One morning early he showed up at the Shull's bungalow with some rabbit, cooked, curried, and ready to eat for breakfast. Sometimes he tried to help out on committees even though he wasn't a member of that committee. He seemed to feel that his advice was needed. He wanted to help. However, sometimes it became a problem.

"No, Kaliben. Philip still does some work for the government forestry office, I think. Why did you think that he was working for the school?"

"He stays over at the new teachers' house some nights, so I thought that he must be working for the school."

Ernie called Philip into the bungalow office for an explanation. Lois served them each a cup of tea, then taking a cup for herself she sat down to listen. After a while Ernie broached the subject. "Philip, have you been visiting the new teachers late at night?"

"Oh yes, Sahib. I thought it was the right thing to do, since I'm a deacon. You see, the girls are afraid to be alone here in the jungle, and I'm an officer in the Church and it's really my responsibility. But you don't need to worry. I'm taking care of it. The teachers are very nice," said Philip."

"We can't have this, Philip. You can't go to their house after dark. You know these are young, unmarried women and they cannot be visited by a man alone, especially at night. They have to be protected. You must not go there any more alone." Ernie knew that the Indian culture would not approve of what Philip was doing.

"Well, if you say so, Sahib. I was just doing my duty. I didn't want them to be afraid."

"No, Philip this is not your responsibility. This is the responsibility of the school. We will take care of the teachers. You are not to visit the teachers any more at night. We appreciate your help on many things, but this is not one of them." After that there was no difficulty with Philip going over to the hut of the young teachers.

Once every three months it was necessary for Lois or Ernie to make a trip into Bombay to get supplies for the school and community and personal supplies for themselves. In addition they needed to replenish certain medicines from the Dahanu Hospital which was out along the main rail line to Bombay.

It was July and the monsoon was heavy. The school crops had been planted and the gardens looked good. As Lois planned her supply run to Bombay, she realized that since the train would be going through Dahanu Road, the Hospital staff there could meet her train with the needed medicines for the Ahwa dispensary. She had already written to Louise Sayer, the American nurse at the Hospital, and given her the Ahwa order.

While Lois was working in the dispensary at Ahwa the day before her Bombay trip someone came onto the verandah and cleared his throat.

"Madam Sahib, Salaam. I need some help. Is it true that you are going to Bombay tomorrow for supplies? " he inquired.

Lois recognized Wilson's voice. "Yes, Wilson. I'll be leaving early in the morning and will be gone about three days."

"I wonder if you would do something for me while you are there," he asked with a big smile.

Lois wondered what Wilson could be wanting from a place so far away from his own village. "Of course, Wilson, I'll be glad to do some shopping for you in Bombay" she agreed picking up her list of things to be purchased in Bombay. "I like to shop, for all the stores are so interesting. What do you want me to get for you, Wilson?"

"Well, Madam Sahib, will you please bring me back a wife?" Wilson shifted from one foot to the other. "I don't know when you or Sahib might go to Bombay again, and I'd like to have a wife now."

Lois's mouth dropped open in astonishment. She couldn't believe she had heard correctly. "Did you say a wife, Wilson? You want me to bring you a wife?"

Wilson moved his head from side to side in agreement. "You see, I'm an orphan and I don't have anyone to make an arrangement for me, so I want you to do it."

If Wilson hadn't been so serious, Lois would have laughed. What a strange request. "I have never chosen a wife before, Wilson. I don't know what kind of wife you want." Lois was playing for time while she thought how best to handle this situation.

"That will be very easy, Madam Sahib. Anyone you like, I'll like," said Wilson.

Lois walked over to the young man and put her hand on his arm. But, Wilson, you see, I don't know what kind of girl you might want," she explained.

Wilson brushed her objection aside. "Any that you like, I will like. Just bring me one. I'd like it if she had a light complexion." That was an interesting suggestion since Wilson himself was rather dark.

Lois knew that the Church officers should get involved in taking care of this kind of problem. "I'll tell you what we should do, Wilson. Let's talk it over with Shull Sahib and Parlak Chowdri and let them help us choose a wife for you. That way you can tell them more about the kind of girl you would like for a wife. I think you would be happier if you could explain more about the kind of girl you would like to marry."

"But, Madam Sahib, that will take so long and I wanted a wife in a couple of weeks."

"I'm sorry, Wilson. Some arrangements take a longer time than that. If you say so, we will start working on it now."

"Very well, Shull Madam Sahib. If that is the best that can be done. I just thought that since you were going to Bombay you could just bring me one."

Lois patted Wilson on the shoulder. "Now that you have told us, we will start working on it immediately. The Parlak and Shull Sahib will be talking to you about it."

The next morning, loaded with her bedding roll, small tin suitcase, and a big, black umbrella Lois left for Bombay. It was pouring rain which made people happy, because heavy rains meant good crops and plenty of food. Ernie took her in the jeep down the mountain twenty miles to the village of Waghai, the station where the logging train began its daily run, transporting huge teak logs out of the jungle to enormous sawmills along the coast. A coolie helped Ernie move Lois's luggage from the jeep to a narrow-gauge, third class train car standing on the track.

Making this trip to Bombay was always fun. Lois sat back on the leather seat and pulled a book out of her bag. The little engine blasted a warning whistle and Ernie stepped to the door of the car. Lois slipped an arm around his waist.

"I wish you were going with me, honey. It would be so much more fun if we could go together," she sighed. "I know it is better if one of us stays at the station to carry on the work. But I can wish, can't I?" Ernie gave her a last quick kiss and stepped down from the car to the station platform. Already the train was starting to move. Ernie walked a few steps along with the slow-moving train, then moved back and waved a final goodbye as the train picked up speed.

It took the train until noon to reach the coastal town of Surat where she had an hour's wait before she could catch the train going south to Bombay. When she got off the train in Surat she noticed an increase in political activity. The dormant Hindu-Muslim tension, never far below the surface in India, seemed to have erupted again. Large groups of Hindus wearing Gandhi caps and Nehru shirts, and Muslims with their own characteristic clothing were moving up and down the platform yelling political and religious slogans.

As she sat on her upended suitcase beside her bedding roll she watched a group of military people move to a spot next to the track and prepare to wait for the train. A group of nicely dressed people escorting an important-looking politician of the Congress Party came down the platform. They brought many garlands and put them around his neck. Through all the excitement the familiar political and patriotic slogans rang out, "Congress Party ki jai!" and "Jai Hind!" ("Victory to India!"). It was almost like watching a theater performance. She found it exciting and interesting and, as an American, relatively safe.

When the train came puffing onto the platform, Lois's coolies picked up her luggage and helped her climb in and stow her luggage in a third class car. Just behind her several fisher women climbed into the car pushing a large cloth bundle of dried fish ahead of them on the floor. There was no doubt about what was in the cloth-wrapped bundle, for the smell was so strong and unpleasant. It was worse because it was wet from the rain.

The rain was so heavy it was difficult for people to get on and off the train. The fields on both sides of the train were so filled with water that it was difficult to see where the bunds (rice field walls) were. Usually people could walk along on the top of those walls, but as Lois looked out the train window she thought, *There is no place to walk to get from one village to another.*

The city of Bombay is built on five islands. To get there the train had to cross over a long bridge. As the train approached that bridge it stopped, then started again, then stopped. The forward progress was slow and halting. As Lois watched out the window she saw only water filled with swirling, moving debris, whole trees and small pieces of branches. Once she saw the roof of a house drifting by.

Lois felt as if the train were floating on the water. The water level was usually far below the train, but as Lois looked it seemed that the water level was up even with the wooden ties that supported the train. Someone was yelling, "We can't make it! We are going to back up! The train has to go back!" The train did start to reverse, but for only a few feet, then it changed direction again and inched along toward Bombay.

Finally someone yelled, "We are almost to Bombay! I can see buildings!"

The train picked up speed and moved forward to the Victoria Terminus. They had made it! When the train finally stopped people breathed a sigh of relief. It wasn't until the next morning that Lois discovered what a close call they had had; their train was the last train to make it across the long bridge. When the next train started across, a section of the bridge was washed away and two cars fell off the tracks and into the water.

When their train pulled into Victoria Terminus, Lois was not surprised at the amount of political activity going on. She didn't see any violence but there was much shouting and parading with signs and placards. She thought she might have trouble getting a taxi outside the station, but there were several waiting at the curb. She chose one and watched the coolies load her luggage. Then after paying the coolies she directed the taxi driver to take her to Raj Mahal, the Church of the Brethren Mission apartment which was just a block from the Arabian Sea. The Minnichs, who now managed the Raj Mahal, welcomed her and showed her to her room.

Because the rains were now very heavy, Lois had some inconvenience getting around in Bombay and finding the supplies she needed for the school. As she left one shop she saw an empty tonga standing on the street in front of the shop. She made a mad dash for it, pulled back the rain shield and climbed in, sitting back against the seat with a sigh. She waited for the tonga to start moving and for the driver to ask where she wanted to go, but all was quiet. Finally she pulled back the rain shield and looked for the driver. She was amazed. There was no driver! As she looked she realized there wasn't even a horse! Thoroughly disgusted, she gathered together all her packages and climbed out of the tonga. Spotting another tonga that had both a driver and a horse, she climbed in and gave directions to where she wanted to go. Some of the streets where the school supply stores were to be found were in crowded, run-down areas of the city, but she had no trouble finding them. She enjoyed even more shopping down in Crawford Market, where the food section alone covered several blocks. In addition to a wide selection of fresh and processed food, one could buy exotic birds, reptiles, and mammals, books, clothing, and a huge selection of imports from over seas. She took most of the things she bought from the various markets to Cheap Jack's, a shop where they crated everything carefully in three huge boxes in anticipation of rough handling on the upcoming trip north by rail.

She went into the section of the bazaar that sold cloth and saris. She bought some pretty cloth that later could be made into articles of clothing for some of the little girls in boarding who needed them badly.

On the second day of her Bombay visit Lois was walking along a crowded sidewalk looking for a school supply depot when she was stopped by a woman and two children, all dressed in old, faded clothing.

"Madam Sahib! Madam Sahib! Help me! My children are hungry. Will you buy a child?"

Lois stopped and stared at the woman. She was used to seeing beggars, but never before had she been asked to buy a child. For a moment she was speechless. Then to see if the woman was really trying to sell a child Lois asked, "Which child do you want to sell?"

"Madam Sahib, you choose. If you take one child and feed her, then I will have some money to buy food for the other one. Please, Madam Sahib, buy one child," pleaded the woman as her large, black, sad eyes looked earnestly at Lois. Fighting to keep back the tears, Lois shoved two rupees in the woman's open hand as she went past her and on down the street.

The homeless problem was too great! Hundreds and hundreds of people were living on the streets. There was nothing that she could do to solve the basic problems but pray for God's guidance to show her how she could help. Lois had heard that there were places in Bombay where people could go for help, but hundreds were falling through the cracks and going without. Lois found it almost impossible to pass by people who were so desperately in need.

By the time she had taken care of what she had to do and had come to the bottom of the list of things she had to buy, Lois had spent three delightful days in Bombay enjoying every minute of it. On the morning of the fourth day she made an early start for home and the Dangs. She had five large boxes of supplies and a big bedding roll to manage.

She sent Balu Singh, the Minnich's cook, out to call a Victoria and four coolies to carry her luggage. With her purse looped around her neck by its strap and an umbrella in one hand she climbed into the Victoria while the coolies loaded her many packages. She had eight annas apiece ready, so she paid the coolies and called to the Victoria driver to take her to Victoria Terminus. It was a busy time of morning and the streets were full of people hurrying to market and to work as they dodged the many cars, taxis, carts, and push wagons stopping traffic in some places.

At the train station three times as many coolies as she needed came running asking to carry her boxes. Selecting four she told them which train she wanted and moved toward the gate. Inside the gates the train was still dripping from the scrubbing it had gotten since the train had come into the station a couple of hours earlier. She watched the sweepers cleaning up the last of the cars.

Finding a third-class car still empty about half-way down the row she climbed in and directed the coolies in the stowing of her luggage under the benches as near the door as possible so there would be little trouble getting it out when they came to Dahanu where she intended to stop overnight and get a supply of medicine for her little dispensary back at Ahwa. She didn't want her luggage covered up by other people's packages so she wouldn't be able to get hers out when they arrived at the Dahanu station."

Lois sat back on the seat and slipped a book out of her purse getting ready to read and relax. She had had a successful time in Bombay but rather tiring. Her fingers touched a small paper package in her purse. Balu Singh had given it to her before she left the Minnich's apartment so she could open it on the way home and have some nuts to munch on. But before she had really gotten settled a group of very noisy Muslim women with several children banged on the car door pushing it open. Packages and bundles were pushed into the car, coolies were ordered to shift luggage around and children were pushed and shoved into tiny spaces. Two men climbed into the car and gave their orders over the general confusion, then climbed down again to the platform.

Before this confusion had settled itself the whistle blew signaling that it was time for the train to leave. The two remaining men climbed out of the women's car, and leaving the children for the women to contend with, they went to their own car where they could have peace and quiet.

Observing that there would be little time or opportunity to read Lois decided to watch the human drama going on around her. She slipped her book back into her purse.

Outside the car a group of noisy people were shouting and putting garland after garland over the head of a man who was obviously a Muslim politician. "Pakistan zindabad! (Long live Pakistan") they shouted.

Before long the three women in the car were busy making the eight children quiet and happy. One woman sat cross-legged on the bench nursing her baby. Another lady peeled bananas for two little boys and fed them peanuts. A third lady was digging in her bundle of luggage to try to find something.

They looked so casual, totally unconscious of the tension that was again surfacing between Muslims and Hindus. Ordinary life must go on as it had for hundreds of years. Yet down underneath, the tension existed, a constant foreboding of impending catastrophe. The morning paper told of two attacks occurring in villages where, as far as most folks could remember, there had always been peaceful existence between the Hindu and Muslim communities. Lois sighed. What would she find when she arrived back at Ahwa? There were far more Hindus in their village than there were Muslims; but as Lois had been able to tell in the short time she and Ernie had been there, there was very little tension between the communities, at least not deep enough to be felt by Ernie and her as Americans.

Lois had decided her second day in Bombay that she would not have time to stop long at Dahanu Hospital on her way home to Ahwa, so she telegraphed Nurse Hazel Messer that she would like for someone from the hospital to meet her train with a new supply of medicines for her little dispensary in Ahwa. As their train was pulling into the Dahanu station Lois looked out between the window bars to see if someone had come from the hospital.

The platform was crowded as usual with embarking and disembarking passengers as well as families and vendors and loafers and beggars and ever present cows and goats. Also there was a political demonstration going on. The demonstrators were very noisy but they were not violent. Lois watched closely to see if she could see any of the activities she had read about in the Bombay papers, for in some papers the violence was reported as happening out in the villages.

Suddenly Lois caught sight of a worker from the Dahanu Hospital running along beside the slowing train. She called out, "Lahanu! Lahanu! Here I am, in this car!" as she waved her hand and lower arm out the window.

Lahanu smiled broadly and waved as he trotted along beside the slowing train. The wheels squealed making a terrible racket as the train car finally came to a grinding stop.

Holding a package carefully Lahanu slipped into the car before the women and children could get organized enough to block the entrance. He handed Lois the precious package and a letter from Hazel, then, with a friendly smile he was gone the way he had come, before Lois could do anything more than thank him.

It was disappointing to Lois to not have time to stop over for at least one night and visit, but she needed to get home. Perhaps she could come later and stay longer. She knew how anxious Wilson was to have his marriage arrangements made.

Chapter 21

———— ·•· ————

Politics and Resources

In a country with such a high population ownership of land was an important issue. People were divided into groups along religious and language lines. A Hindu group headed by Chotubhai, a local leader, was seeking land to build an ashram, a Hindu commune. Such ashrams had increased in popularity as the result of the Gandhian movement and offered opportunities for living, teaching, and learning for devout Hindus.

One day Chotubhai sent a request to the Mission asking if the bungalow where Dr. Davi had his offices was going to be empty when he moved out, stating that he would like to request the privilege of living there since the building was going to be empty.

Ernie wrote that he was sorry, but when the bungalow was vacated by Dr. Davi the Mission was intending to make use of all the vacated space. Chotubhai was disappointed but was able to find other nearby land and he placed his ashram there.

Another group that was trying to move into the Dangs District and begin working there was called the Dangs Sava Mandal. They were a group who had their origin in Maharashtra which was a Marathi-speaking area. The group headed by Chotabhai was from Gujarat, a Gujarati-speaking area. It became increasingly apparent that a conflict was brewing.

Lois found this very interesting because Dangs district had always been considered a hardship post to work or live in by the British and now also by the Indian officers. Why suddenly had Dangs become so important?

"I can tell you why," said Ernie when she asked him about it. "Every person in government has his eyes on the very valuable lumber in this state! Look at all that perfect teak wood and all the bamboo. There is a British company in here working now trying to gain rights to the bamboo. Since India's independence there has been a growing scramble for control of all of these resources.

Lois remembered the admonition not to take part in any politics. In thinking about that, she wondered whether they could live in India and not do things that would have political repercussions.

The Ashram and the Dangs Sava Mandal, both groups from outside Dangs, were in direct competition with each other. Both wanted the wealth of the forest. Lois had the feeling that the Ashram, especially, would like to acquire the Mission land and also take credit for education of the children and for the rural uplift successes of the Mission over the years.

The aboriginal people of the Dangs understood little about the growing battle. The British had called them "Children of the Forest," for they considered the Dangis a simple people who lived off the forest, the rivers, and the small plots of land they cultivated. Some fished with bows and arrows. Their contact with the outside world was very limited. Some had heard of Gandhi, but knew little about him. The religious practices of these tribal people were a mixture of Hinduism and animism. A few Muslims lived in the district capitol of Ahwa. The Christian community numbered only about three hundred.

India was facing another hard year and crops were failing in some areas. Many people were hungry. The last monsoon had been very light and the crops had not done very well. The grass had turned brown and crumbled to dust. The dust in the paths and the roads had gotten deeper and deeper until people walking along sank down until their feet were covered. Large fissures appeared in the earth so wide across that little children had to be careful or their feet would get caught in the cracks. People across India were praying for the monsoon to start and to be heavy for wide spread famine was a distinct possibility.

The people in the village of Ahwa, like the rest of India, faced sever hardship. Getting food for the Mission Boarding School was a problem. The school had a big garden five miles down the mountain where a full-time school gardener lived and cared for the water buffalo that powered a Persian wheel which lifted water in many small cups up from the river bed below. The water was emptied into an irrigation system of canals that carried the life-giving fluid to all parts of the garden. The result was a virtual Garden of Eden which not only produced a bounty of fruits and vegetables to supply the boarding school, but supported large flocks of parakeets, destructive bats, troops of rhesus monkeys, and villagers who helped themselves when they could, in what would otherwise have been a desert of dust. Several times a week Ernie took boarding school students in the jeep and trailer down to the garden where they worked the land and held agricultural classes.

Even with the garden produce, however, the limited school budget made getting enough food difficult so Lois contacted Church World Service. This organization sent shipments of food to the Dangs Mission Boarding School. All of the food except the powdered milk was saved for the school only. The powdered milk was for small children in the community and especially for babies. Other food that arrived included dried beans, cooking oil, rice, corn meal, and wheat.

The shipment would come up the hill by narrow-gauge railroad as far as Waghai, then Ernie would bring it the rest of the way--about twenty miles--by jeep and trailer.

It was a day of thanksgiving the first day that a shipment of food arrived. Although the diet was adequate, this meant the children could eat as much as they liked.

The powdered milk day for families that were eligible went well. However, Ernie found out later that some men took the powder meant for the babies and traded it in at the tobacco store to get cigarettes or other things they wanted—the babies went hungry.

Therefore, the next time a shipment came, Lois had the workers mix the milk powder with the water, then distribute it to each family. The trouble with this method was that the milk had to be distributed each day because of the intense heat. It took so many people to do this job daily that it became a hardship for the school. But, since lives were at stake, Lois found that the trade off was worth it. The school children did much of the distributing. As the hot season advanced the situation seemed to grow even worse.

One day when Ernie and Lois were on the train going to a retreat in South India they were again reminded of how serious the situation in India had become. The train was stopped at the little station of Vyara. They unwrapped the newspaper from around the small lunch they had brought along and ate all but the bananas. When they started to peal the bananas they found them squashed and brown, not fit to eat. Ernie took the four rotting bananas and tossed them out the train window. They landed in the deep dust beside the train. Then almost before anyone could see what was happening, four or five people scrambled for the food. Two people got to the bananas first and struggled to keep the others away. Each ran off with his prize, stuffing the filthy bananas, dust and all, into his mouth. Death had been postponed for a few more hours.

Starvation was nationwide and Lois was concerned about having enough protein in the Ahwa Boarding School diet. They ate chicken now and then. One night Ernie went hunting for wild hares, long-eared mammals that are close relatives of domestic rabbits. These were large "rabbits," however, for they dressed out at about five pounds each.

He asked Wilson, a friend and fellow hunting enthusiast, if he would like to go along and work the search light which ran off the jeep battery. Wilson was delighted to go on the hunt, in fact, over the years, it was to became one of his favorite activities, partly because he enjoyed the hunting and partly because success meant he too, would have meat to eat.

When they arrived home they had three hares. Ernie gave Wilson one to take home, while he dressed out the other two, one for his own use, and the other one for the boarding school. He cleaned the hares out by the back garden fence. The heads and leftover "throwaway" parts were left lying on the ground where wandering animals would soon clear it away.

The next morning the hostel boys told Ernie that, after he had gone to bed, the boys had sneaked over to the back fence where the rabbits had been cleaned and salvaged most of the parts Ernie had left on the ground as inedible. The boys had decided that these parts would make a good curry.

In many ways the school children followed the Hindu ways of thinking. To an orthodox Hindu, cating meat is taboo. However, the Dangis, not being orthodox Hindus, were meat eaters. Consequently, Ernie began sharing the meat that he brought in from hunting trips. This included various kinds of deer, wild boar, and, of course, the hares. This supplemental meat helped to balance the diet of the boarding school children.

Then the rains came. What joy! People ran out of their huts and stood with their hands outstretched, their heads held back, their eyes closed and mouths wide open to catch the precious raindrops. Their skin seemed to drink up the moisture as their clothes became wet and the deep dust became deep mud. What a wonderful feeling. Of course, it didn't last very long, but it would come intermittently, again and again until they were soaked to the bone and prayed for the drying sun.

One morning Lois was sitting at her desk in the bungalow office writing to some people in the States about the shortage of food in their Dangs area of India. The officials of the country were hoping for a strong monsoon so more crops could be planted and there could be relief for the starving masses in the villages. She wanted to paint a true picture of what it was like to be a parent and to have to tell one's nearly starving children that there was no food for them to eat.

As she sat before her desk staring absent-mindedly at the large picture of Solman's "Head of Christ" hanging just above her desk top, she suddenly became aware of two little, unblinking eyes staring at her. A long, slender body extended almost the entire length of the upper edge of the picture. A snake! A deadly one—a Russell's viper! Could it be?

In fright she jumped backward, throwing the chair over with a bang as it hit the cement floor. She jumped to the back of the room where a set of wooden double doors separated the office from the back verandah. Just beside her desk was an open but barred window separating the office from a flower garden where Railu, the school gardener, was working. She stood trembling as she yelled for help. "Help! Help! Snake! Snake! Snake!"

Railu came dashing through the front doors.

"Where, Madam Sahib! Where is there a snake?" Railu asked in a trembling voice. Indian people knew how dangerous snakes were.

"There! On top of the picture! Don't you see it, Railu?"

"Oh, I see it! I'll get it. Just let me get that bamboo stick the Sahib has in the corner." Without turning his back to the snake he worked his way to the corner of the room. Then grasping the stick he went carefully toward the snake. In the meantime the snake hadn't moved a muscle. Cautiously Railu worked the bamboo stick under a loop of the snake's body. With a grunt he flipped the snake up in the air and flung it over his head.

Lois, pressed against the back verandah doors, saw the snake come sailing through the air at her. Railu had miscalculated where the snake would land. Fortunately it hit the wall just beside her head and fell to the floor. Instantly Railu was after it, pounding it until it was dead.

"The villagers say first he kills the patient . . .
then the big boys pump and pump new life right back into the patient."
Collector

Chapter 22

—•—

Surgeries by Flashlight

During the monsoons, snakes are very common. In fact, during that year, snake bites were listed as the second highest cause of death in India; malaria was listed as number one.

Along with the beginning of the monsoon came sore throats, runny noses, fevers, increased snake bites, and many other medical problems. The sore throats became such a serious problem, that on one of her trips to Bulsar, a town along the coast of the Arabian Sea, Lois talked to Dr. Lloyd Cunningham located at the Mission hospital there to see what might be done.

Lloyd shrugged his shoulders is such a way that Lois got the feeling he wasn't quite sure what they should do about it. "Lois, the Ahwa school has not had a medical check for a couple of years. What should happen is that you should bring the children in here and let us check their health. They especially need to have their tonsils checked. It sounds to me like you have a lot of tonsillitis. What you need to do is bring them in here to the hospital and let us examine them," Lloyd declared.

"Oh Lloyd, be practical! You know that I can't do a thing like that. I'd have to bring one hundred fifty children out of the jungle, catch the narrow-gauge train out of Waghai, go out to the coast, change trains, get a big train that runs from Delhi to Bombay, and go down the coast as far as Bulsar to the Mission Hospital. Then I would have to get you to examine all the children, and then bring them back. Anyway, the parents who live out from the village of Ahwa wouldn't allow their children to be taken out to a 'foreign country.'" Lois smiled, for the Dangi people thought of any place beyond Waghai as foreign country. "Lloyd, just think about it for a minute. What do you think about the possibility of you and a team of workers coming out Dangs way? 'If the mountain won't come to Mohammed, then Mohammed must go to the mountain!" Lloyd didn't respond, for the moment, so the problem remained unsolved. Lois had to return to Ahwa.

The day after returning home, Lois received a letter from Dr. Lloyd. "You know, if we are going to do a checkup of the Ahwa Boarding School children's health, we had better do it right now in Ahwa since people are out working in their fields and don't have time to come to Bulsar. Later we will be very busy here and I won't be able to leave. How about my arriving one week from today for the first checkup?" Lloyd wrote.

Lois was surprised when she read this, for she had not realized that Lloyd would think such a thing was possible. She and Ernie talked it over. "Of course he must come. We will make our schedule fit in with that of the hospital. It will be the best thing that can happen to our school, to have a checkup immediately," agreed Ernie. "I'll go over to the government office building in the bazaar and ask them to let me call out to the hospital. I'll confirm the arrangements immediately with Dr. Cunningham."

Lois started making arrangements with the head master and the teachers. They must all work together to get things ready for the doctor's visit. She wanted to send word out to the villages around Ahwa from which the school children came, that a good doctor from the Mission Hospital in Bulsar was coming to examine the children.

On the appointed day the army surplus jeep from the Mission Hospital came rolling into the Shull compound in Ahwa. Everyone was excited and looking forward to it. They had heard about the examinations that they would be having, but they didn't known exactly what to expect. There were a number of people in the Bulsar Hospital team. Not only the doctor came, but he brought a nurse and a registrar as well as an assistant and a driver. For three days they worked examining one hundred fifty-one students and also the teachers. When the task was finally finished, the staff met in the Shull bungalow to talk about their findings.

Lloyd dropped the bombshell when he announced, "You have forty seven students that need their tonsils out. Apparently these children have never been treated for tonsillitis. What I propose is that two weeks from today we arrive here with a surgical team in a van with most of the equipment we will need. "What do you think about that, Ernie? Lois?" Lloyd looked expectantly from one to the other.

Lois was still trying to catch her breath. How could they possibly get ready for such a big project in so little time?

Ernie wasn't about to let an opportunity slip away, to have the children's health checked. The sooner the better. "We'll be ready, Lloyd. Just tell us how to go about getting things ready for you."

Lloyd was relaxed. After all, he had been through this routine many times in many schools. "Don't worry. We'll do the setting up when we get there. We'll need something to use for an examining table and a desk to write on. We want to get all this finished the first part of the monsoon because the three rivers we have to cross will be too high to ford later. So we'll see you in a few days."

Lois found staggering the mountain of things that had to be done during the next two weeks before the Mission hospital team was to arrive. First, the parents of the students who were to have surgery must be contacted and their permission sought. There was reluctance among the jungle people to try anything new, but the faith that the villagers had in the Mission and the missionaries was heartwarming. The general reaction from the parents was, "Yes, we want you to do it if you think that is the best thing for our son or daughter. We know that you will do the best thing."

Their complete faith in us makes our responsibility even greater, thought Lois. "Dear God, guide us through these many decisions that have to be made. Give us clear vision and correct judgment," she prayed as she worked.

Sleeping arrangements and eating accommodations had to be provided for all the workers coming in. They would all eat together from the same menu in the Shulls' dining room . Nurse Louise Sayer promised to bring her cook along to help Gopal Mistri, the Shulls' cook, in the kitchen. Several other helpers were going to lend a hand wherever they could. As many as could would sleep in beds. When the beds were all taken the rest of the visitors could sleep on mattresses on the floor with mosquito nets tied to rafters above their heads.

Lois decided that on the day of the surgeries the best arrangement would be to bring the students who were the patients in the back door of the bungalow and have them wait their turn while sitting on bamboo mats on the floor of the verandah. She herself would stay with the patients, talking to them and giving them confidence for what lay ahead. She would keep their minds occupied with other things.

She wished she could foresee the problems that the surgical team would meet so that she could be prepared. She knew they would be needing a big supply of water, so she had the school girls carrying water from the well and filling huge earthen pots ready for use.

On the day agreed upon, the Mission medical van from Bulsar pulled into the Ahwa Mission compound. They had not had any trouble fording the rivers to get into the Dangs area, for the monsoon was only a few days old.

As they pulled in, Lois rushed out of the bungalow to greet the medical team and bring them in for a cup of hot tea. They had been traveling for about four hours so they were ready to move about and work on getting set up for the next day when they would begin the surgeries. Everyone was excited about this big project and sure that what they were about to do would make a big difference in the health of this big boarding school.

Dr. Lloyd Cunningham took charge. "Let's begin by making an operating table," he said. "I'll just take a look around and see what we can use."

The operating theater was to be the front verandah. Lloyd and Ernie, with two big school boys to help, began by moving two study tables to the operating area. They set them end-to-end in the best place to catch what light there was. The rain was heavy, making a dull drumming sound on the tile roof. There were a few observers already in the front yard standing under the roof-overhang out of the rain, curious about what was going on over at the Mission.

"Our next problem is light," said Lloyd. "We don't have the luxury of electricity here in Ahwa. Ernie, did you say you have a five-cell flashlight that we could use somehow?" He turned hopefully to Ernie, who was supposed to have answers to all their problems since he now lived here in the jungle.

"Here it is, Lloyd. I have it already. I even have a good idea about how to suspend it from the rafters just under the tiles of the verandah. The boys and I worked on this yesterday and we have some good, strong hemp ready to tie the flashlight so it will hang just over the operating area."

Next Lloyd started working with some kind of pump arrangement to one side of the table. At the back wall of the verandah were two wide double-doors. Lloyd went over to the one nearest the head of the tables and opened them. "Ernie, we need to open these doors and put this manual suction pump just inside this door. Since we don't have electricity to run a suction pump, we have to use a manual one. I'd like to suggest that you take charge of the suction machine operation and see that we get suction when we need it. This is a hard job and more than one person will have to work on this, taking turns to be sure that we have access at all times when we need it. Can that be arranged?"

Ernie grinned and his blue eyes twinkled. "Oh sure! No problem with the manual part. The boys and I will take care of that." When the machine was finally set up it looked like a glorified manual bicycle pump. The boys and Ernie tried it out and felt they could handle the problem with just the three of them.

Then Lloyd tackled Lois's end of the arrangements with Nurse Louise's able assistance.

"Lois, do you have a pressure cooker?"

"Yes, I do. It's a big one," said Lois. Louise checked it out and agreed that it would work just fine as an autoclave for it could sterilize the instruments very well. Bandages were to be ironed with a hot iron and some were to be placed in the oven of the wood-burning stove until they were nearly toasty brown.

Nurse Louise asked Lois, "Where had you thought that we would put the patients for recovery after their surgery?"

Lois picked up two big, black umbrellas from a corner rack by the front room door and handing one to Louise said, "Come along with me and I will show you where they will be." They opened their umbrellas and ran down the few verandah steps to the compound path, through the swinging gate to another path that took them to the main school house which was a series of five rooms with tin sheet walls and roofs. The second room was set up with bamboo mats lying side by side on the floor with enough room between mats for a nurse to walk and care for a patient. In one corner was a huge earthen pot standing two-and-one-half feet tall, filled with water.

"Will this be all right?" asked Lois anxiously. "If you need something else I'll try to get it for you."

"No, this looks just fine," complemented Louise. "But how are we going to get the patients over here from your front verandah in this downpour of rain?" she asked.

Lois laughed, "Oh, we've taken care of that! We have an umbrella brigade! We have six big students, each with an umbrella, four to carry the stretcher and two to carry umbrellas, one over the patient and two over themselves."

By this time Louise was laughing too. "This is great. It looks as if you really do have everything taken care of." Then she hesitated. "Oh, by the way. I'm afraid we don't have any stretchers. Can you think of anything we can use for that?"

"Of course. I've had to make do before. We'll take a couple of sturdy bamboo poles, wrap some saris around them and we have some good stretchers. Anything else you need?" she laughed. This was really exciting. She was praying that they would be able to find whatever was needed and that each surgery would be successful.

Louise and Lois took their umbrellas and, feeling quite pleased, went walking through the rain back to the bungalow.

As they walked up the steps of the verandah, Lloyd called Louise.

"Sister Louise, where is the ether mask? I've checked, but I don't seem to find it."

"Doctor, its right here," said Louise, hurrying over to the supplies prepared to be picked up. "Well . . . I was sure that it was right here! Do you suppose that in worrying about doing things without electricity we forgot to put in the ether mask?"

Lloyd was grinning, "Nursebai, I wouldn't know about that," he teased. "That is your department. It wasn't on my list. Lois, come to the rescue. What do you have that we can use for an ether mask?" With his hands on his hips he turned to Lois for a suggestion.

"Well, my word and honor, Lloyd! I don't have anything that would do for that."

"I just thought you might have . . . some kind of wire netting or something," he suggested in fun.

"Well, I don't have a thing!" said Lois. "In my department, I wouldn't have anything but a tea strainer . . . Say! A tea strainer wouldn't do, would it? Come to think of it, I do have a kind of big one . . . how about a tea strainer?"

Lloyd took his hands out of his pockets and exclaimed, "A tea strainer! Hey, let's see it."

Lois ran to the dining room and took a fairly large silver tea strainer out of the drawer. "I use it when I am making tea in my large tea pot for a number of guests. Look, Lloyd! Will it work?"

Lloyd took the silver tea strainer in his hands and examined it. "You know? I think it will work. In fact, I'm sure it will! Lois, I was sure you would come up with something that we could use! As far as I know, I think we are ready to go tomorrow morning. I'll see you later. I have some paper work to do."

Surgery day arrived. Lois went to check with the headmaster and the teaching staff who were acting as lieutenants in organizing the children and sending them to the waiting area on the back verandah of the bungalow. They had already seen that the children had been fed and were lined up in the proper order for surgery.

When Lois was sure that everything that was her responsibility was completed and ready she went to the staging area where the children were waiting. Lois walked through the bungalow to the mat on the back verandah where the first three children were waiting to be called for surgery. Premilabai, one of the teachers, was sitting with them, reading them a story. Lois reached over to Rama and took his hand in hers. He moved over closer to her and she smiled at him.

"I don't want to be first, Madam Sahib," he whispered.

"Why not, Rama? If you are first, then yours will be finished and the others will still be worried about theirs."

Nurse Louise came through the dining room door. "We are ready for the first one, Lois. Is it Rama?"

"Yes, it's Rama. He's going to hold my hand, and I am going to stand beside him while he's lying on the table. He is a brave boy and in sixth standard!" Lois stood and gently led Rama through the house and out onto the front verandah where the team stood ready to receive him, and a crowd of villagers filled the lawn standing in the rain under their primitive bamboo and matted leaf umbrellas just beyond the surgery area.

As one of the team lifted Rama up onto the table he began to cry. Lois squeezed his hand. "I'm right here beside you, Rama. You are going to be just fine!"

The doctor patted him on the shoulder as the nurse held his head steady and began to fit the tea strainer over his nose and mouth. Rama began to struggle and cry as he tried to shove the mask away. Then as he breathed in the ether he suddenly went limp and lay quietly on the table. The crowd gasped as they thought the patient had gone limp and then died.

The doctor and the nurse proceeded efficiently with the surgery. The doctor worked in the patient's mouth a few minutes. Then he called out, "Suction please!"

At the back of the verandah, just inside the bedroom, the suction pump was set up. Ernie and three big boarding school boys were ready to take turns pumping. Ernie started working the pump with a steady rhythm and each one of the boys took his turn as the doctor directed him.

The doctor took something out of Rama's throat and dropped it into the kidney pan that the nurse was holding ready to receive it.

After a few minutes the doctor said, "Stop the suction, please." And the pumping team followed directions.

After a long few minutes, Rama's foot started to move and the crowd began to murmur. He moved his head and began to fuss showing that he was beginning to come out from under the anesthetic. The doctor patted him on the shoulder and said, "You're just fine, Rama. It's all over and you are going to be okay."

The crowd of villages which had been watching, fascinated with what was going on, began to whisper and talk excitedly.

Under the direction of the nurse, four school boys stepped forward with the improvised stretcher. They lifted Rama from the operating table, placed him on the stretcher, then with two other boys holding the bamboo and leaf umbrellas over him, carried him off the verandah, down through the compound, out the gate, through the rain, over to the school house, and into the schoolroom set up for recovery. Rama's crying had subsided to a mere whimper by this time. With a last word of comfort, Lois left his side and went to help with the next patient.

The surgeries went well patient after patient. The team took time off for the noon meal. After the first successful day of tonsillectomies, Lloyd was about to leave for a rest. Louise stopped him before he had a chance to escape. Word had spread through the villages that something was going on at the Mission and new patients were arriving by the minute.

"Doctor, there are three patients and their families waiting to see you and they have been

waiting since early morning. What shall I tell them? That you don't have time to see them?"
Lois asked.

Lloyd shook his head. "You had better not tell them that. We are very conscious of the fact
that we need to have good community relations. Let me take a quick look at them. Maybe it
won't take long."

"I thought that is what you probably would say, so I have set up a place you can interview
them in the office at the other end of the verandah," said Louise as she led the way to the
office.

After the examinations were over, Louise announced, "We have three more surgeries to
do--tumors, no less. Lloyd said that if they aren't removed shortly the women's chances aren't
good, so he has consented to do them when the tonsillectomies are finished. It may mean that
we will be here longer than we thought. We can't stay too much longer or we won't be able to
ford the rising rivers and get back to the hospital. Dr. Lloyd didn't seem to be worried, so I
think that I shouldn't be either."

It took three days to do all the tonsillectomies, but they went well. Each day the crowds
in the compound grew larger. When the tonsillectomies were finally finished it was necessary
to set up for a different kind of surgery. The next ones were to be abdominal--D and C's (a
procedure which dilates the cervix in order to scrape the uterine wall) in fact--and since privacy
was needed, they were set up in the office out of public view. Observers kept trying to see what
was going on, pushing their way up to the three windows or the blocked door. Lois knew that
the villagers were filled with curiosity that had continued to build through the three days of
the visit by the medical team. Wild rumors were flying through the nearby villages bringing
even larger crowds.

On the final day, about 3:00 in the afternoon, before the last few surgeries were completed,
they had a very important visitor. The Collector, whom some had remembered from the mass
wedding, came calling. He came through the compound gate accompanied by his personal
servant. The servant came onto the verandah first and announced that the Collector Sahib
would like to talk to the Missionary Sahib.

Ernie invited the Collector to come into their front room and sit down. Lois, after folding
her hands in greeting, hurried away to prepare hot tea.

As they drank tea and visited, the Collector commented, "Some villagers have been coming
up to my bungalow and telling me some very strange stories! I thought that I would come
over and find out if there was really any truth to the amazing rumors! They told me that some
wonderful things were happening over here at the Mission. They report that there is a marvel-

ous doctor here. He can do fantastic things. First he kills the patient. Then he takes a knife and cuts something out of the patient's throat. The villagers say the doctor puts something in a pan. After a while, the Sahib and the big boys at the back pump and pump, pumping new life right back into the patient, and he lives again! I thought I would come over and see what was really happening over here."

"Collector Sahib, some wonderful things are happening! We do have an excellent doctor here who is performing a number of surgeries. As a result our school children will have much better health through the rainy season and the cold season. We are so glad that you came over and we invite you to watch a surgery if you wish to put on a mask," Ernie suggested.

"No, I'm just very glad so see the good work going on. Just keep it up," he said with a twinkle in his eye, "and now I understand how patients are brought back to life." He finished his tea and then took his leave.

At the end of the third day, about 8:00 in the evening, Dr. Lloyd pulled off his gloves and mask and went into the bungalow from the front verandah. There he had folded his hands in a final "salaam" to the people waiting outside and Ernie pulled the big front double doors shut. The big venture was over except for the nursing care of the patients still on mats in the school rooms. All of the surgeries had gone well. Over fifty patients were now in recovery and, under the supervision of nurse Louis Sayer, were being cared for by their families at the school.

Lois and the cooks had a big meal ready for the team as soon as they could get cleaned up, but when they sat down to eat, they seemed almost to be too tired to swallow. They sat talking over the many things that had happened. As they gathered around the table they prayed in deep thankfulness to God for His guidance and help every step of the way in this huge venture. Every surgery had been a success. Every difficulty had been met and overcome satisfactorily. So many things could have gone wrong, but they didn't, thanks to God.

The next morning, after a good breakfast of cereal, buffalo milk, papaya, and chapatti breads the medical team was ready to leave. A runner brought in the word that the three rivers they would need to cross were still fordable. The van would be able to make it through.

Just before they climbed into the van the compound gate opened and a big crowd of people came through carrying armloads of garlands. They went up to the team, one after another, and placed garlands of jasmine and roses around the necks of each of the team members. There was much joy and gratitude and many farewell "salaams" as the van pulled out through the compound gates. Many villagers had been blessed by the visit of this skilled medical team which had given of themselves. Needs been met, the health of over 50 people had been improved, and God's love had been manifested once again.

Chapter 23

———•———

Rashmuk Encounters a Devil

"I'm going over to the supply room to check the rice supply for the hostels with Dalvi Master," Ernie told Lois as he picked up his huge, black umbrella and headed for the compound gate. "I'm concerned about our boarding school supplies! With the famine conditions in the whole of India so bad, I'm not sure that we can get grains when we need them." Ernie turned toward the hostel supply rooms. He looked worried, shaking his head.

Lois retrieved her umbrella, which was draining on the front verandah, and fell into step beside him. "I'm headed for the girls' boarding myself for the usual Saturday hair-washing routine, so I won't be back for quite a while. I've discovered that Matronbai usually has some things she wants to talk about while I am there."

Outside the compound gate Lois turned right toward the long building that housed all the girls in the boarding school, while Ernie turned left to reach the supply rooms.

Lois was still learning about the routine of hair washing that needed to be done every Saturday morning. First, she had to do something about the head-lice. Following the practice of other mission boarding schools, DDT powder needed to be sprinkled on each girl's head, left for one hour only, then washed out again and the hair dried. It was not until many years later that it became general knowledge that DDT was hazardous to the health of people and was dangerous for the environment. During the hot season when water was scarce the easiest thing to do was to take all the girls in boarding on a one-mile hike down the hill to the Sun River where all the girls could wash their hair at the same time, rather than trying to carry all the water necessary for washing so many heads back to the hostel. Now, at the beginning of the rainy season, the girls would try to catch rain water for general use by filling huge earthen pots.

Even so, the girls preferred to go down to the river to wash their hair and bathe. The matron always went with them for safety and brought them back. There was the ever-present danger of animals down by the river. Although most predators were nocturnal, or hunted at twilight, there was still some danger even at midday.

The DDT supply was always kept locked up and the key was in Lois's hands. She called to the girls to get ready to be powdered. One of the girls brought a wooden stool and set it on their verandah where there would be the most light on this dark rainy day. Then the matron took the can of powder and while one girl sat on the stool another girl divided her hair and the matron sprinkled the powder on the girl's head while Lois watched to see that no more powder was used than was necessary. "Hold your nose and don't breathe in any of the powder," she warned.

When they were all powdered, the matron reminded them, "Girls, find your soap. Don't take your clean clothes along. You can put clean clothes on when you get back from the river. If you put them on down by the river they will only get dirty coming back up the hill."

When they were all ready, the housemother picked up her own supplies and started toward the gate with the girls following after like a flock of pretty ducklings.

Lois worked in the hostel while the girls were down at the river taking baths. After an hour or so she heard them coming back long before they came through the gate. They were laughing and teasing each other. Now, the fun time over, they would need to work together on the daily chores of cooking and cleaning, each one having her assigned job for the day.

The boarding school children loved being in the Mission Boarding School. Here they had enough to eat. At home they would probably be hungry much of the time. Food was scarce and famine was the condition all over India.

When Lois got back to the bungalow she sat down at her desk to write some letters. She was in contact with several organizations which handled relief supplies from America. These included Church World Service which already had donated milk for babies, the Church of the Brethren which sent supplies from New Windsor, the Catholic Relief service, and several others. She wanted to find out if any of these organizations might be a source of relief food specifically for their boarding school since their supplies were running so low and the people in the village were nearly destitute.

Lois was appalled when she discovered that kitchen scraps such as potato peelings and onion tops that she was throwing away, were being salvaged and used by people in the village. People were picking up what she was throwing away! She felt she had to do more to improve the situation for as many of these hungry people as possible.

It took two months and much red tape before the next shipment of relief food arrived at the Waghai "toy train" station. Ernie took the jeep and trailer loaded with six of the huskier boarding school boys to help with the moving of the supplies and drove the twenty miles down the mountain to get the precious food. There were wheat flour, cooking oil, dry beans, and powdered milk.

Ernie and the headmaster took out enough of the supplies for the school, then set a day when the remaining supplies would be distributed to the villagers with children. There wasn't nearly enough to meet the need. The entire powdered milk supply went to the school and the baby clinic.

Not a week had gone by before Lois discovered that she shouldn't give a week's supply of powder to the mothers and expect the powder to be used for the babies only. It was too easy to exchange milk powder for other commodities resulting in the babies going hungry.

Six weeks later when the next shipment of supplies arrived Lois found the flour and the beans to be full of meal bugs. Nevertheless, the school children sifted out these beetles and beetle larvae the best that they could and used the rest for food. People in the village used the flour and beans as they received them. During the rainy season, at least, they didn't have to worry about having enough water for cooking and for household use. Now their worries were more about keeping their bedding and clothing, and also the cottage cow-dung-and-clay floors, dry. Even the clothes they were wearing were damp most of the time.

One night toward the end of the rainy season when there weren't so many puddles standing around and once in a while the moonlight actually peeped through the clouds, three frightened boys from the boys hostel came hurrying up onto the front verandah of the Shull bungalow. They cleared their throats excitedly to signal Shull Madam Sahib that they were there and that they wanted help as soon as possible. Lois could tell by their voices as they talked among themselves, that they were very excited. She dropped the letter she was writing and hurried from the office out toward the verandah.

"Are you there, Madam Sahib? Oh, please come with us if you can," one of the boys yelled when he saw Lois approaching. "Come over to the hostel quickly! Rashmuk is sick! Come right now if you can!"

Lois saw that the boys were not just excited; they were shifting from one foot to the other as though they couldn't wait to get back to the hostel. As Lois looked at each of the boys she thought every one of them appeared to be very frightened.

"What is it? What has happened to Rashmuk? Did he fall?" she asked.

"No! No! A devil has him! There is a devil in him! He can't talk! His eyes are back in his head!" All of the boys were talking at once wanting to explain how bad the situation was and why they needed her to come immediately and rescue Rashmuk from the devil.

Lois couldn't tell from their excited explanations what had really happened, but she knew it was an emergency. She ran back into the office to get her medical kit, then headed back to the verandah and down the front path over toward the boys hostel. The boys rushed along with her, telling her how Rashmuk had been making funny noises, then just fell over and wouldn't talk to anyone. They said that there was no doubt that there was a devil inside him.

"How do you know there is a devil inside him?" Lois asked as she ran with the boys toward the hostel.

They all tried to answer at once. "Why, because that's the way people act when they have a devil inside! Ask anybody!"

Lois hurried up onto the verandah of the boys' hostel, past some of the boys who were anxiously waiting for her to come inside with them. As Lois entered the room she saw one lantern was standing on the floor beside Rashmuk who was lying on a bamboo mat on the floor. Two other boys were sitting on their own mats sniffling and crying.

"Madam Sahib, please do something! The devils will get us all! Stay with us, will you? Help us!" cried one boy and others joined in pleading.

"The devils will get us like they have Rashmuk!"

Lois dropped down on the floor beside the unconscious boy lying on his mat and tried to pick up his hand, but it was so stiff that she couldn't lift it. She tried to lift his leg, but it too was stiff. She tried to turn his head from side to side but it was immovable. His pulse was so slow and weak that it was hard to detect.

"Rashmuk! Rashmuk!" she called in his ear, but the boy showed no sign of hearing her voice. Unpinning a safety pin from her blouse she pricked his arm, but he didn't react. Then she stuck him harder with still no response.

"Lord, I don't know what I need to do to help Rashmuk. I have never seen a case quite like this before. This I do know: whatever it is, You can heal it! Show me how I can help these boys in this very frightening situation," Lois prayed.

Then turning to Rama she said, "Rama, please go over to the Parlak's house and call him to come and help us."

Rama slipped out of the hostel door quickly and was gone only a few minutes before he returned bringing the Parlak back with him.

The Parlak was dressed in a dhoti and a white Nehru shirt. He was carrying his Bible.

"How can I help, Madam Sahib," he asked in a soft voice as he patted one of the crying boys on the shoulder.

"Parlak Sahib, we want you to be with us and pray with us for Rashmuk. The boys say that the devil has taken possession of him. But we know that whatever evil has happened to Rashmuk, God is more powerful than that evil. God can heal this boy. He can cast out any other spirits that are making this boy sick. We want you to pray with us for God to be with this boy and to heal Rashmuk." Lois could feel the confidence the boys had in the Parlak.

Parlak Choudhari asked the boys to fold their hands then, closing his eyes, he began to pray.

"Oh, most powerful, holy, loving Heavenly Father, You who love us more than we can know, You whose son gave up his life so we could know Jesus and follow his teachings, be in our midst just now. Rashmuk is in trouble, Lord. Enter into him and drive whatever evil is in him out again so he can get well! We know that you are all-powerful and that you can heal him. Fill him with your loving, Holy Spirit. Be in our midst! We believe what Jesus told us. Amen."

"Boys, I'm so glad you and the Madam Sahib called me to be with you, for it is always wonderful to see what the Lord can do in our lives," he said. He rose to his feet and began walking around among the boys who were still filled with fear.

"But Parlak Sahib! What do you mean? Rashmuk is not healed! Look at him! He is still filled with the devils! He's still stiff as a board. He can't move! Why didn't God heal him when you prayed?" asked Doulet, a fourth standard Hindu boy with large brown eyes and a desire to learn more about what Jesus taught.

The Parlak went over to Doulet and, sitting down beside him, laid his hand on the boy's shoulder. "I don't know the answer to that, Doulet. All I know is that God answers our prayers in his own good time. Meanwhile we need to go about our normal business and let God work. Isn't it about bed time for you boys? Shouldn't you be getting some sleep? Morning will be here before you know it." The Parlak rose to go. As he went toward the door he touched each boy giving each an assurance that he would be with them in spirit and that he would come back if they called for him. Lois, too, went out the door and toward her bungalow.

As Lois prepared for bed, she thought she was so glad that Ernie would be home the next day so she could share with him the strange experience with Rashmuk and the boys. She wasn't sure what the next step to help Rashmuk should be. She wanted to talk to Ernie in the worst way. In the mean time she turned the lantern flame down low, crawled into bed, tucked in her mosquito met securely all around the edges, making sure there were no gaps where some hungry mosquito could work its way under the net and get at her, then turned over, closed her eyes, and went to sleep.

The first thing Lois thought about the next morning when she opened her eyes and looked up into the thin covering of the bed net, was Rashmuk. How was he? Had he gotten better? Was he worse? Was he dead?

She pulled the bed net loose beside her, reached down to the floor, picked up first one chappal (sandal), shook it out in case some little, undesirable creature might have crawled into the warm spot, then shook out the other. She slipped her feet into the chappals and proceeded to drape on her sari. On days when she had to hurry she could drape a sari on in three minutes. This was one of those days. The sari seemed to go on very smoothly. The pleats fell into place beautifully and the "padar"--the colorful end of the blue, cotton sari--fell gracefully over her left shoulder, revealing a fascinating elephant design done in black and red.

She picked up the medical kit that she had left beside the front door and opened the big double doors that led out onto the verandah. She went down the steps, along the front path to the gate. As she stepped out onto the road that ran from the bungalow to the boys' boarding house, she saw some boys skipping as they came toward her.

Rashmuk! What was this? Could this really be Rashmuk walking toward her? Could he have been healed so soon?

"Rashmuk! Is it really you? Are you really feeling this much better? You were really so sick last night!" Lois exclaimed.

"Madam Sahib, I was so sick. I didn't know what was happening to me! I didn't know anything. There was a devil in me! But the Parlak and all of you prayed for the power of God to come into me and I was healed. Thank you, Madam Sahib!"

"Rashmuk, don't thank me. Thank God who healed you. We're all so happy that you're well again. God's love is so wonderful! He is with us always. Go with God, Rashmuk."

Later, as Lois was trying to tell Ernie about Rashmuk, she shook her head in bewilderment. "Ernie, it can't be explained logically. What happened to Rashmuk? I believe God works through natural laws. But somehow I can't find them in this case."

Ernie laughed. "Maybe you just don't know all the natural laws. Why don't you put this question with the others we don't have answers to yet. You can work on it as you gain more knowledge and understanding." Ernie gave her a sympathetic pat on the shoulder as he thought about the fact that everyone has many unanswered questions. It felt to him that, no matter what the circumstances in life, questions about God's ways are to be expected.

Chapter 24

———— ❧ ————

Rabbits and a Snake

Lois had grown up in a town where the nearest thing to wild life was the neighbor's pet dog. Ernie had a little more experience. He and his family lived on a farm where they raised cows, horses, rabbits, and chickens. Ernie was interested in wild animals and had read widely about them and their characteristics.

One evening Ernie made arrangements to go with some of the young men to hunt something for the boarding school children to eat the next day--a couple rabbits, a barking deer, or something bigger like a sambar, a large deer, or a wild boar. The trouble with hunting a wild boar was that these animals could become extremely dangerous. The boys, however, weren't afraid as long as they had Shull Sahib and his gun with them. They had watched Shull Sahib before and they knew he was an excellent shot. He had brought in meat for the boarding school many times.

On one of these hunting trips, after about an hour's search from the open jeep, one of the boys leaned over Ernie's shoulder and said, "Sahib, I saw two little eyes in the bamboo back there. Let's stop and get it!"

Ernie braked, but he didn't stop the jeep.

"Anand, I could shoot that rabbit, but it is so small and we need more meat than that for four boarding school rooms. We should have four rabbits at least or you won't even be able to taste the rabbit. I was thinking that a small deer or a peacock would be a better size for our needs."

Anand was getting anxious. "But, Sahib, we don't have a peacock or a deer, and there is a rabbit in that clump of bamboo back there! Let's get it, Sahib. Maybe there might even be two if we looked!"

"Let's try to get it!" urged the other boys. They didn't want to pass up a chance to have some meat in their curry if they could get the Sahib to look a little longer maybe there would be a larger rabbit or even more than one. They could just hear the shouts of anticipation of the taste of curried rabbit from the other boarders once they saw the results of the successful hunt.

"Let's go, then," said Ernie, as he slowly backed up the jeep toward the bamboo thicket. The boys grew quiet.

Ernie stepped out of the jeep onto the ground and carefully shouldered his gun. He deliberately aimed between the two shiny eyes and pulled the trigger. The eyes disappeared.

"You got him, Sahib! Right between the eyes! But I think there is another one almost in the same place!"

Again Ernie aimed and pulled the trigger. Again the glow in the eyes of the rabbit blinked out. The boys dashed into the bamboo thicket, and in a few seconds rushed out triumphantly with two rabbits.

"Let's go home now, Sahib. We have enough rabbit to make a good curry. Let's go so we can get our food started cooking. This will be the best curry we have had for a long time."

The boys didn't have to ask twice. As Shull Sahib backed the jeep around onto the road ready to head for home, the boys began to sing and shout happily. They always had food, but to have meat to flavor the curry was a special treat.

By the time the hunting party reached home, they had shot two more rabbits. As the time arrived to start preparing the evening meal, each of the boys took off to carry out his own particular work assignment. They had shot enough rabbits for one for each hostel room and one for the Shulls. Ernie stopped at the back of his own compound to clean and skin the one he had kept. He left the skin, the head, and the entrails by the back fence. The rest he dropped off in the kitchen for Gopal Mistri to wash and fry for the family's supper. The boys who had been with him took the rest of the rabbits for the evening curry. One rabbit went to the girls and the others went to the boys.

The rabbit dinner was delicious for the Shulls--fried rabbit, mashed potatoes and gravy, egg plants grown in their garden, deviled eggs, and lettuce which had been soaked in chlorine water and then rinsed, boiled buffalo milk, and plenty of boiled drinking water.

Rabbits were not the only creatures which moved about at night. In fact, because of prowling wild animals which sometimes left the jungle and wandered through the village and a few times up on the Shulls' verandah, Lois and Ernie tried to not schedule any appointments late in the evening. One exception was the "gayansaba"--or "sing"--they would hold on their front verandah on Sunday evenings. People would come and go in groups to these meetings, which made it safer.

One night there was trouble in the village and Ernie was late getting home. Lois and Ernie sat at the table talking for a while after they had eaten dinner. They were discussing the need that the Ahwa school would have very soon for two more teachers. It was going to be necessary to hire some qualified teachers from some other mission since none were available from the Church of the Brethren Mission.

"Well, we can't do anything about it tonight. It's getting late. Let's go to bed," said Ernie.

"Of course. You may have to visit another mission to interview some candidates," Lois replied.

"I think that is a good idea. I believe that I will begin searching tomorrow for the time is getting short."

When they were getting ready for bed Lois was still thinking about the boarding school diet. She took the undersheet off the bed and soaked it in water from the well; the she put the wet sheet on the bed, then lowered the bed net which was tied at each of the four corners of the bed on wooden posts. Then she tucked the edges of the net under the mattress pad on every side. Hopefully as the sheet dried it would cool the air under the net. It felt cool to Lois as she climbed under the net and tucked it under the thin mattress pad.

How she missed Linda, Jimmy, and Danny who were away in the Himalayan Mountains in Woodstock, an American boarding school.

Ernie came in from the office carrying a lantern. He got ready for bed and turned the lantern down low, leaving it burning just in case someone needed help during the night.

As Ernie tucked in the net on his side to thwart the mosquitoes Lois said in a sleepy voice, "Good night, honey. I love you." And soon she and Ernie were sound asleep.

About 1:30 Lois felt the whole bed give a big jerk. It was so startling that she sat straight up! She found herself staring up through the top of the bed net where some creature was twisting and turning, coiling and slithering, its heavy weight pulling the net askew.

"Ernie! Quick! There is something coiling around on the top of our net. Ernie! Quick! Do something! Oh, Ernie! Wake up! Ernie, oh ... oh ... oh!"

"Huh . . . what?" he mumbled as he came up on one elbow. He looked up and saw the twisting, writhing snake! "Oh, look at that. A snake! I wonder what kind it is!" he said, his eyes now open.

"What kind is it? Honey, you make me so mad.! What kind is it? Who cares! Just get it off this net!" Lois said with a mixture of amusement and irritation and fear. It was so typical of

Ernie to worry about the reptile's classification more than its presence.

"It's okay! It's okay! I'll get it off. I've got a bamboo pole over in the corner of the bedroom by the door. I'll get it!" Carefully he loosened the net from under the edge of the mattress and stuck one foot out to find his rubber chappal, then the other one. He ran to the corner of the room and retrieved the bamboo stick.

Lois watched as he came back to the bed where the snake was still twisting and wiggling. Ernie put the point of the stick in a coil of the snake and gave it a big heave, but it was awkward and the stick slipped. He tried again, pushing the stick farther into one of the coils. This time the heavy snake was lifted over the edge of the net and flipped to the cement floor where it landed with a heavy "plop." It started to slither away, but Ernie gave it a big blow. That didn't seem to stop it. It slithered in another direction. There followed a big battle. In the end the snake was dead, although its body kept twisting and turning, even with a smashed head. Ernie raced for the door.

"Ernie! Where are you going!" Lois yelled.

"Don't worry, honey! I'm just going to get a tape measure so I can tell how long this snake is. It might be a record," Ernie explained.

"But, Ernie, it's not dead! It's still moving," she warned.

"Oh, it's dead! It just doesn't know it yet!" Ernie explained.

The snake proved to be a kind of rat snake, 85 inches long, and nonpoisonous. It was not a record but, through the net, it had certainly looked like a giant.

Lois had learned much about wildlife since she married Ernie. One of Ernie's majors in college had been biology and he had a natural interest. She had take basic zoology and that was all, but Ernie had taught her much. Living in the Dangs jungle would teach her even more because they would be living close to many wild animals. Occasionally Ernie sent shipments of bird skins and insects to the American Museum of Natural History in New York. Lois took a certain amount of vicarious pride in Ernie's knowledge of wildlife.

Chapter 25

⎯⎯•:•⎯⎯

Leopards and Hunters

"Mother! Mother!" called the boy happily. "Look what I brought us to eat tonight! I was fishing in the hole in the river that father showed me is the best. It's under that big clump of willow branches close to the path."

"Let me see, Tukaram." she exclaimed taking the string of fish and counting them. "That's fine! This is just the right number to make the curry good! We'll all eat well tonight." Taking the fish she went outside the hut to clean them and to begin preparing the evening meal.

"The reason I have so many fish is because father taught me how to fish with a bow and arrow. I stand on my favorite rock and aim carefully before I let the arrow fly. My father knew many things, Mother."

Mother Sitabai stopped working and looked thoughtfully at Tukaram. "You are right, my son. Your father was a very clever man. But times are changing and I am worried about you. You will have to know more than your father knew. Did you hear the teacher that was in our village a few days ago? I'm convinced, Tukaram, that you are going to need to go to the Mission School and learn many things. In fact, I think we had better go to Ahwa where the Mission School is and talk to the missionary tomorrow."

Tukaram listened to his mother with mixed feelings. He had heard the missionary a few days ago and when he thought about attending a school it sounded exciting, but he didn't want to be away from his hunting and fishing and all the things he could do in the jungle. But if his mother wanted to go to the village of Ahwa and talk to the missionary then he would go with her.

The next morning Tukaram and his mother entered the mission compound and asked to see the missionary sahib.

"I want my boy to learn things in school," Sitabai told the missionary. "I don't want him to have to stay in our village all his life. What do I have to do to get him into the school?" Sitabai asked.

The missionary explained that the boy would need a bamboo mat to sleep on, a change of clothes to wear while one set was being washed, a cake of soap for bathing and seven rupees a month to pay toward his board and for a slate and chalk.

"Here are the first seven rupees," said Sitabai counting them out on the missionary's desk. "I will try very hard to find more money for next month. I want him to get as much learning as he can until I don't have any more money. I will do my best, Missionary Sahib."

So the arrangements were made for Tukaram, the first person from his jungle village, to enter the Mission school. He was assigned a place in cottage number two with seven other boys and his school life began. It was quite different from life in his home village. One thing he liked especially, was that the students in boarding school ate food regularly, every day in fact. At home, they ate when they had something to eat.

Tukaram felt very uneasy the first night he was in boarding without his mother and without the familiar gods he usually worshipped. During the first night he was awakened as he lay on his bamboo mat, by a peculiar squeaking and moaning sound that would swell and then disappear. It wasn't normal—unlike anything he had ever heard. It came and went like an evil spirit threatening him just outside his window. It seemed to be telling him that he was displeasing the gods and he would have to pay for it. He was quite sure that his gods from home were angry at him for leaving them back in his home village of Mahal! But how could he bring them along when the people of his village wanted them to stay with them! He began to shiver for he didn't know what to do.

Finally he tapped the boy next to him on the shoulder and managed to whisper, "Deshmuk, do you hear that devil in the tree just outside our window? I think it is one of the devils from my home village of Mahal. It is angry because I have left the village, I think."

Deshmuk opened his eyes and began to listen. Sure enough, there was some kind of creepy, sinister noise outside the window. Finally he said, "Tukaram, do you know what? I don't think that it is a devil. Let's call the housemaster and have him listen."

Together they crept over to the housemaster's mat and touched him. "Dalvi Master, we are afraid that we are hearing a devil in the tree just outside our window. Will you come and listen with us?"

Dalvi Master stood up beside his mat. "Come on with me, boys. Let's listen."

After a few minutes Dalvi Master began to laugh. "Do you know what you are hearing, boys? It's a couple of branches rubbing together in the mango tree just outside your window. Deshmuk, Tukaram hasn't been with us very long, so maybe he doesn't know about the power of the true God. But you should remember, Deshmuk. If there were a devil out there in the tree, you still don't need to be afraid. Pray to the true God for his presence with you. He will help you. Let's pray and then you won't be afraid."

They all closed their eyes and began to pray, "Dear God, we pray that you will be with us. We know that you are the most powerful spirit in the world and if you are with us no other spirits have any power. Amen."

Dalvi Master gave each one of the boys a pat and told him to go back to sleep for they were in God's care.

On the hillside not far from the Mission was a little cement temple about five feet high. It had an opening for an entrance and the top came to a peak. The whole structure was white-washed. Lying on the ground around this little building were bits of food, leaves, and other things the Hindus use in worship.

One day Lois asked some Hindu worshipers at this small shrine what or who they were worshipping. They told her that in this little temple a snake lived and they were worshipping the snake. They told Lois it stayed curled up at the end of the tiny room inside and it could grant good luck and protection to the worshiper. Sometimes the Hindu boys in the boarding school would slip away and worship the snake, especially when the parents came from other villages to visit their children who were in boarding school.

Early one morning while Lois and Ernie were still in bed they heard a commotion at the compound gates.

"I'll get up and see what the trouble is. You just sleep another hour if you want to. If I need you I'll give you a call," Ernie said as he pulled the bed net loose from under the mattress and slipped out the side. "It could be that some of the parents from Mahal need some help. Some Mahal people were here in Ahwa last night."

The people at the gate were, indeed, from Mahal, Tukaram's village, and his mother was in the group waiting at the mission compound gate. These people had stopped at Tukaram's hostel and asked him to come along with them to convince the Mission Sahib to help them.

"Shull Sahib, these people are from my home village. They have come with great trouble! During the night a leopard sneaked into the headman's hut, snatched his little son and then leaped out the door and ran away into the jungle. Please, Shull Sahib, bring your gun and get his son back again. Come now before the leopard kills the little boy!" Tukaram pleaded.

"I'll come, Tukaram, but I'm very afraid that it is already too late to save the life of the little boy! Come with us, Tukaram, while we search for the little one," said Ernie.

It was a twenty mile trip farther into the jungle to the village of Mahal. Twenty two huts made up the village. In the center of the group was a large hut where most of people could gather at once. The headman lived in this hut, the largest in the village.

When the missionary and the villagers arrived in Mahal, they heard that the little boy still had not been found. They told the missionary just what had happened.

They had fixed a metal pan with burning charcoal in the center of the hut. The mother, father, and four children were each sleeping on a bamboo mat near the metal fire pan to keep warm. Soon after they had all gone to sleep, a leopard came up to their doorway, smashed down the bamboo mat they had hung over an opening that served as a kind of door, leaped the few feet to where the little boy was sleeping, grabbed him in its teeth, bounded back through the doorway, and disappeared into the thick, dark jungle. They had searched near at hand, but had found nothing. Now with more lanterns, the coming daylight, and a gun they hoped that the little boy could be found. However, by mid-afternoon all that had been found was some bloody cloth and bones.

The men of the village built a machan, a hunting platform in the trees, about seventeen feet off the ground where Ernie said he would sit and wait for the leopard to return. He stayed there until about 3:00 in the morning, then decided that the leopard wouldn't come any more that night. He took the light walla and the Ahwa men and went back home to try to get some sleep.

For three nights the men sat on the machan waiting for the leopard to come back for another meal, but it didn't show up. On the third night the missionary told the headman of Mahal, "I'm sorry but I can't wait any longer. It is interfering with my work."

"But Sahib," the headman pleaded. "If you don't come back tonight the leopard is sure to come and someone in our village will be killed. Please, Sahib. Come one more night."

Finally the missionary agreed to come the fourth night, but explained he would not be able to come any more after that.

Ernie and the Ahwa hunters were there at early dusk waiting quietly on the machan in the trees. It was dusk when they heard the familiar breathing sounds of the leopard as it approached the village. It was barely visible in the increasing darkness. Ernie slowly raised his gun and took careful aim. The big cat was headed toward the smashed door of the headman's hut where it had already obtained one easy meal.

Ernie aimed for the heart and pulled the trigger. With the sound of the explosion, the leopard fell into the tall grass.

"You got it, Sahib! You hit it! It won't kill any more people! That's sure!" The villagers began to come running out of their huts singing and shouting with joy, "Our enemy is dead! Our enemy is dead!"

The men climbed down off the machan and walked cautiously over to where they thought the leopard had dropped to the ground. Sure enough, the huge animal lay there, lifeless as a stone. With gun cocked Ernie slowly approached the leopard. He threw a big rock to see if he could get the animal to stir, but it didn't respond. They made sure the leopard was really dead, and then they moved in.

As Ernie was finding several men to help him lift the dead animal up into the jeep, Tukaram touched him on the arm. "Shull Sahib, the headman and the villagers want to touch and worship the leopard before you load it into the jeep. Will you let them do that, please?" he asked.

"They may touch the leopard if they wish. It can't hurt anyone ever again," Ernie answered.

The villagers gathered close around the dead animal, trying to reach out and put their hands on the beautiful coat of cat fur that just a short time ago had been the greatest threat to the village.

Some mothers brought their babies to where they could brush their eyes with the tip of the leopard's tail, believing that this touch could prevent eye infections of the babies for one year. Many people just wanted to touch the animal, thinking that this would cure whatever was wrong with them.

"Sahib," said Tukaram. "These men want something special. Tell him, Rasham. What do you want?"

Rasham was a young man from Tukaram's family. "Sahib, when you skin the leopard please give me a piece of the fat from the shoulder so that I can prepare it and eat it. If I do that I will become as strong and powerful as the leopard."

Tukaram translated, "Shull Sahib says you may have it if you wish."

Very carefully the skinners worked, making sure that every bit of fat was removed from under the skin so there would not be any hair loss as the fat rotted. When they arrived back at the mission compound they stretched out the skin and cautiously tacked it to the side of the woodshed and left it there to dry.

Tukaram led his mother over to see the leopard skin stretched out on the woodshed wall. "Do you see, Mother? The leopard god isn't a very powerful god. Even Shull Sahib can kill him and save our village. I'm not going to pray to the leopard god any more!"

"Don't talk like that, Tukaram. The leopard god can bring trouble to our hut!" his mother told him. But Tukaram was thinking his own thoughts.

Danny, barely able to handle an air rifle which was almost as large as he was, had quickly lost interest in all of the talk of leopards and gods. He had spotted game of his own.

"Mom, where are you?" called Danny as he came rushing in the back door of the bungalow. Gopal Mistri glanced up from the mixture he was stirring on the stove in the kitchen to see what all the excitement was about.

Lois, who had been working in the office, came through the big double doors into the dining room. She wanted to arrange a center piece of flowers for the evening dinner table.

"Oh, there you are! Mom! Guess what! I just saw a bandicoot! It was out in the chicken pens, and it was huge, Mom! It was a giant! I wish I could get one of those! If Dad gives Jimmy and me four annas for each mouse we can shoot with our air rifles, I'll bet he would give us eight annas for shooting a bandicoot rat!"

"You had better be careful of those big rats, Danny Baba. One of them bit Boulu Singh, my son, one time," cautioned Gopal Mistri. He shook his head and turned back to the mixture he was stirring.

Lois had a feeling that Gopal was right to caution Danny about the rat. "Why don't you wait until you can ask Dad about the bandicoot? I'd hate for that creature to bite you, Danny!"

"Aw, gee, Mom. I'd probably get it with my first shot and wouldn't have to worry about it biting me. I'm going to tell Jimmy about it and tell him to get his gun and come with me!" he decided as he started across the verandah to find his brother. Two guns would be more likely to get the bandicoot than just one. Danny thought himself to be a pretty good shot, but it wouldn't hurt anything to have a back-up. When Jimmy heard that Danny had sighted a bandicoot he grabbed his air rifle and joined the hunt.

They found several large rat holes in the ground out in the rabbit pens and the chicken cages.

"Dad says that the best way to drive the rats out of their holes is to smoke them out. Let's smoke them out with burning dry grass," suggested Jimmy. While Danny stood at the ready with his gun, Jimmy stuffed smoldering brown grass down the biggest rat hole. Very soon smoke started to pour out some of the other rat holes which showed that they were all connected by underground passages.

"I see a nose, Jimmy! Help me watch the holes!" shouted Danny. "Come on!"

The next fifteen minutes were very exciting. The bandicoots would only stick their heads out, then go back into their holes.

"Stop shooting!" yelled Danny. "There are a couple rats outside of the holes. Let's see what we have!" They found two big dead rats with twelve inch long bodies and twelve inches of tail lying outside their holes.

"Oh boy! Wait 'till Dad sees these! Maybe he'll pay us for killing a big rat today! Let's throw them into the chicken house so no other animal will carry them off and eat them before Dad sees them!"

A few minutes later Ernie came into the pens getting ready to feed the animals.

"Hey Dad! Look what we shot! We think they should be worth more than four annas each because they are so big!"

"I agree," said Ernie as he reached into his pocket and pulled out two eight anna pieces. "It is worth that much to me to have those big fellows killed and out of here. Throw them out by the back fence," he suggested.

The boys felt quite rich with eight annas each. A few hours later the boys were playing a game with stones in the road in front of the bungalow when they saw Hari carrying something wrapped in banana leaves. He laid the package against the brick wall of the house.

"Why are you doing that, Hari," asked Jimmy of the garden worker.

"Well I didn't think you would care if I took the bandicoots. You threw them away, didn't you?" asked Hari

"Of course!" said Jimmy

"We like to eat them! They will make good curry! So I put them by the brick wall to stay cool until I go home from work this evening. I didn't think you would care."

"That's okay. You can have them if you want them. It's just that I don't think rats would be good to eat," explained Jimmy as he turned away feeling a little sick. Hari took the bandicoots and put them back along the brick wall where he hoped the dogs or other predators would not find them.

"What do you have?" asked Jimmy's and Danny's friend, Viju, as he came through the compound gate. "I thought I heard your guns go off. What did you shoot? You aren't leopard hunting, are you?" Viju laughed as he pulled the banana leaves back so he could see the huge rats lying up against the brick foundation to keep them cool.

Danny started to clean his gun. "Not my gun! You didn't hear my gun," he said. "I'm glad to let my dad shoot the leopards. You know, Viju, he got a big leopard last night?"

"Someone told me that he did. They said it was down in the village just ready to attack somebody. Arrae! I'm glad he is a good shot! I know what we can do," said Viju "Are they going to bring the leopard back here to the bungalow? I'd like to see it, and see how big it is. I wonder if it is as big as the last one he had to kill down by the well. While we are waiting lets go into your house and see if your mom would let us have some ice cubes. I just love to suck ice cubes! Your mom doesn't care, does she?"

"It's beginning to get dark and it's still very hot. We can go in and get some ice cubes if we take them to the sink on the back porch so we don't make a mess. You do it, Danny," Jimmy suggested. "I'm going out to see Dad a minute. I want to know something about that leopard they are bringing in to the bungalow."

It was dusk and the day was beginning to cool. Jimmy pushed open the back screen door and went running out toward the chicken pens to help his daddy with the daily routine of feeding the animals. The chickens were making an awful racket. Ernie was near the grain bins getting ready to feed the chickens when he saw that something had torn a hole in the heavy expanded metal mesh that was around the pen of a pair of four-horned antelopes that had been given to him when the mother had been shot. Ernie had raised these unique animals since they were fawns. Found only in this area of the world, these antelope had never been thoroughly studied. They fascinated Ernie and he studied their behavior as best he could. In fact, their gestation period was unknown until the pair produced a fawn in captivity. Ernie reported his findings to the scientific community. Although the antelope were now "pets" they remained essentially undomesticated. The male actually had four horns, two short spikes in front and two sharp four-inch spikes behind. One had to be very careful when cleaning the cage because the male would lower its head and charge with little warning.

Ernie discovered that the commotion was apparently because the male antelope had gotten out of its cage and was loose in the compound. Jimmy and Hari, who sometime helped with the feeding chores, rushed to the scene to try to get it back in its cage. Daylight was rapidly changing to twilight as Jimmy ran to shut the compound gate and Hari moved toward the antelope. Without warning, the antelope charged Hari and, before he could react, had shot between his legs. Fortunately for him, his legs were bowed like a cowboy's. Before he knew it, the antelope had wheeled around and charged back between his legs from behind. Both charges completely missed, more than a major bit of good luck for Hari! In the corner of his eye, Ernie caught a glance of Jimmy shutting the gate, but the ominous shadow of a bounding animal was also heading for the gate.

"Go to the bungalow, Jimmy! Go back! Go back!" Ernie yelled in sudden terror. Seeing Jimmy running toward him, he realized what could happen in the next few seconds if he didn't act fast. Ernie yelled to Hari to forget the antelope and get in the bungalow.

Jimmy ran for shelter and was almost to the bungalow when a black shadow shot between him and his dad. He couldn't tell exactly what it was, but he knew it was fast and he sensed it was dangerous.

"Dad! Dad!" he screamed. By this time Ernie had arrived by Jimmy's side and had his arms around his son.

"What was it, Dad? I thought it was going to jump on top of me," cried Jimmy.

"Let's hurry into the house, Jimmy, so I can get my gun! Hurry!"

Lois saw them rushing into the house and called, "What's the matter? What's wrong?"

With his arm still around Jimmy, Ernie said, "Some very big animal jumped between Jimmy and me out in the compound. I think it was trying to get the four-horned antelopes. I've got to get my gun."

"You aren't going out there with you the only person with a gun, are you?" cautioned Lois.

"Of course, you're right! I can check the 'pug' marks in the morning. Big paw marks like those of a tiger or leopard will be easily identified. I'll wait until morning. Maybe I'll go out later yet tonight to see if I can get the male back in its cage or maybe, at that, I'll wait 'till morning."

Everyone was almost too excited to eat, but Lois thought she would try to break the tension. "Just now dinner is ready. Go to the table, everybody," urged Lois.

When they were all seated Ernie prayed a sincere prayer of thanksgiving not only for their own lives but for the lives of other people in the village. It seemed pretty clear that a hungry leopard or tiger was wondering much too close to civilization on this night and that it was probably frightened enough to not appear again soon. With a smile and a shudder, Ernie was especially thankful that Hari, who never really realized what had happened, was safe.

"We believe that it should start with us."
Tukaram

Chapter 26

Splendor in the Dust

The Dangs had become very important politically and economically. Teak wood and bamboo were the source of much wealth. The states of Gujarat and Maharashtra both coveted these natural resources. The Dangs Sava Mandel continued to work for Maharashtra's ownership, while the Ashram sided with the State of Gujarat on all political and economic issues.

The competition had escalated over the years and now was bitter. The petty rivalry even showed up on public occasions with disputes over which faction should be assigned seats of honor. The Christians, however, were largely not a part of this rivalry.

As March and April came and went another hot season was in full swing with its thick dust everywhere. Big zigzag cracks in the dry earth appeared, evidence of no rain for the last six months. The sun seemed to beat down with merciless heat and tempers ran high.

Newspapers that were brought in from the capitol cities of Gujarat and Maharashtra carried articles that were about the competition for ownership of the Dangs timber area. Politicians from both groups visited Ahwa. Rumors were circulated that someone was going to set the jungle on fire.

One day an official from the forestry department came to the Shulls' bungalow. Ernie was gone on a three day journey to Palghar which was located out along the main railroad line.

The official cleared his throat loudly, then waited for someone to answer. Lois called from the back verandah, "Who's there? What can I do for you?"

The forestry officer folded his hands before his face, in respect and said, "Madam Sahib, the forest department has sent a message to warn you that the jungle is on fire in the southeast corner. We are working to control it, but we thought that you should know and think about the safety of the boarding school children. We will keep you informed."

"You will keep us informed in time so that we can get the children down the hill to Waghai to the train before we are cut off by fire?" asked Lois. "Can you furnish us with an escort?"

"No, there will not be an escort, but, yes, we will keep you informed," he stated as he turned and left the compound.

Lois breathed a prayer as she started an emergency preparation to move the whole school the twenty miles down the hill to the railroad station at Waghai.

The first thing to do was to organize the teaching and boarding school staff. How she wished that Ernie was at home! She gave each staff member a specific job to do and everyone swung into action.

Food had to be prepared to take with them. The children had to be prepared to meet this unusual emergency. They had been working a half hour when three children came hurrying in talking excitedly. "Madam Sahib, there are burning leaves falling in our compound! Look there!"

Lois ran out to see the burning leaves. Smoke was rolling in from the south. The air was heavy with the smell of smoke. Lois checked on the different points of action to see if they could move immediately if orders came from the forestry department.

The next five hours were torture as they fought the smoke, burning leaves and excited children as they worked to prepare to move the whole school down the mountain, walking to the nearest train station which was twenty miles away.

The next morning by first light they were nearly ready to leave. First the children must be given their breakfast, and then dishes packed. Finally the word they had been praying for came from the forestry department that they thought they had the fire under control. Government orders came to the Mission that they should not plan to leave the school, but stay where they were until further notice.

The teachers decided to wait two hours to be sure that the news they had received was true, for they didn't want to have the students eat all the prepared food and then be told that they must leave the Mission compound after all. When there was no change of orders from the forestry department, the teachers, working together, supervised the distribution of the food that had been prepared. They hurried to make hot tea to go with the chapattis and they celebrated the joyful news that they didn't have to hurry down the mountain to escape the wildfire. But much valuable timber had been burned and the destruction of animal life was great. This was tiger and leopard habitat. No one knew how many of those had been killed directly, but definitely their jungle home had been diminished considerably. Eventually, the fires were extinguished and the smoke cleared. After months, the political fallout too was over, and the Dangs was awarded to Gujarat State.

As the years went by and Linda, Jimmy, and Danny grew older, Ernie and Lois began to think seriously about how long they should stay in India. Their goal was to see the Church firmly established, that it should become self-propagating and self-supporting. When the time came that the Church could continue with its own leadership, that would be the sign that the time for them to leave India had arrived. They agreed that to stay beyond that point would be to stand in the way of the development of the Indian Church.

It was an important day when Linda graduated from Woodstock High School in Mussoori. It meant immanent separation for the family. For Linda, it meant not only leaving the family, but going to live in a strange country that she had visited only two short times before when her parents were on furlough in the States.

A week later it was time for Linda to leave India and go to Manchester College in Indiana for four years. It had been arranged for her to travel with other missionaries from another mission who were also going back to the States for furlough. It was planned for them to fly to Italy, then Germany, where they would be attending the 1960 Passion Play at Oberamergau. Later they would fly to Amsterdam, then London, and finally New York, Chicago, then Fort Wayne, Indiana, where she would be met by Lois's brother Don, who lived there.

It looked like a perfect arrangement for Linda, but on the morning when Linda was to leave their temporary home at Prospect Point on the mountain top, Lois held onto Linda until the last minute. She watched with tears rolling down her cheeks as Linda, smiling and waving her last goodbye, went around the last curve in the path and disappeared beyond the rocky cliff. For Lois, it felt as if her heart would break. She prayed that God would go with Linda every step of the way as she left India and started her college career. God had seen her through some very serious bouts of malaria when she was only a little girl, repeated cases of dysentery, close calls with snakes, and a potentially deadly encounter with wild dogs. Surely, He would see her through the next four years as she made some of the most important decisions of her life.

The next morning, Jimmy and Danny went down the mountain to go back into boarding school at Woodstock, and Lois and Ernie left the Himalayas to return a thousand miles to their station at Ahwa. It felt like such an isolated place now—so cut off from the children they loved—yet God's call was clear and the work to be done was a challenge. Faith alone could sustain such a sacrifice.

Lois and Ernie still had four years left in their term of service. They had already spent fourteen years as missionaries in India. To allow Linda to return to the States without her parents was the hardest thing Lois had ever had to do. It felt as if the next four years would likely bring a thousand emergencies and momentous decisions which Linda would have to face alone.

Lois and Ernie quickly slipped back into the busy routines of village and school life in Ahwa. There was little time to consider their own loneliness with Linda in the States and both boys away at school. One evening, Tukaram, who was still adjusting to life in the government high school, stopped in to see Lois and Ernie. He wanted to tell them how glad he was that he and the other six Christian high school boys from scattered jungle villages could live in the Mission boarding school while they attended the government high school. It was almost like a home away from home, for they had lived in the Mission boarding hostel for years while they attended the first seven standards.

Tukaram didn't get to see any of his family very often, for it was a twenty-mile walk to Mahal. He could go home only at vacation time, which wasn't very often. He especially missed seeing his mother, Sita. He was the only person from his village who could read and write and his mother was very proud of him.Fortunately she had brought Tukaram to the Mission boarding school to be admitted when he was just seven years old, and there opened up for him a new world--the world of science, of literature, of other cultures--the whole world of education. No longer did he believe in the power of the thousands of Hindu gods, for he had found the one true God who made and orders all, a loving Heavenly Father to whom he prayed every day. He tried to help his mother to find the truth but she would have none of such ideas.

Since the government of India considered the Dangs forest a backward class area, it was a favorite tactic of politicians to sponsor high visibility projects for the people living here. It made good publicity, increased prestige, and thus furthered their own careers. Probably it was in this spirit, it was decided in New Delhi that the Dangs should have a high school. Space was made in the government buildings in the center of the village, a staff was hired, and a high school was established. Tukaram and the others were benefiting from this decision.

Students graduating from the Mission seventh standard school were eligible to enroll. The first year, seven boys, all graduates of the Mission school, entered the government high school. They did very well in their classes, ranking at the top.

Evening deepened as Lois and Ernie stood with Tukaram under the large Gold Mahor tree off the front verandah of the Mission bungalow. He began to speak of some of the problems he and the other Christian boys were facing at the high school.

It was Divali, the Hindu festival of lights. Over at the high school in the government building the teachers had set up a Ganpati god. Its huge body and elephant head were highly decorated for the occasion. The teachers were demanding that all of the students pay homage to the idol. All students were instructed to bow down and worship Ganpati. Tukaram, however, refused, and the other Christian boys followed Tukaram's lead.

The next day was to be a special festival day and everyone in the village of Ahwa was invited. The principal told the boys that if they wanted to attend this high school they must take part in the ceremony and worship the Ganpati god.

Together the boys went to the Shulls' bungalow to see Shull Sahib. Seeing how worried the boys were, Ernie sent for Parlak Choudhari to come to be with them. The group sat in the Shull's front room on the floor and talked over the situation. Lois and Gopal Mistri brought them each a cup of tea as they talked about what would be the Christian thing to do.

Shull Sahib reminded them that the constitution of the nation of India guaranteed religious freedom to everyone of all religions. Each person has a right to worship or not to worship according to his belief. This is a guaranteed right.

Parlak Choudhari led them in a discussion of what they should do. They asked God for guidance. What were they to do and how were they to do it? They didn't want to be expelled from school. They didn't want to lose their opportunity for an education. If they were expelled from this school they would probably never be admitted into another one. They prayed earnestly for God's help.

If the teachers or the principal made an issue of this, Parlak Choudhari or Shull Sahib would go over to the high school and have a talk with the authorities. Lois and Ernie both believed that the Indian people should be encouraged to do their own negotiating as much as possible. Because it was a sensitive point with the Indian Government, the less done by foreigners, the better for Indian citizens. Parlak Chaudhari and the Shulls all agreed that the Indian people should be encouraged to not depend on Americans any more than was absolutely necessary. Ernie and Lois would enter into the discussion only in the case of an emergency.

The group spent an hour deliberating and earnestly seeking God's guidance. Finally it was decided that the boys should go to school the next day the same as usual and that they should be courteous but firm, and when the others went to worship they should just sit and refuse to take part in the Hindu ceremony. The law was on the side of the Christians.

The boys went to school the next day with fear and trembling but with determination. They sat in their accustomed places and took part in school as usual. Crowds of people had come to attend the festival. When it came time for the worship of Ganpati the other Christian boys looked at Tukaram and he just sat still, so the other boys remained seated. All the Hindu students did the worship of the Ganpati. The teachers decided not to make an issue of it and went on with the festival. They ignored the sitting Christian students. They weren't quite sure until the day was over, but the Christian boys, by standing firmly for what they believed to be right, had won their right of freedom of religion.

About a month after the confrontation over the Ganpati idol worship at the high school, Tukaram and the other high school boys stopped in to visit Shull Sahib and Madam Sahib.

"Shull Sahib, we'd like to talk to you a little while," said Tukaram, who seemed to be the spokesman of the group.

"Of course," answered Ernie with a smile. "I've been wanting to talk some things over with you boys anyway." They went into the front room of the Shulls' house and ignoring the chairs sat down on the bamboo mats scattered on the floor where they felt more comfortable.

Tukaram picked up the conversation. "You see, Sahib, we all feel that God is calling us to do a special work here in the Dangs area. We want to tell our village people the truth and give them a chance to become Christian like we have."

"I feel I must go back to my own village and tell the people about Jesus and the Christian way of life!" Rama agreed. "It will be a long time before anyone from the Church here at Ahwa gets to my village. In the mean time the people who are my neighbors have not heard. I feel that I must go and tell them."

"I'm concerned most of all about my mother," said Tukaram. "All these years that I have been in the Christian Mission School, she was still doing daily worship to her village gods. Even when I became a Christian she turned away from the truth and kept her Hindu gods. I want to go back to my village and help my mother."

"We Christian high school boys have talked it over and we feel that since we have more education than anyone else in our villages that it is really up to us to tell the others the truth. Our goal is to make the entire Dangs area Christian. We believe that it should start with us. What do you think, Sahib?" Tukaram leaned closer to Shull Sahib. He was excited by his dream for the Dangs, and for a new opportunity for his mother to hear again about Jesus. Maybe this time she would really believe the truth and accept the way of Jesus.

Listening to the boys talk about their dreams for the Dangs area filled Ernie, Lois, and Parlak Chaudhari with great joy! This was what they had been working toward for years! This was the seed that they hoped would grow into a movement toward the acceptance of Christ as the answer to their search for truth.

Ernie moved among the boys and touched each one on the shoulder. "Yes, God is leading you. Your call to save your people is a wonderful calling. I'm glad that Parlak Choudhari is with us and could hear about the inspired dreams that you boys have for the future, because the Ahwa Church will want to be a part of your dream. Together we will pray and plan for this wonderful work that is to be done in the Dangs."

Parlak Chaudhari was filled with joy as he listened to the boys discuss their dreams. "I want you to know that there are some others in the Ahwa church who are wanting to open some preaching points out in other villages. We must not keep this good news just for ourselves or we'll lose it. It must be shared with other villages. You can count on the Ahwa church to help out in this sharing of the good news."

The boys remained in high school until they finished. Tukaram had become convinced that he wanted to become a minister in the church, so he applied for entrance into the seminary in Poona and was accepted. Three years later he graduated and came back to the Dangs area to work with his own people.

With Tukaram now prepared to work in the area, Parlak Choudhari continuing to pastor the Ahwa church, and an evangelist named Prabakar working part time at Mulchond, the Church had the good beginning of an outreach program.

As Ernie and Lois talked it over they sought the will of God for their lives and for the Church of Ahwa for they were beginning to sense that the church had matured to the point that it could thrive on its own. They prayed together for guidance as they tried to come to a decision about what they should do now. What did God want them to do?

As the days went by they became more convinced that they should leave India at the end of the school year at Woodstock when Jimmy would be ready to enter Manchester College and Danny would be ready to begin his sophomore year of high school. It was a difficult decision to make, for the Indian people were begging them to stay.

As Ernie and Lois thought about the Church at Ahwa and the whole Marathi speaking area they recognized that the young leadership in the Church had grown much stronger, and there were people anxious to do things in the Church. They must answer the question whether their staying on in India might hinder the development of the indigenous leadership and so harm the growth of the Indian Church.

Life in the villages seemed to go on as it had for hundreds of years, each generation passing on its way of doing things to the next. In her village of Mahal, Sita would sit in her hut and wait patiently for her son to come home from Ahwa and be a part of their village again. One particular evening word came to Sita that her son would be coming home the next day. She sat excitedly by her small wood fire making preparations to cook an especially good meal. How she longed for her late husband who would have been so proud of Tukaram, their only son.

She remembered the day she had taken her little seven-year-old son to the Mission School hoping to have him admitted. It was her effort to break the endless cycle of doing things the same old way as they had been done for centuries. By breaking this custom she had become an innovator in her village. No one else had become interested in schools or education or changing anything. Somehow she wanted her son to do things better. She thought that if she could help him to learn about things beyond their small world, he would find a better life. She didn't know what that life was, but she wanted him to have a chance to find out.

As she sat cross-legged on the floor by her open wood fire preparing some food for her noon day meal, she was happy, for she was expecting Tukaram any moment. Sita was deeply concerned about some decisions she needed to make, and she needed to talk to Tukaram about them. He was always so gentle and loving with her. He was always ready to listen and help her if he could.

The second year that Tukaram was in high school, he had come home for the Christmas vacation and had joyously told her that he had found the true God. He told her that God is a Father who loves every single person in the whole world, and that heaven is a place that He is preparing for all true believers to be taken after they die. He was so thrilled with this God of Love that he couldn't wait to share this wonderful news with her, his loving mother.

But she resisted. How could everything that she had been taught all the years of her life and everything all the rest of the villagers of Mahal thought, be wrong?

Whenever Tukaram came home for a school vacation he would share with her about his experiences in this new knowledge he had about the true God. She would think about it and wonder about her own worship of Ganpati and Shiva and Krishna and other gods. She didn't want to be left out if what Tukaram had told her was the truth. As the years went by and Tukaram graduated from the seventh standard, Sita became convinced that he was right and she decided she would talk to Tukaram about how to become a Christian.

Finally Tukaram would be coming home, for his academic career was over. He had graduated from high school and had finished his course of study in the seminary. Several villages were asking for him to come and start work in their villages, but first he wanted a time at home.

The last ten miles he walked most of the way. Twice he had gotten rides on logging carts pulled by a pair of bullocks. The oxen were so slow, and he was so eager to get home, that several times he climbed down and walked beside the cart. Finally he came to his own village of Mahal. He walked past a number of huts until he came to his mother's hut. His mind flashed back to one night seven years ago when Shull Sahib had shot a leopard just outside one of these huts. That shot, no doubt, saved someone's life.

`Now he approached the hut. He hoped that his mother would be inside. She hadn't known exactly when he might come, of course, and was squatting near her fire cooking. "Ai, I'm home," he greeted her.

"Oh, my son! Are you really home! I am so glad! Are you hungry? Here! Have a chapatti. They are just ready," his mother said.

"Yes! I'm starved! I haven't eaten since early this morning. Oh, this tastes good," said Tukaram

Sita patted him on the shoulder. "Lots of folks want to see you, my boy. Now since you are educated they want to ask you many things. But mostly I want to talk to you."

"And I want to talk to you, Mother. We have so much to talk over and we don't have to hurry."

"Sitabai, Sitabai! Are you there?" called a voice from outside the door of the hut. "Are you in your hut? May I come in? I heard something very bad and I want to tell you. My husband has just been to Ahwa and he knows the whole terrible story. May I come in?"

Sita started toward the bamboo door of the hut. "Yes. Come in, Ratanbai. My son, Tukaram, is home from school. He is finished now with his schooling."

"Oh, yes, Tukaram, you have been in Ahwa, haven't you? Did you know Bima? She lived in Christiparda (the Christian sector)."

Tukaram had known Ratanbai since he was born, for she lived in a hut next to theirs.

"Yes, Ratanbai, I knew who Bema was. I saw her in the bazaar sometimes. What is the terrible story you heard, bai?"

"Well," Ratanbai took a deep breath before she started her story. "You know that Beemabai's husband works for the forestry department. He had to walk twenty miles down the mountain to Waghai to pick up his money for the week of work. That was very good, but on the way back he was suddenly attacked by a tiger that jumped on him from a bamboo thicket by the side of the road. It killed him and ate part of him. But they say that Beema had followed him, and on the way home she changed herself into a tiger and killed him. She wanted his money. All the villagers around are saying it's true, so I think it must be."

Tukaram smiled in disbelief. "Ratanbai, that's just someone's made-up story. It's not true. You can be sure that it never happened. You don't have to be afraid of that."

Ratanbai was half-insulted that Tukaram didn't believe her story. "How can you say that, Tukaram? Her husband is dead. And she had followed him. She wanted his money, I think. They didn't get along very well anyway, people say."

"Ratanbai, during my seven years of school I have been living in that community, and never have heard that anyone could change themselves into an animal and attack someone. There is nothing like that in their religion. Their religion is about a loving God. I'd like to tell you about that God sometime," Tukaram said.

Ratanbai smiled and turned toward the door. "Alright. I'd like to hear that. I like stories."

Ratanbai's story about Beema didn't die out in the village of Mahal. Apparently it had spread all around town and it was being believed.

Back in the district capitol of Ahwa, there were repercussions. One morning Ernie was holding a teachers' conference in his office in the bungalow. They had just settled down over cups of tea as they were considering some new text books when there was a commotion on the front verandah. Lois left the group and went to find out what was going on.

Beemabai was on the verandah, being kept there by the cook, Gopal Mistri. "What's the trouble, Mistri? What is she yelling about. I can't understand her because she is yelling so much. What is she saying?"Lois asked.

"She is saying that she has to see the Sahib right now, that some people are lying about her. She won't stop until we let her in. I told her that Sahib is in conference and that she should sit and wait."

"You are right, Mistri. Tell her again from me that she should sit down and wait until the meeting is over." Lois left Gopal to try to communicate with the hysterical woman then she went back to the meeting in the office.

However the yelling continued. Bema ran down off the verandah, around the corner of the house and stopped just outside the back verandah. The entire back verandah was protected by a wall of expanded metal fencing. Bema began to climb the back wire by thrusting her toes and fingers in the holes of the mesh and climbing up the wire as high as the roof.

Lois, coming out to the back verandah, was amazed to see the screaming woman hanging on the wire and yelling at the top of her voice. At first Lois was frightened, then disgusted at such a stupid way to handle a problem. Then the funny side struck her and she couldn't keep from laughing. Looking up through the fencing she called, "Beemabai, come down. Will you drink a cup of tea with me while we wait for the meeting to be over? We can talk. Come down please."

Bema stopped yelling and began to climb down the wire fence. Lois sat down on the step and Bema sat down beside her.

"Do you like tea, Beemabai?" asked Lois in a soft voice.

"Oh yes," she answered.

Lois continued to ask questions about the way Bema made different food dishes and so was able to avoid any more hysteria. Before long the meeting in the office came to an end and

Ernie was able to see Beemabai in the office. He helped her to recognize her problem as one of village gossip, and to realize that you cannot legislate against gossip.

Back in the jungle in the village of Mahal, Tukaram was again getting acquainted with the villagers, for he had been gone most of the time for the last seven years in boarding school at the Mission. As he listened to people visiting and just talking he was appalled at how many objects around their village and in the jungle the people believed had evil spirits in them. They were afraid to go by certain bushes, or to touch certain rocks. They thought the tiger was a god and would do them harm if they didn't worship it. He was sad at how many people lived in constant fear.

One day as Sitabai and Tukaram were sitting on the floor by their fire eating rice and curry, Sita said, "Tukaram, I have been thinking for a long time about gods and I heard how you and the other boys stood up to the school officials and told them that you wouldn't worship Ganpati. I admired you so much! I just knew that you were right, and I wanted to go and sit with you boys and tell the school principal that you were speaking the truth. I could tell inside of me that you were speaking the truth. Tukaram, I want to become a Christian. I want to follow the way of Jesus. Will you help me?"

Tukaram put his arm around Sitabai's shoulder, "Mother, you have made me the happiest person alive by what you have said! For years I have been praying that you would become a Christian! Now it is actually happening! I am sure there is rejoicing in heaven with what you have just said! I will contact Parlak Choudhari in Ahwa and he will arrange to come out here and baptize you in this very river! My dear mother, next to my own becoming a Christian this is the happiest day of my life."

The rains of 1964 grew less and less and the lovely cool season descended on the jungle. The plants were lush and green and peace seemed to reign between the different antagonistic groups of people.

"Listen!" said Ernie in a low voice as he tilted his head to one side. "I think I hear someone coming along the jungle path!" Just then a horse came through the trees and riding on its back was a nice-looking young man who called out to them, "Salaam, Sahib! Salaam, Madam Sahib! I was looking for you!"

"Manaji! Salaam! It is good to see you! We haven't seen you for some time."

How well they remembered Manaji and his wagon.

"What have you been doing?" Ernie asked.

"I would have come to see you sooner, but I have been looking for a job, and I found one. The government has hired me to be a teacher in a village school. I am very happy. The Mission

School taught me well. I passed all my tests, and then passed the teacher training tests. I will begin teaching at the first of the next session. I saved some money and I was able to buy this horse. Since I am crippled I had to have the horse to get to school from my hut." Manaji explained more about his new position, then said his "salaam" and rode away.

"There goes a young Christian teacher out into a village to teach. He is just typical of so many of our students. They are becoming leaders in this young, old country of India, and their influence is going to be felt as this nation grows," commented Lois.

Ernie agreed with her. "That's so true! Look at the central government, and also the various state governments. A number of Christian men and women have been appointed to positions of influence. It is good to see this country growing and becoming stronger. I'm sure India is on the verge of a great future. I pray that God will give her guidance," said Ernie.

Lois and Ernie sat one evening on the flat top of a low stone wall that surrounded the government compound up at Lookout Point, and mused about their years in India coming to a close. The scenic overlook was located on a bluff just outside the village of Ahwa and presented a misty, panoramic view of three ranges of low hills of the Western Ghats which they had come to love. A rhesus monkey appeared, scampered along the top of the wall, and stopped a few feet from where they were sitting. He cocked his head to one side and began to scratch himself while he studied them—guarded, mildly curious, wild.

Seeing the monkey seemed to pull together so many threads that had become the tapestry of India to Lois—the wildlife that fascinated Ernie and brought both dazzling beauty and great misery to its people, the hardships and unpredictability of day-to-day village struggles, the fear and superstition surrounding jungle life, and the inertia of customs long honored yet now strangely incongruous with an emerging modern nation. They would be leaving—and soon. Life would go on here—in the mud of the monsoons and the dust of the dry season—in the splendor of lives transformed by Christ's message. Young leaders in the church, educated and capable, bode well for India and cushioned the blow of leaving home.

ABOUT THE AUTHOR

Lois Shull balanced three careers—mother, missionary, and high school teacher. She is the mother of a daughter and two sons, and with her husband Ernie, spent from 1946 to 1964 as a missionary for the Church of the Brethren among the hill people of the Western Ghats in India. There she was a pastor's wife, school principal, and nurse. Upon returning to the United States in 1964, she embarked upon a high school teaching career in English, dramatics, literature, and speech. She retired from teaching in 1982 and soon began this book. She has written numerous articles and a filmstrip called "A Chance to Live." Lois wrote the scripts for, and directed three movies called <u>Shepherd of India</u>, <u>To Meet the Sun</u>, and <u>The Turn of the Tide</u>. She wrote a radio play entitled <u>Valley of the Sun</u> and a book called <u>Women in India Who Kept the Faith</u>. Home is now in Timbercrest, a retirement community in North Manchester, Indiana.